Meet the Hybrids

by

Miguel Mendonça
and Barbara Lamb

About the Authors

Miguel Mendonça is an Anglo-Azorean writer based in Bristol, England. After gaining an honors degree in geography and history he studied social science and environmental ethics at postgraduate level. He then worked in the sustainability field, becoming an authority on renewable energy policy. While serving as Research Manager for an international NGO he wrote textbooks, articles and papers, providing an evidence base for campaigners around the world to push for better renewable energy laws in their jurisdictions. He lectured internationally and worked with campaigners from NGOs, politics, finance, industry and civil society. Miguel now writes fiction and non-fiction on politics, relationships, spirituality, consciousness and ufology.

Barbara Lamb is a licensed psychotherapist, hypnotherapist and regression therapist in Southern California. She has counseled and regressed over 1,700 people to 2,600 extraterrestrial encounters. She is a leading expert and presenter in this field. She has done extensive research into the ET-human hybrid phenomenon, and has given presentations on this subject at major conferences including IUFOC. She personally knows and interviews a dozen people living among us who have enough ET DNA, heritage and continuing contact with the beings who created them, to be considered ET-human hybrids. Barbara has co-authored two previous books: *Crop Circles Revealed* and *Alien Experiences*.

About the Cover Artist

Christine Kesara Dennett has been illustrating for investigators, witnesses and documentaries since 1986. Like a police sketch artist, Kesara creates illustrations from actual events and descriptions from eyewitnesses. To this day new reports come to her from around the world to be illustrated. Kesara is updating and adding to her collection everyday.

Archives of her work are available at kesara.org.

First published November 2015 by Miguel Mendonça
and Barbara Lamb through Amazon CreateSpace

Copyright © 2015 Miguel Mendonça and Barbara Lamb

All moral rights reserved

This book or any portion thereof may not be reproduced or used in any manner whatsoever without the express written permission of the authors except for the use of brief quotations in a book review

Cover artwork by Christine Kesara Dennett

Cover design by Miguel Mendonça

A catalogue record for this book is available from the British Library

ISBN 13: 978-1518741012
ISBN 10: 1518741010

www.meetthehybrids.wordpress.com

To the seekers.
MBM

To the cosmic beings who create benevolent hybrids, and to the hybrids who have the courage to live on Earth and teach us, inspire us, and lead us into Oneness and Ascension.
BML

If you want to find the secrets of the universe, think in terms of energy, frequency and vibration.
Nikola Tesla

We're supposed to keep evolving. Evolution did not end with us growing opposable thumbs. You do know that, right?
Bill Hicks

My soul is from elsewhere, I'm sure of that, and I intend to end up there.
Rumi

The Way is not in the sky; the Way is in the heart.
Buddha

Acknowledgements

I wish to express my gratitude to Barbara, for her contributions, companionship, perspectives and the endless hours of fascinating transatlantic conversation, often into the small hours. It's been a joy and a privilege to share this journey with you.

I am grateful to numerous people for their assistance.

My father, for buying me my first book on UFOs, and taking me to see Star Wars as a child. You started all this.

Mary Rodwell, CristiAnne Quiros and Joanne Summerscales for sharing their views, contacts and humor as this project germinated.

David Saunders, for helping me get my priorities straight.

Joe, Matt and Charmaine for helping out with the transcription.

DB for the moral support; Tim, Jim, Sam and Rick for the tech support; Hannah Batten for the legal advice; Peter Urpeth for the range of advice, and for introducing me to pleonasm.

As always, Louise. I have a feeling this book explains a few things about the depth of our connection.

And Dexter. I miss you every day brother, but you are always with me.

Miguel

Cynthia Crawford and Fran Harris, for validating my intuition that they are hybrids, and for assisting me in trusting the reality of ET-human hybrids. And Miguel Mendonça for originating the idea of writing this book, for inviting me to collaborate with him, for being so open to and inspired by our hybrids, and for doing the lion's share of the work with enthusiasm and delight.

Barbara

We wish to express our profound gratitude to our extraordinary friends Tatiana, Cynthia, Charmaine, Robert, Juju, Vanessa, Jacquelin and Matt. Your spirit, bravery and wisdom is a constant inspiration.

A special thanks to Grant Cameron, Linda Moulton Howe and Mary Rodwell for their time and perspectives.

Also to Christine Kesara Dennett for her beautiful artwork.

And to Jennie Thomas for proofreading the manuscript.

Contents

Contents 9
List of Box Texts 11
Foreword 13
Part I – Ground Work 17
    Introduction 17
Hybrids in Human Culture 23
Hybrid Discourse in Ufology 29
Part II – From the Inside 37
    Introduction 37
        Glossary 39
Tatiana Amore 41
Cynthia Crawford 51
Charmaine D'Rozario-Saytch 71
Robert Frost-Fullington 95
Jujuolui Kuita 117
Vanessa Lamorte 141
Jacquelin Smith 163
Matthew Thomas 185
Part III – Crossing the Threshold 199
Short Summaries of Part II 201
    Backgrounds 201
    What is your ET component? 201
    How did you learn you are a hybrid? 201
    Do you have your own hybrid children? 202
    How do you reconcile the multiple aspects of your identity? 202
    Do you have physiological differences to humans? 203
    What protocols govern ET interaction with humans? 204
    Earth changes and the New Earth 205
    What is your take on the takeover thesis? 206
    Have you had contact with the military or intelligence agencies? 207
    How do you feel about the global hybrid community? 208
    What would you most like to discuss with other hybrids? 209
    How can humanity best work with you? 210
    What are the best and worst things about being a hybrid? 210

How do you conceptualize 'God?'	213
What is the most important lesson you've learned?	214
Methods of Creating Hybrids	217
Purpose	221
Introduction	221
Frequency	223
Ascension	231
Bridges and Ambassadors	239
Missions, Abilities and Services	243
Guides and Star Family	247
What roles do they play?	247
What kind of connections do they share?	250
How do they communicate?	252
How can they be contacted?	253
The Heart	255
Can Anyone Have ET Contact?	259
Personal Journeys	263
Miguel's Journey	263
Barbara's Journey	272
The Big Picture	279
Recommended Reading	285

List of Box Texts

Manifesting protection 62
Manifesting love 98
Holographic healing technique 106
Contact protocol 106
Manifesting protection 111
Lesson from a Grey on sending love energy 122
Raising your vibration 129
Manifesting protection 136
The four key stages of hybridization 147
Calling in your guides 172
Opening the third eye 188

Foreword

On October 16, 1962, Arthur Lundahl, the top photo analyst at the CIA, walked into the oval office to brief President John F. Kennedy. Lundahl was also the top expert on UFOs inside the CIA, and the man who briefed the President on the subject. He ran 'the weird desk' at the agency, where reports of UFOs and all paranormal phenomena were stored. The photos that Lundahl showed Kennedy that day were of missiles and missile launchers in Cuba, and they would be used to determine Cuban intentions. Kennedy and his military advisors were forced to consider an invasion of Cuba and a potential nuclear exchange that they estimated would cost 80-100 million American lives.

In the end, the decision was made to negotiate rather than add to the 200-plus million people who died in the 20th century because they were determined to be evil by one group or another. Years later, on July 20, 2015 to be exact, the evil that was seen in Cubans in 1962 had evaporated. The American flag was raised in Cuba and diplomatic relations were established. Now, like the Japanese, Germans, and North Vietnamese before them, the Cubans became good guys who would buy American imports and provide winter sun for Americans.

The search for evil, however, never ends. Like the 1962 Cuban situation, in 2015, UFO researchers are debating questions such as, 'Are ETs evil?' and 'Can we talk with them and learn, or will it be necessary to kill them?'

Within ufology there are researchers who believe that ETs, like the Cuban leaders of 1962, are up to no good. The proponents of the 'evil ET' evaluation say ETs have violated our rights, raped our women, and may be planning to steal our planet's resources. The ETs, through an army of hybrids, are planning to take over and enslave us at best, and eat us at worst. The proponents of this idea have been warning for decades that the end is nigh, and that we must do something before it is too late.

Miguel Mendonça and Barbara Lamb have not come to the evil ET conclusion. They, like a growing majority of researchers, see the ETs in a more positive light. Their conclusion has come from extensive evidence they have gathered from working with experiencers and hybrids. It has led them to the conclusion that the beings we are dealing with are "extremely benevolent, altruistic, and are here to serve and upgrade humanity, to help usher the world into higher consciousness and Ascension."

The book *Meet The Hybrids: The Lives and Missions of ET Ambassadors On Earth* tells the stories of "eight people who we have good reason to believe are hybrids and who are living on Earth among us." Their stories are some of the most important that will be told in the 21st century, and Mendonça and Lamb deserve high praise for bringing them to the public.

The authors' conclusions are, I believe, about to be strongly supported by the first major poll of experiencers. The good/evil ET debate will enter the scientific arena and the authors will be shown to be very close to the reality of the situation. I also believe that many of the other conclusions raised by the authors of this book will be strongly supported by future experiencer polls.

I suspect that the hybrid phenomenon may not be that rare based on research I did on modern musicians and their strong connection to the UFO phenomena. Many modern musicians have written songs with UFO-related lyrics. Many have had sightings, and dozens either affirm they are experiencers or appear to be. The list of those who claim a hybrid-type connection to outer space are numerous. They include Afrofuturism originator Sun Ra, glam rock originator David Bowie, electric guitar pioneer Jimi Hendrix, dub reggae pioneer Lee 'Scratch' Perry, the 'godmother of punk' Patti Smith, P-funk originator George Clinton, singers Vince Taylor, Marc Bolan, Michael Jackson and Elvis Presley, and John Denver, who wrote a song called *Spirit* about his origin near a ring nebula in the constellation of Lyra.

People identifying themselves as experiencers and hybrids are critical to solving the UFO mystery. For the past 70 years we have logged UFO sightings in the sky but we are no further ahead than when we started. That is because very little can be learned by compiling statistics on color, speed, behavior and so on.

The only chance we have to solve the UFO mystery is to talk to the people who have interacted with those behind the phenomena.

The government and military may know what is going on, but they are not about to tell us. Experiencers and hybrids on the other hand, will take us inside the craft and into the motivations, intentions and behavior of the ETs themselves.

What the eight hybrids in this book have told Mendonça and Lamb goes to the very heart of reality, saying that the world is not composed of physical nuts and bolts bounded by time and space, but is rather a more spiritual, etheric place where everything is connected and conscious.

Their descriptions of how things operate are lining up with what the new paradigm, defined by biology and quantum physics, is telling us: the universe is self-organizing, entangled and aware.

Experiments such as the double-slit experiment have shown that consciousness is the primary element of the universe, and that the physical world, along with time and space, may be nothing more than an illusion. As Max Planck, the father of quantum physics, defined the new understanding, "I regard consciousness as fundamental. I regard matter as derivative of consciousness. We cannot get behind consciousness. Everything that we talk about, everything that we regard as existing, postulates consciousness."

In 2012 I had a moment of insight that came with absolute certainty. The message was simple. It said that the solution to the UFO problem was connected to nonlocal consciousness, and that idea is a big part of the message in this book.

In that moment of insight I was reminded that the Canadian government had been told by 'American officials' back in November 1950 that 'mental phenomena' were part of the flying saucer phenomenon. I was reminded that a former defense official—and later president of Penn State University—had told myself and others in 1991 that ESP was a key to the UFO phenomenon and that we would go nowhere without an understanding of it. Finally, I was reminded that Ben Rich, who headed Lockheed Skunk Works, had stated in 1993 that the mechanisms that facilitate ESP are central to how UFO propulsion works.

Suddenly, my belief in the nuts and bolts of the UFO phenomena collapsed like Newtonian physics did the day they ran the double-slit experiment. I realized I had to quit watching the lights in the sky, and the screen-imaging puppet, and start listening to the message.

Almost immediately I came across dozens who claimed that ETs had allowed them to fly the craft—which seemed like a strange thing for evil ETs to be doing. (There is at least one such story in this book). When I asked how this was done, 100% of the people replied, "You do it with your mind."

The nuts and bolts of the UFO story really fell apart when I suddenly realized that the ET encounters on board the ship really lack any of the physical things that appeal to our left brain ego minds. They don't have designer clothes and sometimes no clothes at all. There is no fancy furniture on the ship. They are almost never reported eating. They have no sex organs. Despite the claims they might be here for our gold, I can't recall anyone describing them wearing any jewelry. Most importantly, unless they are very good with makeup, it appears that the main ET each experiencer deals with never gets any older. This led to the question: if they are not tied into physical things, why are they here?

The message I heard from experiencers and hybrids is exactly the same message as told by the eight witnesses in this book. It is a message of expanding consciousness, and moving from fear and victimhood to love and understanding. It is a program of beings behind the UFO phenomena moving humanity from a mentality of a swarm of locusts that have descended on the Earth singing, "Me me me, I I I, self self self," as the world goes off the cliff, to an expanding consciousness where we perceive the big picture that everything is alive, sacred and connected. We are being told where we are from, where we are going, and what our connection to the universe is.

If stories were games, the UFO story would be the Super Bowl of all stories. It is the biggest and most important in history, and the hybrids are key players. If we are to have any chance of understanding what is going on, we must listen to those who have been on the ships, interacted with the beings, or—as hybrids—are the beings themselves.

This book tells us part of the big story, and is required reading. As beings told Barbara Lamb when she was about to publish an earlier book, "It is time to get the material out and let the people know."

Grant Cameron

Grant Cameron is a researcher, and author of Alien Bedtime Stories
www.presidentialufo.com

Part I – Ground Work

Introduction

The modern UFO phenomenon has persisted in the public consciousness for almost 70 years. In that time it has maintained a doggedly mysterious, nebulous quality that can frustrate as much as it excites. The coming of the internet has seen the subject explode into new life and expand in every possible direction, covering matters physical, metaphysical, psychological and political. Along with understanding our own consciousness, and figuring out how to live peacefully and sustainably on this planet, it may be the most complex and important subject facing humanity at this time. The excitement and frustration are interwoven around the central offering of ufology: a larger reality.

This book seeks to explore the meeting point of all of the above, perhaps the most material product of ufology—ET-human hybrids living on Earth. While crashed ET craft may well have become the energetic focus of the defense industry deep within secret bases and laboratories across the United States and beyond, a new race of humans may simultaneously have been under construction on board more fortunate craft. These people, part-human and part-ET, have been created to help humanity and the Earth evolve, and in pursuit of that mission, eight of them—made up of more than 15 ET races—are willing to share their experiences, knowledge and practices.

If this idea stirs you on any level, you will undoubtedly find material here that you have never before encountered, which may expand the realms of the possible for you—and even give you some much-desired answers.

It is not our objective to 'prove' this reality. For some, no amount of proof would suffice. If we had everyone DNA tested, and found that they did indeed have mystery genetics in apparent agreement with the amount of ET DNA they understand they have, some would argue that we would need to repeat the testing with another laboratory. If the results matched those of the first process, they may protest that it proves nothing, it's a coincidence. The mechanics of denial are well-oiled in that kind of person. Some of this resistance may come from fear, and we often deny ideas that disturb us. We may not understand our fears, and may have no desire to unpack them.

So we do not seek to inflate the fears of the unwilling, but to illuminate for the curious. We tend to accept that which serves us, so if the material in this book is in alignment with your values and goals, you may find it of great personal benefit. This information may well change you—in various ways. Speaking from experience, we can say that the person who begins reading this book will not be the person who finishes it. If you embrace change, and growth, this is available in abundance.

The original intention of Part I was to provide a substantial introduction, scene-setting in various ways so that any reader might be conceptually equipped to venture into these realms. However, after all but completing the interviews, three key things became clear: First, that no amount of preparation would be enough; second, that a wealth of material was being generated; third, that their information was far more interesting than any kind of external speculation. Consequently, it only made sense to cover the bare essentials in Part I and get to the information for those who are ready.

It is likely that every reader will find material in this book which challenges them, triggers them, even upsets them. This is a radical reorientation of the possible, of the cosmic order—of reality itself. Mainstream Western science says most of it is impossible, it cannot be. It says that whatever is going on here, it is explainable in conventional material terms, and there is no such thing as non-human races visiting Earth from other star systems. The argument seems to be that it is impossible because humans cannot currently do it or explain it.

So, how to read this book? If the reader is a materialist, and feels confident that the above assertions on behalf of the contemporary Western scientific model are entirely valid, one suggestion might be to treat the book as a guide to living well. Even if you believe you are no more than flesh and blood, a single-use brain on legs, you may still find renewed pleasure in connecting with nature, with plants and animals. Most of the hybrids share beautiful stories of connection with the living world around us, and a profound care for it. Seeing the world through their eyes is a joy, and grants new perspective for our own experiences.

If you are uninterested in non-human intelligences but are spiritually open, you may find much richness here. These people are, perhaps above all else, spiritual teachers. It is humbling to attempt to do justice to the level of understanding they have about the interconnection of all aspects of reality, and to the spiritual ideals they live for.

For those who are strictly here for the ETs and UFOs, and are perhaps determined to understand the big picture, you will find many more pieces to add to your collection. Do they all fit together neatly? Are there contradictions? Certainly there appears to be contradiction, within and between accounts, and the hybrids themselves cannot always account for that. The entire human trip is full of apparent contradiction and paradox, so should we hold the hybrids to a different standard? The hybrids own both their understanding and their ignorance, they offer what they experience, think and feel as their truth. We present this work as simply that.

Each reader will take from this material what makes immediate sense to them, but other things will sink in over time. And it may be that those contradictions resolve themselves with greater perspective. Or they may cease to matter entirely.

So Part I is a brief introduction only. It surveys examples of hybrids in human culture, from mythology to science and technology, to the treatment of the ET-human hybrid subject in film, television and literature. What does the latter suggest about agenda, purpose and methodology in the 'hybrid program?' And why is it that humans across all cultures have a fascination with hybrids of various kinds?

We then look at some examples of how ufology has discussed the same questions, and the schism between those with 'positive' and 'negative' research findings. Is it possible to reconcile these apparently contradictory views?

Part II is the core of the book, in which the hybrids discuss their experiences and understandings. They have a chapter each, produced from a questionnaire format. The sessions were done mostly via Skype conference calls involving both authors, and totaled around 50 hours. As the lead author and editor, Miguel then spent at least the same again in conversations with them as he sought clarification or expansion in developing the manuscript—though many hours were spent simply connecting in growing friendship. The methodology is set out in more detail in the introduction to Part II.

The information shared by the eight hybrids was often beautiful, sometimes troubling, always mind-expanding. There is, naturally, a vast array of other questions that we did not have the time and space to explore here. Future books may pursue those.

Part III offers thematic summaries which analyze and synthesize as we compare across testimonies, looking for commonalities and differences within each subject area.

We look at the 'how' of the hybrid program, its various modalities, and which races are involved with our participants. This includes supporting anecdotes from regression work done by Barbara over the last 25 years.

The 'why' is the biggest question of all: the subject of purpose. This incorporates many physical and metaphysical aspects. Key questions relate to the concept of 'Ascension.' What is it, and how does it affect us? What can we learn from it, how can it improve our lives and how can we pursue our own Ascension? What are the hybrids' missions, and the abilities which help them fulfil those missions? Who are the guides that support them, and do we all have guides?

'The heart' is a feature of the hybrids' language, and we explore its various meanings and applications.

After the interviews, the question came up: can anyone have ET contact? Differing understandings of this are set out.

The project has been so personally affecting that we discuss how we got here, and something of our experiences of working with these beings.

We close by standing back to look at the big picture. What have we learned here? Where can this information take us?

For those wishing to delve deeper into various aspects of this and related phenomena, the authors and the hybrids share some recommended reading at the end of the book.

The material itself can be extremely challenging, and when the reader reaches the chapter on our personal journeys as authors through this process, they will get a sense of how challenging it was for us. But as with any book of such complexity—and in our view, wisdom—it will repay multiple readings, and take time to integrate. Few readers will skate effortlessly across this work, and we believe that none will have heard it all before. We have allowed each hybrid room to explore their ideas, processes and experiences in unprecedented detail.

You may find, as we did, that the most useful way to approach this material is to eliminate judgment as early in the process as possible. Depending on what stage of your own exploration you are at, your mind may to a lesser or greater degree attempt to impose itself on the information, and make determinations on what is true and what is not. You may even encounter one or more seemingly insurmountable conceptual barriers, yet with sufficient determination to understand, you may find that by letting go of preconceived notions of what is, you become light enough to rise above those barriers. It is clear that the hybrids themselves have undergone this process over the months, years or decades, and they have sympathy with those attempting to make sense of their information—especially when new to it. Even for us as authors, despite decades of combined interest and research, we have learned a great deal, and will continue to do so for as long as we do this work.

In the spirit of disclosure, this is not a work of dispassionate scientific enquiry. These individuals, whether before or during, became friends of ours. In some cases we seem to be bonded in ways we don't necessarily understand. To an extent it may simply be a matter of kindred spirits meeting, people with a shared fascination for uncovering deeper truths about reality.

As opaque as the UFO subject has always been, the hybrids grant access to parts of it that could change human understanding in a revolutionary way, and we are privileged to share their stories with the world.

Hybrids in Human Culture

What do Mr. Spock, a Labradoodle, edutainment and a Toyota Prius have in common? We could add to the list brass, margaritas, the Greek god Triton and Napoleon Dynamite's favorite animal, the Liger. In nature, science, technology and culture, hybrids have either arisen naturally or been produced through deliberate human activity.

Human mythology is replete with hybrids, whether gods, races or individuals. Most cultures tell stories of such creatures, but the Greek, Egyptian and Hindu traditions in particular have specialized in them.

Athena, in a fit of pique at losing a weaving contest, turned her opponent into Arachne the spider-woman, who had the consolation of being the mother of all spiders. The centaurs and centaurides—male and female respectively—were a race of half-human half-horse people. Less well known is the Hippalectryon, a rooster up top and horse down below. Those imaginative Greeks of old really let themselves go with the Chimera, a triple-headed nightmare—lion, goat and snake—with the front legs of a lion, hind legs of a goat and the tail of a snake.

The Hindu pantheon features Lord Ganesha—the elephant-headed lord of knowledge and destroyer of obstacles, Hanuman, a humanoid monkey—devotee and messenger of Rama, and Narasimha, the Great Protector, with a leonine face and claws, and human torso and lower body.

The Egyptians had a great enthusiasm for hybrid deities with animal heads and human bodies. Khepri had the head of a dung beetle. Anubis, a jackal. Khnum, a ram. Others hybridized animals include crocodile, lion, hawk, cat, ibis and hippopotamus.

The Chinese Fenghuang is an exalted bird, symbolizing the union of yin and yang, among other things. Today is it commonly depicted with the head of a golden pheasant, the body of a mandarin duck, the tail of a peacock, the legs of a crane, the mouth of a parrot, and the wings of a swallow. These elements represent qualities and values: virtue, duty, propriety, credibility and mercy.

Bavarian folklore gives us the Wolpertinger (AKA Poontinger), a creature of the alpine forests commonly depicted with the head of a rabbit, the body of a squirrel, the antlers of a deer, and the wings and legs of a pheasant.

Words entirely fail to do the appearance of such beings justice, but the point is clear. For many thousands of years, diverse human cultures have been creating and venerating hybrids.

If you asked most people today what they associate with the word 'hybrid,' the answer may well be cars. In a global economy challenged to reduce fossil fuel dependency, hybrids are a step in that direction. Since the late 1990s there has been a steady market deployment of gasoline-electric hybrid cars, with sales of toward ten million vehicles, but the first was in fact the Lohner-Porsche Mixte Hybrid, developed way back in 1901 by Ferdinand Porsche. Today there are even hybrid aircraft in development, expected to decrease both noise and take off distance.

In language, hybrid words, or portmanteaux/frankenwords, have been in use since Lewis Carroll began constructing them in 1871. In *Through the Looking-Glass*, Humpty Dumpty explains to Alice the genesis of the bizarre words in the poem *Jabberwocky*. For example, 'slithy' means 'lithe and slimy' and 'mimsy' is 'flimsy and miserable.' Far from being a product of the 1980s, 'brunch' was coined in 1896 by the magazine *Punch*. Some people have a spontaneous gift for portmanteaux, such as Sarah Palin with "refudiate" (refute and repudiate) and George W. Bush with "They misunderestimated me." They may be genuinely funny, but they also stick (and boy are they compelling, I just lost half an hour of writing time reading lists of 'Bushisms' online). In fact, one could be forgiven for thinking that the internet's core purpose is to disseminate new hybrid words. Go through the latest and greatest words on urbandictionary.com and you will find plenty. Today's top word was 'insipiosexual,' deriving from the Latin 'insipiens' (opposite of 'sapiens') and 'sexualis' (sexual), meaning: attracted primarily to fools.

In biology, a hybrid is a genetic blend of two animals or plants of different breeds, varieties, species or genera. As well as human breeding programs and genetic experimentation, hybrids have also arisen through nature taking its course, as in the grolar bear, a mix of grizzly and polar bears. One theory suggests they have arisen through climate change forcing polar bears south. Although a mysterious specimen known as 'MacFarlane's bear' came to light in 1864, the modern grolar was made famous in 2006, when an odd-looking bear was shot by a licensed hunter in the Canadian arctic. The killer would have had the sweats during DNA testing—as he faced up to a year in jail if it turned out to be a grizzly—but it was deemed a legitimate hybrid, the progeny of a polar bear mother and a grizzly bear father.

Nature has also given us the wolphin—a mix of dolphin and false killer whale, and an array of others including hybrids of iguanas, rhinos and owls.

Humans have been hard at work with hybrid projects covering all areas of the animal kingdom, breeding for characteristics such as increased meat production and better temperament.

The same is true of the plant kingdom. For thousands of years many species have been cultivated and crossbred to produce novel, beautiful flowers, or food crops with higher yields, disease resistance or drought tolerance. Kew Botanical Gardens in England are spearheading a global project to build a stock of 'crop wild relatives'—wild relatives of common crops—for a hybridization program. They intend to produce new varieties which can offer food security in a changing global climate, and believe this offers a safer route than genetic modification. The GM debate continues to rage, seemingly between the safety-first and profit-first camps.

Humans have been breeding across racial lines for millennia, but the subject is among the most toxic in human discourse. Racists of all stripes still like to warn of the dangers, and miscegenation (race-mixing through marriage, cohabitation, sexual relations or procreation) was a crime in the United States between 1691 and 1967 (though in some states it remained on the statute books until 2000). Nazi Germany and Apartheid-era South Africa also outlawed the practice. Around the world, due to the age of exploration and the colonial era, mixed-race groups proliferated, particularly in Africa and South America. The modern era of globalization and cheap air travel has further increased the blending of the gene pool. When literal horse-power was the only game in town, the marital/sexual sphere of availability was a few miles at most. Today, nowhere is more than 24 hours away.

The liminal being is another concept related to hybrids. This anthropological term derives etymologically from the Latin līmen, meaning 'a threshold,' and refers to the disorienting middle stage of a ritual wherein the participant is neither what they were, nor what they will become. The ritual may shift the nature of a number of fundamentals, including their identity, community and time. The term has now extended semantically to incorporate political and cultural change, such as impacts on power structures, traditions and cultural trajectories.

Liminal beings are to some extent representative of duality, ambiguity and the lack of fixed boundaries in nature. During ritual, the shaman stands between the physical and metaphysical worlds. Mythological liminal beings hold dual states, thereby offering wisdom and unique perspectives, such as Chiron the centaur, mentor of Achilles. And they can come in many forms, and inhabit different realms. Merlin the wizard is the progeny of a human mother and an incubus. The Green Man is both human and vegetable. Ghosts are both alive and dead. Robocop is a cyborg, both human and robot, and a Christ allegory. Jesus Christ Himself was, in his time on Earth, considered both human and deity. Artificial intelligence may already be considered as somewhat human, and it is feasible that at some point in the future it may demand its own constitutional rights.

Most people experience a state of liminality twice daily, as they cross between waking and sleeping, but when it comes to the embodiment of liminality, this neither-nor state may provoke the fear of the unknown. Myth and legend across the world features therianthropy, the ability for a person to turn into an animal. Native American legends speak of skin-walkers, people who can transform into animals, such as a coyote, fox, eagle or crow. The werewolf has roots in classical antiquity, and came to represent, among other things, the initiation of men into the warrior class. The vampire has a history extending back millennia, and remains as popular a cultural figure as ever. All such creatures are open to psychological and political interpretations, but at their root they have a pull through the mix of fear and desire that they evoke.

This is captured in Clive Barker's 1989 film *Nightbreed*: "[We are] the last survivors of the great tribes. We're shapeshifters. Freaks. Remains of races that your tribe have all but driven to extinction. To be able to fly? To be smoke? Or a wolf? To know the night and live in it forever. That's not so bad. You call us monsters. But when you dream, you dream of flying and changing and living without death. You envy us, and what you envy, [you] destroy."

As tribal beings at heart, humans tend to look for similarities and differences upon meeting strangers. When people are neither one tribe or another, however, that may present a challenge to a fundamental part of our programming. So it is not surprising that we are endlessly fascinated with duality, and that so many of our cultures create beings which are both more than human, and less than human. *Star Trek* has thrown up numerous examples. Mr. Spock is human and Vulcan, a being who tries to bring logic and emotional restraint to his human nature, which in turn offers a degree of emotional insight. Seven of Nine is a half-human, half-Borg woman whose journey focused on adjusting to being severed from the Borg hive mind.

Alien: Resurrection, the fourth movie in the *Alien* franchise, features a hybrid storyline in which the protagonist, Ellen Ripley, is cloned by military scientists after her death. She had committed suicide because she had an Alien growing inside her. The scientists know it was a queen and want to grow and extract it so they can breed Alien soldiers. As Ripley's DNA was mixed with that of the Alien, her clone has increased strength and reflexes, the alien's acidic blood and a psychic link with the Aliens.

There are many treatments of the hybrid idea in general in science fiction, going back to the 1897 German novel *Auf zwei Planeten* (*On Two Planets*) by Kurd Laßwitz. One of the protagonists, Friedrich Ell, is the son of a Martian explorer stranded on Earth and a German governess living with a family in Australia.

The most detailed treatment of the subject of ET-human hybrids in popular culture—and the most commercially successful—is in *The X-Files*. Although it has a new mini series forthcoming at the time of writing, the main run of this prime time TV show was between 1993 and 2002, over six seasons, and around a third of the 202 episodes focused on a story arc involving alien abduction and hybridization. It explores all the staples of the phenomenon as reported in the ufological literature, including various conspiracy theories. It is the heart of the plot, involving both protagonists—Fox Mulder and Dana Scully—and their families. The recent human aspect of the story goes back to 1973, but the true scope is vast, reaching back to a time when early humans first appeared on the planet Earth. There are various types of hybrids in the plot, playing different roles within the factions and power structures. In general, the subject, and the ET and human conspirators, are treated as malign. There are 'good' hybrids in the mix, but betrayal and murder are constant, and the competing agendas of the various groups threaten everyone in some way. It could all be read as a Cold

War parable, but may have gone a long way toward implanting negative connotations of the hybrid subject in the public mind.

In literature, one of the most pointed takes on the subject is Whitley Strieber's 2011 novel *Hybrids*. It goes a similar route to *The X-Files*, with a storyline featuring a nefarious alliance between ETs and government, supersoldiers and a plot to destroy all humans. Is this increasingly standard plotline entirely fanciful?

'Otherkin' are in some senses another cultural product, but are far more material. They are individuals who self-identify as not entirely human. Their otherness may be spiritual or symbolic if not physical. The subculture grew online from 1990 and includes elves, fairies, angels, vampires, dragons and aliens. The community is studied in a 2012 paper in *The Journal of Alternative and Emergent Religious Movements* by Joseph P. Laycock. He begins by quoting Albert Camus in *The Rebel*, 1951: "Man is the only creature who refuses to be what he is." He argues that the Otherkin community has strong religious elements, and is an expression of existential and social needs.

Humans are obsessed with our own nature, in all its aspects. We are animals, and are challenged to both transcend the worst of our animal nature and embrace the best of it. We are tribal, yet economic forces are dissolving the boundaries between cultural groups. Increased mobility has tended to decrease heterogeneity, and the internet has facilitated further cultural shifts, particularly in language development and community-building, by reducing contact distances to zero. It has also allowed for information to move at speeds simply unimaginable even fifty years ago. Whatever we are, we are always changing on some level, and the conclusion might be, at this stage, that whatever is incoming in terms of ET-human hybrids, it is another aspect of the cultural and genetic churn.

Humans have long created hybrids of all kinds, whether for utility or artistic expression, creating things that are more than the sum of their parts. Apparently we are not alone in this enterprise. If the ETs are creating hybrids with humans, one would imagine it is a matter of utility rather than art—although that is an intriguing idea.

But what do we really know of them at this point? For those who have investigated the subject previously, what have they concluded? In the next chapter we examine the discourse within the field of ufology to see what kinds of narratives have arisen thus far.

Hybrid Discourse in Ufology

The written study of ET-human hybrids has been thin up until now, with only two researchers dedicating themselves to the subject. Their entry points, methodology and findings have been markedly different.

The earliest major work on the subject was *The Threat* by David M. Jacobs Ph.D (1988). He examines the ET agenda, detailing what he understands of the hybrid program, and concludes that its objectives and implications are "chilling" and "profoundly ominous," making him "fear for the future of [his] own children."

So what is his understanding, and from where does it derive? According to his website bio, he began researching the UFO phenomenon in the mid-1960s. In 1973 he completed his doctoral dissertation, which he published in 1975 as a book entitled *The UFO Controversy in America*.

In the opening chapter of *The Threat*, Jacobs lays out the history of the field and his own activity within it. It is a fascinating journey, beginning with the largely technological era, which then became more sociological in nature, bridging into the xenopological—the study of ET cultures. He notes that, in the 1960s and 70s, the more researchers learned about the behaviors of ETs, the less they understood about their motivation, but there was little reason to conclude that their evasiveness represented anything other than a neutral attitude. However, with the Betty and Barney Hill abduction case in 1961, a new era—the biological—was born. When it became known that the Greys had taken reproductive material from Barney, and from a string of other male and female experiencers, the plot thickened.

In 1981, Budd Hopkins published *Missing Time*, a study of the experiences of seven abductees, which included missing time/memory loss and physical marks. Hopkins used hypnotic regression as a means to subvert the memory erasure, and gained access to a variety of experiences. In his conclusion, Hopkins deploys logic and instinct to make his way into the biological aspect of the phenomenon. He notes that the evidence for sample-taking is clear, which he referred to a genito-urinary specialist for an opinion. The getting of reproductive material seemed to be the goal.

When Jacobs met Hopkins in 1982, he became convinced that the abduction phenomenon was not—as per the view of J. Allen Hynek—simply "eccentric," it was "important." Thus he broke with the standard approach and followed the evidence. Four years later he had learned the mechanics of hypnotic regression, and he conducted his first regression in August 1986. By 1992 he had conducted over 300, and wrote up his research in the book *Secret Life: Firsthand Accounts of UFO Abductions*. Drawing on the retrieved experiences of abductees, the work sets out the range of reported examinations and procedures, both mental and physical, including reproductive activities. The book also describes a typical abduction scenario from beginning to end.

Jacobs and Hopkins were putting together a picture that included abductees being required to interact with "odd-looking" children that appeared to be part-ET and part-human. In further elaborating the picture over the next few years, Jacobs' conclusions became inescapably disturbing, as set out in *The Threat*.

The book lays out his research in three key chapters, dealing with hybrid children, adolescents and adults, and independent hybrid activity. He shows that there is a clear motivation to create hybrid beings which look human and can live among us. Some of the material is as disturbing as the title suggests, with regard to both the methodology and implications of the activity.

How does all this jibe with the idea that the hybrid program is a way to upgrade humans and make them less aggressive and warlike? It appears not to. It makes the picture yet more nebulous. The reader is encouraged to read *The Threat* as it is full of fascinating detail on Jacobs' research and evolving conclusions.

As the title makes clear, his 2015 book *Walking Among Us: The Alien Plan to Control Humanity* doubles down on his 'threat' thesis. The picture that has emerged from his research is that the whole purpose of abductions is 'The Change'—the replacement of humanity as the dominant species on planet Earth. ETs are creating human-looking hybrids—'hubrids'—which can live undetected among humans and use their advanced neurological capabilities to control the minds of regular humans.

In 1999, research in the subject of hybrids had a watershed moment. Leading up to that were two key events. CristiAnne Quiros, a psychology Ph.D candidate, was considering what to do for her dissertation. She had in mind a study of the implications of enforced communal living. But in May 1995, one Sunday afternoon after classes, she sat on the beach at Carpenteria, California, gazing out over the Pacific Ocean. What happened next changed the course of her life. A holographic image of a typical Grey ET appeared over the ocean, and suggested she do her dissertation on ET-human hybrids living on Earth. Having neither a framework for the experience, nor an interest in the subject matter, she laughed it off. Five months later however, the second event occurred. Sat in her dissertation development class, the students were each announcing their chosen topic to the professor and the rest of the class. She intended to declare her original topic of communal living, but instead her mind went blank and she saw a marquee sign flashing 'HYBRIDS' over and over. She was, by this point, in a place of sufficient metaphysical understanding to recognize the signs. She refers to it as "cosmic choreography," the intricate design weaved by higher Source to encourage people to answer their call, which may derive from a soul agreement before incarnation.

Quiros answered, and found that her institution, the Pacifica Graduate Institute, was supportive of her proposal. This was due to it being a strongly Jungian school, and Carl Jung had made UFOs the topic of his final major work in 1959. *Flying Saucers: A Modern Myth of Things Seen in the Skies* explores the psychological significance of the phenomenon and suggests that it may be a replacement for God in a time of deep uncertainty. His work, and its relationship to the institute, opened up the subject for this rare academic venture into ufology.

Four years later, Quiros produced a dissertation titled *Exo-Psychology Research: A Phenomenological Study Of People Who Believe Themselves To Be Alien-Human Hybrids*. The rationale was simple enough—the research would help broaden the scope of psychological understanding, helping the field to familiarize itself with the beliefs of this group of people, and develop ways to support them and those close to them. An understanding that such a belief is not an automatic signifier of mental disorder is vital for practitioners.

The research was intended in part as a baseline account, given that nothing similar existed at the time. In terms of methodology, she took a phenomenological approach, focusing on the lived experience of the subjects, and excluding cultural and other biases of the researcher and reader.

Six hybrids participated, all North American women. They had responded to adverts in UFO newsletters and journals, a website call for subjects, and flyers and an announcement at two UFO conferences. The requirements were that they be over 18 years of age, believe themselves to be an 'alien-human hybrid,' and be willing to tell their story. Respondents were asked to complete a screening questionnaire, and six were chosen, based on their coherence, sincerity and credibility. Their anonymous responses were given a section each, followed by a summary of findings and a discussion.

The study was guided by two central questions. Firstly, how did the subjects come to believe they were hybrids? And secondly, how has that affected the way they think, feel, and live their lives? These were broken down into ten questions:

1. How did they come to know this (at what age and under what circumstances)?
2. With whom have they shared the information?
3. What has been the response of others?
4. How has it affected their worldview, their cosmological beliefs?
5. What influence has it had on their feelings about the human race, this planetary environment, their family of origin, their religious and political views?
6. Has it changed their career path, their choice of mate, their circle of friends?
7. How has it altered their thoughts of having children or how they think about the children they have and how they parent them?
8. Do they know other hybrids?
9. How often and in what format do they interact with their ET parent?
10. How do they assimilate and make sense of their belief that such an incredible, extraordinary thing is true of them?

The resulting study is not just recommended, but mandatory reading. It offers many insights, from the daily lives of these people to the future of life on Earth. Quiros' neutral perspective elicits a rich data resource that created the first true baseline study of hybrids living on Earth. The hybrids themselves saw the work as a contribution towards human evolution, through the expansion of human consciousness. The discussion is a highly astute, intelligent analysis, evidently the product of deep reflection. Without giving away our findings up front, they are remarkably similar to those of Quiros in terms of the journeys, missions, values, thoughts and experiences of the participants. The only major difference is the fact that our group did not wish to be anonymous, though they shared the cautious attitude of the first group toward how they share their story and with whom.

To a lesser degree, other researchers have written on the subject.

The late John E. Mack, M.D., a professor of psychiatry at the Harvard Medical School, explores 'experiencer' experiences of the hybrid program in his 1999 book *Passport to the Cosmos - Human Transformation and Alien Encounters*. In this study he struggles to determine the extent to which it may be a conventionally material phenomenon. His conclusion tends toward seeing it in the context of the ecological crisis which the ETs were at pains to impress upon experiencers. Critically, Mack says that he found no psychological explanation for the 'reproductive narrative' suggestive of deception or fantasy.

He discusses the views of some who believe they have contributed to the hybrid program. Jim Sparks and 'Andrea' believe that the hybrids are a backup plan in case humans destroy themselves, while 'Nona' sees them as a less emotional, more intelligent race that will not destroy themselves and their home in the first place.

Mack lays out the basic components of the program: 1) reproductive material is taken, 2) an embryo is implanted and pregnancy is experienced, 3) the fetus is removed, 4) the woman, or occasionally man, is presented with a being which appears to be half-human and half-ET, which the women are commonly urged to hold, feed and energize.

In his view, if the program was material, its characteristics could give rise to a dark 'colonization' interpretation such as Jacobs', but if it is metaphysical or interdimensional, it could be seen as a vehicle for spiritual evolution. He cites some of the women involved in the hybrid program, who have an ambiguous view of the reality of the phenomenon. Throughout his discussion of the subject, Mack is clearly torn between interpretations. On the one hand there is no material proof, yet on the other, he states that the level of intensity and detail in the recounting suggested that it was just as they described.

For all his ambivalence, Mack compiles a fascinating body of information. He looks at the problems of health and emotion in the hybrids, the efforts to create viable bodies with emotionality. He then discusses the successful integration of both alien and human components, in particular the case of a seven-year-old boy called Kiran. Andrea, his mother, said he "is going to live and be beautiful and be extremely gifted and have a sense of himself."

Taking the two together, one can sympathize with Mack's difficulty in accounting for such material and spiritual perfection arising from the preceding section on genetic and emotional missteps. In his end of chapter discussion, he cites 'Isabel,' who herself is uncertain on where to place the various actors on the spectrum between spirit and matter. She suggests that humans are both spirit and matter, but identify far more with the material. The ETs, by contrast, are more spirit than matter. The hybrid children are more material than the ETs as they need physical connection and the nourishment of breast milk. Even the nature of the sexual activity gives a sense to both men and women that there is something less material than we are used to at work. This includes the nature of the sex organs, orgasm and conception. Our research has revealed similar experiences.

The mentally and spiritually expanding nature of the experiences caused Mack to think of the whole enterprise as "an outreach program from the cosmos to the spiritually impaired." By contrast, Budd Hopkins saw the opposite. He saw the ETs coming here to absorb what they could of our humanity: our love, caring, sensuality and humor.

This distinction in viewpoints is vital as we move forward in this book. Contrasting the resources humans possess with those of the ETs may give us insights into what this union is about, and what it can do for both sides if we are open to it.

This is not to ignore the shadow side of the phenomenon. Firstly, this relates to the accompanying trauma for some experiencers, and the potential for a malevolent streak in, or purpose behind, some aspects of the enterprise. Secondly, there may indeed be an alternate program aimed at supplanting human beings as the dominant intelligence on this planet.

Galactic Diplomacy - Getting to Yes with ET by Michael Salla (2013) presents a guide to establishing diplomatic relations with ETs, particularly via 'track two' citizen diplomacy. It gives only two brief paragraphs to the hybrid subject and refers only to David Jacobs' viewpoint.

For a book on diplomacy it is surprisingly undiplomatic. Salla divides the races he discusses into two largely discrete camps: good and bad. The good guys are covered in chapter four, 'First Contact: the Galactic Community Introduces Itself to Humanity.' These ten races are, or hail from, Alpha Centaurians, Lyra, Vega, Pleiadians, Procyon, Tau Cetians, Andromedans, Sirians from Sirius A, Ummites and Arcturians. The next chapter, 'Extraterrestrial Races Cooperating with the Military-Industrial Complex,' covers seven races: Greys, Tall Greys/Whites, Praying Mantis, Reptilians, Draconians, Sirians from Sirius B and the Anunnaki. Contrast this, if you will, with the testimony relating to these races in Part II of this book.

Taken - Inside the Alien-Human Abduction Agenda by Karla Turner (1994) surveys eight women on their experiences of abduction. It makes a brief reference to 'baby presentations' connected to the abductees' involvement, but is not a detailed work relating to hybrids.

Raechel's Eyes, books 1 and 2 by Helen Littrell and Jean Bilodeaux, explore the experience of Marisa, a woman who roomed with Raechel, whom Marisa believed to be a hybrid. Raechel had significantly different habits of talking, walking, eating, and always wore black wraparound sunglasses. In Book I it is revealed that Raechel was not fully human, had been rescued from a crashed UFO and was half-human and half-Zeta extraterrestrial. A U.S. Air Force colonel had rescued her, then adopted her as his daughter and tried to integrate her into human society. He was part of a secret Humanization Project that combined extraterrestrial reproductive material and DNA with human eggs, and gestated them either on a ship or in a human mother's womb. The project, a collaboration between humans and ETs, was set up to create hybrids and see how well they could function in human society.

Book II is an unravelling, through hypnotic regressions, of further information about the project. Details emerge concerning the roles and identities of the women involved in the project, and the genetic manipulation that took place.

The written study of the hybrid phenomenon is still in its early stages, but what have we learned so far? Through regression work and personal testimony we have discovered many things about the methodologies of the various programs, and how they affect those involved in them, whether willingly or otherwise.

The products of this activity, the hybrids themselves, have been given the opportunity to share their reality, initially with a view to helping the fields of psychiatry and therapy accommodate those who are awakening to their nature.

Contrasting the work of Jacobs and Quiros, there is an apparent gulf between them. One discusses the hybrids as a threat to human sovereignty, yet the other hears about them helping "increase human consciousness of extraterrestrial existence, and of the potential for evolutionary advancement built into the human race."

Are they talking about different hybrid programs? Salla's work gives us another clue. At first it seems that he casts many of the races heard about in this book as villains, however it has emerged in our work that there are sometimes many varieties of the 'same' race. Some of them are active here in service to self, rather than service to others. Does that make some of them evil? 'Good' and 'bad' are, in general, relative terms.

So it may be that all the researchers are right, in terms of the conclusions they have drawn with regard to ET agendas.

Mack was challenged to determine the extent to which the reported phenomena were material or metaphysical. As you will see, this question applies in the experiences of the hybrids themselves. They are all at different stages of their journey, and each has more to learn about their own nature and their expanded reality. No one has a complete picture of this subject yet, but for those of us called to reveal more of it, we all contribute our piece.

The work that has gone before depicts an array of beings coming here for various purposes, most of which seem to involve tailoring life on planet Earth, much as humans have done for millennia, either actively or passively. And, just as we have, they are creating hybrids, blending various physical, behavioural and even spiritual traits.

This scenario throws up a mass of questions, which eight hybrids have been brave and dedicated enough to help us answer. We are also grateful to those who have paved the way for this study, which we trust will contribute significantly to this important field. We can say with confidence that what follows gives a voice to ET-human hybrids in a deeper and more extensive way than ever before.

Part II – From the Inside

Introduction

We now find ourselves in the heart of this book, in which the hybrids share their experiences, and the understandings that come from them. In seeking to understand their reality from the inside, we endeavored to create a mix of questions that explore both the physical and metaphysical aspects of their lived experience. We wished to understand: how they know they are hybrids; how they and others deal with it; how their human and ET aspects operate and co-exist; how they connect with their guides and star family; why the hybrid phenomenon is happening; what they are here to do; how they connect with one another; if they are safe here; and what we can learn from them.

Given that, as we have seen, the hybrid subject is treated with some suspicion—due in part to the idea of hybrids being a kind of Trojan Horse for an ET takeover of the Earth—we have asked them for their thoughts on the matter. As ever, the answers are unexpected and illuminating.

Let us say a few words about our methodology. Each of the eight hybrids has their own chapter, built from the transcripts of the interviews, which generally ran to around eight to ten hours, over three to four sessions. This was supplemented by many hours of further conversation and dozens of emails and texts.

We asked a series of around thirty standard questions, but introduced some spontaneously in response to the information being shared at the time. When we have done so, unless they are of particular significance they have been folded into the continuing response of the hybrid to improve flow. Otherwise they are marked in italics with a line break.

The questions themselves were modified as our understanding developed. It became apparent that a central narrative was taking shape, revealing a process which they, and all of us, are involved in. Thus we came to focus on the purpose and methods of the hybrid program, and the missions, messages and services of the hybrids within that.

Some questions are almost an opportunistic indulgence, given that as time went on it became increasingly apparent that they could give us new perspectives on almost any aspect of reality. And given our shared appetite for understanding the big picture, it was irresistible to pick their brains on opaque, tantalizing subjects like the nature of God, and the journey of the soul.

There was no obligation to answer every question, and it became clear that each hybrid has their own focus in terms of their journey, so we have gone with that, allowing them to bring out the richness of their experience and understanding relating to certain areas, for example their healing work or their own hybrid children.

Often in answering one question, they would flow into answering another, so the structure is likewise fluid.

What has made it onto the page is close to verbatim, but some work has been done to turn the natural messiness of speech into clear passages. The hybrids have also been given the opportunity to edit their own text in order to express their ideas and experiences as clearly as possible. The focus is always on hearing their voice, and representing them faithfully. While it would have been wonderful to truly capture the dynamics of the lively, funny, often moving exchanges that we enjoyed with them, priority must be given to clarity.

In the edits sent back by the hybrids, they would—for reasons of honoring and emphasizing—commonly capitalize words of their choosing, such as Star Being, Star Family, Love, Light, Soul, Hybrid, Experiencer and so on. However, in editing the work for readers, the decision was made to drop capitalization wherever reasonable in favor of readability, taking as read that we honor these groups and phenomena, and that they are emphasized by the book as a whole. There are so many uses of these words that the text would become too visually noisy with capitals. However we have capitalized Ascension, taking 'the Enlightenment' as precedent, and the 'names' of each race.

The chapters are presented simply in alphabetical order, by surname.

Few readers will understand everything on the first reading. The material tends to come into focus through experience, which is why it is so important to work with it practically. The interviews feature box texts where practices have been shared, and in Part III, in the Ascension chapter, we have drawn out further practices and concepts that can be applied in one's own life.

Given that there is a wealth of jargon operating in this field, we offer a brief glossary, with broad definitions relevant to this context. This does not agree with everyone's precise definition as there can be fine distinctions, but it should be a useful introduction for those new to the subject.

Glossary

3D, 5D	Pertaining to the third or fifth dimensions
Ascension	A process of physical, emotional and spiritual evolution
Akashic record	A metaphysical database of everything; this can be accessed by beings to see all previous incarnations, and can show past, present and future
Come in	Incarnate
Dimension	A realm of existence
Download	To receive information psychically
	Information received psychically
Frequency	A rate of vibration
	A measure of energy
	A unique pattern/identifier for each soul
Guide	A being who helps other beings, often through psychic means
Hybrid	A being which has been genetically altered to be more than one species
Light worker	A being actively working to raise consciousness
Mission	A duty that a being is working to fulfil within the current incarnation
Power	To come into one's power: developing/activating personal capacities
	Ability to complete a certain task
	Ability to prevent others blocking one's activity

Soul agreement	A pre-incarnation agreement made at the soul level to perform a certain role in the next incarnation
Star family	A being's familial relations from realms beyond Earth
Starseed	A soul originating from outside Earth which has incarnated into a form for a specific mission on Earth. This form can be human, animal or other being

Tatiana Amore

Tatiana is a 33-year-old Brazilian-Spanish woman living in Southern England.

How did you learn you are a hybrid?

A few weeks before meeting Charmaine and her mother for the second time, I saw a being in my bedroom. I thought he was a guardian angel. He was a little over two meters tall, with short blond hair, bigger than usual blue eyes and slightly pointy ears. I didn't think about those things before. At the workshop where Charmaine and I met, she and I were discussing spirituality and I told her about the being I saw. She started talking about beings not from this planet, and about her childhood, things that happened to her, and how she always felt different, and I related to that. So I started to wonder and began reading about these things. Then she mentioned your project, and put me in touch with you, and you connected me to Matt, Cynthia and Jacquelin.

    It was when I spoke to Matt that things really started to happen. I told him about the being that had come to me and he said it sounded like a Pleiadian, and when I did a Google image search the picture I saw was exactly the same as the being I saw in my room.

    When I went to do my next kinesiology session after that, I took my usual approach. I don't ask anything, I just ask the woman to tell me what my body is telling her. In the previous few months, my body was telling her that there was something about me that I need to find out about. We were both puzzled because I had no idea what it could be. But in that session my body was saying that I had now found out what I needed to discover about myself. She asked me if anything significant had happened since the last session, so I told her the whole story about speaking with Charmaine, and her suggestion that I might be a hybrid. She did the muscle testing to ask if I am a hybrid, and my body said yes I am, and that I have more than 50% non-human DNA.

Once we found out, I asked, "Why do I need to know? Do I have to open up something, to communicate with them?" My body said yes, I need to investigate, to find out more about this, to find out more about *me*. She suggested that we do muscle testing while pointing to different things in a book she had, to see how to open a channel with them. We got to a page on mandalas and my body said to do that, to start creating and using them in order to strengthen the connection.

So I started creating mandalas, and started feeling the beings who had visited me coming into my bedroom again. And I had a sensation like my body was spinning very fast, or my soul was spinning. I always close and lock my widows at night because it gets cold, and on two occasions after starting to create the mandalas, in the morning I found my windows were wide open. On one occasion my boyfriend witnessed that, and was as surprised as I was.

Mostly things happened during sleep time.

After I spoke to Charmaine I had an episode where I was half asleep in bed, and went into a tube of white light. It ran horizontal then straight up, and as I was going up the doorbell rang downstairs and I came out of it. In the regression with Barbara I went back to this, and I felt my body spinning. When I was taken up, the tube was transparent, and I could see the Earth, and that I was being taken up into a ship. On the ship I saw the man I'd seen in my room, and a woman, and later, from his clothes, a man who seemed to be a captain. I could sense other people around. I was taken to a kind of chamber, and I transformed somehow to wear the same clothes as them. They were showing me that I was one of them.

After this I had an experience while I was on vacation with a friend on the Spanish island of Formentera. I'd been studying these things and looking at Pleiadians and other beings. I was going to a kind of hippy market, and before I entered it, I mentally asked the beings to show me something that would help me to strengthen the connection with them. I had a feeling something was going to happen, and when I was walking around I became drawn to a tent selling jewelry. Inside I saw a guy behind a stall and for some reason I couldn't stop looking at him. He was selling crystals and things, and I went over to look at them. He started telling me about their properties, and my friend asked where he was from. He said Sirius, and that his name was Siri. He asked me my name, and when

I told him Tatiana, he said, "No, your *real* name." I said I didn't know what he meant and he said that I just hadn't been given it yet. Then he asked if I'm from the Pleiades. I was shocked. I asked him how he knew these things and he said he was constantly connected to his people and they told him telepathically that I was Pleiadian. That was a big confirmation for me, especially with the information in the regression. So I arranged to meet up with him the next day to find out more. He was telling me about meditating to help connect to my people. He said it's all telepathic and the more you meditate and be silent, the more you'll be able to communicate that way. In the experiences I've had with them they don't move their mouths, it's all telepathic. He said don't force it, allow it to happen naturally.

What is your ET component?

The main connection is Pleiadian. However, when I did my Star Origin Reading with Jacquelin, she took me back to my first incarnation, and I started as a race without a name we would recognize. They look like dolphins, and are not really from a star. She used the term 'ether.' When my soul was first incarnated it was into that kind of being. Somehow I ended up in the Pleiades, and these were the ones I saw in the regression.

How were you created?

I really don't know at this point. But I had many experiences with sleep paralysis throughout my life, where I couldn't see, but I could hear and feel people around me, and it felt like they were scanning my body or something. I could feel something hovering over me, like an energy field. I don't know if they were checking something. On one occasion I felt a strong pressure on my chest, and my body being pushed down into the mattress. I could hear people in the room, and feel the mattress depressed as though someone was sitting there. I don't know if that was spiritual or if that was them, physically. I had wondered that all my life.

It happened many times but I never got used to it, I just had a panicky feeling because I couldn't move or scream. I didn't feel they were doing anything bad to me, but it made me panic. I couldn't hear them talking, and I couldn't hear anything telepathic. Maybe I was so scared that my mind shut down. I always had a feeling that whoever was there didn't want me to know why they were there or what they were doing and why.

Barbara: That sounds very similar to many reported experiences. Apparently there are many reasons for them doing that. One is that they don't want to worry the person or unduly scare them, but they are dedicated to doing whatever they came to do. Following those experiences, did you feel any changes in the days after? For example, did you feel more intuitive, or have energy coming from your hands?

I've noticed different things actually. Afterwards I feel more intuitive, more sensitive. Physically, I have had some different sensations around my bladder, and what felt like my ovaries. On one occasion the palms of my hands felt like they were on fire, and a friend said I should use them for healing. It wasn't painful but the heat was so strong that I was blowing on them to cool them.

Barbara: They could have been upgrading or enhancing you with other abilities, like healing. The Pleiadians are considered highly advanced and benevolent, and seem to care in a very positive way about humans. Generally speaking they are known as wanting to be in good relationship with humans, and if anything to upgrade us in terms of our consciousness, and develop our telepathy, psychic abilities and so on. You may not have previously connected that with them being there. It's latent within most of us, and they may have been activating that within you.

In the past two years my psychic abilities have been getting stronger. I'm at a very different level with intuition, psychic abilities and my dreams. I've had a lot more of those sleep paralysis experiences in the past two years. I had a strong feeling in the past year or so that something was coming up, that it was my time to do something. My kinesiology sessions were telling me that something was coming. Now I no longer have that. It now feels like it's happening. My body is covered in goosebumps just talking about it.

What connection do you retain with your star family?

Barbara: Have these beings visited you recently?

In that way, I don't think so. But when I meditate now, I get very deep, and have started receiving little telepathic messages.

Barbara: It sounds like you're channeling them, and that could be at a significant distance. Distance doesn't seem to matter at all when they're sending information, they don't have to visit you. It could be that you're transitioning from visits and perhaps enhancements, through meditation, to the point where they can do this telepathically rather than having to do it physically.

It feels like a constant connection, like I only need to focus. I can tune in, sometimes when my mind is relaxed, like while washing the dishes. I receive some thoughts in my head that I know are not mine.

Barbara: Are you connecting these messages/communications with those beings?
Definitely. I know when it's me or them, from the language. It's always encouraging, positive. If I ask something I'm worried about, they come back with very positive messages—more positive than I am generally.

Barbara: Do you take them in?
Yes, because it feels very true. It comes in very deeply, it feels very truthful for me.
Barbara: It seems they're very aware of you, the issues you're concerned about; it sounds like they're good guides.

Miguel: How do you perceive them? Are there particular words, or more a feeling of an idea?
I was talking with my boyfriend, about ideas for our vacation to Spain. Something in my mind said, "Ask him about going to Granada," so I did. He stopped in the street and said he was just about to ask me that. So yes, there are specific words. Those little things have been happening for a while.

How do you reconcile the multiple aspects of your identity?

I always felt different since childhood, but now I feel like I relate more to the idea of that, and feel that it will help in my career, which is in clinical psychology and neuroscience. I won't be telling people about that, but it feels sufficient that I'm in agreement with the star beings, and that I'm doing what I'm supposed to do, in accordance with what I was trained to do before I came here. There's nothing in me saying, 'People have to know.' I will be doing my mission, and won't be telling people unless they're interested. It feels like I found out who I am, like I have remembered who I am and why I'm here. I always felt different, not like other children. I felt like I didn't like being human, or didn't feel human, but now that conflict has gone. I used to feel anger and hatred towards humans for all the destruction and bad things in the world, but I no longer feel that. I feel complete.
Barbara: You saw flaws and dysfunctions before, but now see how to help with that.

Humans destroy because of what goes on in their brains, how their minds work, how they think, so I will work towards helping them with that. In my regression I was hearing that I was on the right path with my studies. That has made a lot of difference to me now.

Do you have a sense of mission?

I had a confusion in me as a child, wondering what I am supposed to be doing, because I knew I was going to be doing something important. I always had certain people being very attracted to me, particularly disabled and special needs kids. I was like a magnet for them. I always had a feeling I was going to help people mentally. In teenage years those things went away for a while. Perhaps I suppressed that, but later I knew I'd do something to do with mental health. Like subconsciously I knew more when I was a child than when I grew up, but I was very sensitive to this as a child.

Are you encouraged by guides?

I always felt looked after, and I've had some protection. There were times when I should have been badly injured or killed. At age nine I was hit by a car and flew about 10-15 meters, but I had no broken bones or even major bruises.

At 18 I had a big accident. I was coming fast down a steep road on my mountain bike when a car came around the corner. I had no time to brake and could only go left, down the side of the mountain and onto the road below. So I threw myself sideways, and I recall nothing until I landed on the road below. I lost a lot of blood and some skin, but when I stood up, I had not one broken bone, no head injury.

A couple of years later, I was going to go out on the back of my ex-boyfriend's motorbike, and an hour before I said I had a feeling we were going to crash. He laughed and said, "You and your feelings!" As we were riding, a guy on a bicycle crossed in front of us and my boyfriend hit him. It was a terrible crash, but I felt something lift me over my boyfriend and I floated through the air and was placed gently on the curb. The cyclist unfortunately died, and my boyfriend nearly had his leg amputated, but I didn't have a scratch. I had not a single scratch or bruise. I felt like I was floated gently through the air, and found myself sat on the curb.

I stopped talking about this, as people just said, "You're lying, that's crazy." So I kept it to myself.

Do you have special abilities?

As a child my mother used to bring dying plants or flowers to me, as she said I gave them new life. So I'd talk to them and caress them as if they were people. She would bring them to me when they were nearly dead, and I would prolong their life. Jacquelin told me in the Star Origin Reading that as a dolphin being I used to make "a world made of flowers." I love flowers, I always have to stop and look at them in the street, but I don't like them being picked—I hate to see them being killed.

If I give people a massage or talk to them when they have problems they say they feel so much better. That's part of why I thought about the field of study I am now entering. People just feel comfortable opening up with me about their problems. I think it's more about talking; I don't really go around massaging my friends, but through talking they feel a lot better.

Are you aware of coming Earth changes?

I understand the Earth is now changing to a new frequency which is meant to be lighter and better for humans.

What is your take on the takeover thesis?

I find that an exaggeration. They have their motives, but that attention is not necessary. In Barbara Marciniak's book *The Bringers of the Dawn: Teachings from the Pleiadians*, she explained that we have to do things to help the world. My feeling is that as long as we keep doing our part, we don't need to focus on the negative stuff. Fearing the Reptilians is not necessary.

How do you feel about the global hybrid community?

It's a nice idea to have a community like that, to join everyone. The point for the beings is for us all to be together as one family. I just wish there wasn't so much worry and focus on what the Reptilians are doing. The Pleiadians call them "the Lizzies." David Icke's work is interesting, but it doesn't resonate with me. It's too exaggerated for me.

Barbara: The people Miguel and I are working with are so much of the light. They are very upgraded in consciousness, very spiritually aware and benevolent. And they are the group we are focusing on. They are wonderful people with benevolent missions. The hybrid community that we are interested in are here to help humanity with Ascension, with spirituality and consciousness. Completely to do good. We haven't focused on the negative types.

What would you most like to discuss with other hybrids?

It was very positive to find out things from Charmaine, but I was scared by the whole Reptilian thing, the conspiracy stuff involving those who are trying to keep everyone under control. I didn't want to know more about that. But Matt calmed me down; he told me about the Pleiadians, and that resonated with me strongly. That instantly attracted me, it felt like it was more 'me.' And with Jacquelin it was very positive and enjoyable doing the Star Origin Reading. I liked it. I feel a lot more secure now. I don't feel I'm going to be depressed about the Lizzie story.

Barbara. I don't know how true it is but in some ways it represents the self-serving aspect of humans. I know there is a variety of species, some are very nice and helpful, but I do hear about the other ones. I don't know how much is sensationalism and hype. One thing that is clear about humans, is that we love drama, particularly negative drama. Some of the nicest people I know love horror, reading and writing about conflict, drama, trouble. I think there are so many people addicted to that. Given that, it makes sense that people would put a lot of attention onto negative Reptilians seeking power and control. But even within Reptilians, there are species which are truly benevolent and don't do the other stuff. I really like your idea that you know who you are and are going ahead with your mission, and will do so even more.

Yes, I don't go for the sensational stuff, it doesn't attract me.

What are the best and worst things about being a hybrid?

The conflict I always had inside me is no longer there. This has opened a new world to me. The best thing is knowing that I can help, that I have a natural mission and I'm going to do it.

As for the worst thing, I don't see anything particularly negative in it yet. But I have learned that when a hybrid baby is born it can be difficult for them, with allergies etcetera. Adjusting to living in a real body as a human on Earth is not easy.

I didn't like always feeling different, but during those times I felt I was right. If there was bullying going on I would defend them, even if others turned against me because of it. I didn't like it, but I felt happy that I was doing the right thing.

Barbara. It sounds as though you had a strong ego. Not in terms of being egotistical, but in terms of having a strong sense of self.

I knew I was doing the right thing. I would never just go with the flow if something felt wrong.

Cynthia Crawford

Cynthia is a 66-year-old American woman living in Arizona. Her human ancestry is German and Jewish.

What is your definition of a hybrid?

One whose DNA comes from two or more planetary races. This is done either through sexual intercourse, insemination or genetic alteration of the fetus in the mother's womb.

What is the definition of a starseed hybrid?

A starseed hybrid is when the soul aspect of a hybrid incarnates into a human body in order to perform a particular mission requiring the best qualities of the various races.

How did you learn you are a hybrid?

My father told me when I was 34. At the time, the only reason I believed him was that my twin sister and I were so different; I even had different blood and tissue types from her and the rest of my family.

How were you created?

My father had served two years in combat during WWII. In 1958, while training to be a doctor in med school, he was approached by a man from the OSS (which later became the CIA), and offered a top secret mission in the Army that his family was not allowed to know about. In the first part of the mission, he was asked to participate in a 'hybrid project.' This required my mother to be drugged and impregnated with a hybrid embryo without her knowledge. My creation required the combination of my mother's egg, my father's sperm and two types of alien DNA.

The second part of the mission required my father to serve in Korea, working with alien technology found on a downed medical UFO. This secret program to create a superhuman race originated when the U.S. government brought German scientists over during Project Paperclip in the aftermath of WWII. The scientists had been creating hybrids and doing cloning for many years prior, and we offered them asylum in exchange for access to their secret programs. Much of this information was given to me by my father after his passing while reading the book *In League With a UFO*, and confirmed during a regression with Dr. Leo Sprinkle in 2000.

What is your ET component?

I am 38% Anunnaki, 34% human and 28% Zeta. The Anunnaki were a race of very tall humanoid beings who were known to integrate with various races in order to maintain control of the universe. The best reference book on the Anunnaki is called *Anunnaki Encyclopedia*, by Maximillien de Lafayette. It contains decades of researched information from documents, scrolls and ancient Arabic, pre-Islamic writings. Although originally written for the government, his books later became available to the public. The two most common Anunnaki hybrid races brought to Earth were hybridized with the Lion People and a race of Reptilians. Sekhmet, known as the daughter of Ra, was on Earth during the 12th Dynasty. She was of the Lion People tribe, half-human and half-Lion. Conflicting research says she was a ruler over her own people somewhere in ancient Egypt, while others say she was the protector of the pharaohs and led them into warfare.

What do you understand to be the purpose of your creation?

The secret hybrid program, which has since been taken over by the NSA, was originally intended to create superhuman hybrids that would perform tasks humans would not normally be able to do. However, in early 2003 my guides explained that my soul had agreed to come into a hybrid body in order to assist starseeds to fully awaken to their true mission on Earth. By 2005, I was making sculptures of benevolent beings that would carry an aspect of the soul of that being to assist the starseeds in what they needed most.

Do you have your own hybrid children?

I have two Earth children, the oldest a daughter who doesn't embrace my beliefs, and a son who is more hybrid than myself because I was impregnated with him on a ship. I've also got other children who were removed as fetuses during early gestation, and dozens of children created from eggs which were taken from me prior to having my ovaries removed in 1990.

Do you have physiological differences to humans?

My muscle tissues have always been more dense than human muscles, my bones are more porous than normal human bones, and I have an unusual blood antigen that prevents me having blood transfusions. Then, in 1994 while having corrective surgery following an accident, I was found to have my intestines and colon growing in the opposite direction of humans. My lungs have always been weak, and when I was 29 they were collapsing from pneumonia. I thought I was going to die, but I awoke the next morning completely healed. In 2004, I learned from my human-looking star family in the Galactic Federation that my healings were done by the Nebulan Healers, and also entailed being taken to Archangel Michael's medical mothership. Other healings I've experienced came from the assistance of my guides instructing me on using natural herbal remedies. One such remedy completely reversed my heart disease, and by my mid-50s, a cardiac catheterization revealed my heart to be equivalent to that of a 30-year-old.

All hybrids have clones so that if there are complications, body parts can be replaced as needed in order that we complete our missions. I had my entire vascular system replaced when I was 18 years old after attempting suicide by taking an overdose of aspirin. The vessels had dissolved and I was hemorrhaging internally, finally passing out when my body became cold. I woke up the next day completely healed.

Do you ever fear you won't complete your mission on Earth?

No, I'm too protected, as are many of us starseeds. There have been numerous attempts by the secret government and NSA to take me out, but every time I'm either shielded, protected or healed and brought back to life.

The only time a hybrid or starseed is allowed to die is when their mission is completed or they are needed to serve elsewhere. For example, a friend of mine was the captain of a mothership, and every night left his body to take command of his ship during his human body's sleep hours. At 58 years old he died unexpectedly of natural causes, but when his sister called to tell me, he communicated with her through me from his mothership, where he had taken full-time command. I've known several people who've crossed over to be back on their Galactic Federation ships, or ships of their star origin. Another friend was a woman on dialysis, and when she crossed over she came to see me and said, "My God, you ought to see my body *now!*" She looked to be in her late 20s. She is now working with the Federation on strategies, and filling them in on what's happening on Earth politically and all the major challenges humanity is going through.

Do you have a sense of mission?

I am mainly here for the starseeds, assisting them in any way they need in order to fully awaken and come into their true powers. Just as it takes humans thousands of lifetimes to experience all the lessons in the third dimension, our souls will likewise experience many thousands of lifetimes on different levels of mastery. According to my star family and guides, this is the last incarnation for humans working on their Ascension from the third dimension to the fifth to start on a new program of becoming Masters.

There are millions of starseeds assisting humanity at this time, and all were selected from masses of volunteers because they had already proven themselves worthy to complete their missions. Earth is not the only third-dimensional planet in the universe, but being human is one of the most challenging of all races. Humanity has failed many attempts at Ascension because they are so focused on the material world—on greed, power, control and karmic payback. There is no helping humanity until first, they realize that the material world is an illusion, and second, they get out of their heads and into their hearts.

Until humanity learns how to live in the 'Christ Consciousness' they are trapped on this prison planet. The simple meaning of Christ Consciousness is to live without fear, greed, judgment or prejudice by looking beyond the physical container to recognize the Source in every living being. It's that simple.

Why do you think hybrids are on Earth?

My guides explained it quite simply: humans have been brainwashed into believing through religion and ideology that humans are the only beings in the universe, and in order for humanity to awaken to their truth, they must release their judgments and prejudices. Therefore, many of the hybrids have chosen to be able to shapeshift between human and other races as needed, so that humans will realize they are not their bodies but their *souls*.

Humans need to understand that every soul is nothing less than a Source-self. To understand this, we must realize that what humans call 'God' or 'Creator' or 'All That Is,' the star people call 'Source.' So from the beginning, the Source *was* all and *knew* all. But the Source wanted to know what it was to come from nothingness to become All That Is, so Source made Source-selves, each an aspect of itself. Therefore, the Source lives vicariously through each and every aspect of its Source-selves. Each Source-self experiences numerous lifetimes as various beings, and between each lifetime, the soul gets to reflect on what it has learned. This is where our Akashic records come in, but we are not shown them until we are nearing the end of each lifetime and/or mission.

How can a person determine if they are a starseed?

Starseeds typically feel as if they don't belong on Earth, and believe that they are here for a specific reason, that they have a mission. In addition, most starseeds have encounters with other star people as needed for healings, assistance, and remembering their agreed missions. People contact me to make sense of their experiences, to remember who they are and why they are here, to learn how to protect themselves, and especially how to activate their DNA to come into their true powers. These days, when such people contact me they have a feeling of urgency.

One example was a young man who had an experience in his early 20s after serving in Iraq. Upon completion of his military service, he and several military buddies were flown into Canada first, then driven the next day by bus into the United States. Since they hadn't been around women for a while, the first night they went to the hotel nightclub for some fun. He was dancing with a woman when his friends noticed he seemed to be talking to someone other than the woman, but they could see no one else. The guy then said he remembered, "Walking outside and seeing the moon on the ground." And the next thing he knows, he's waking up with blood on his shirt in an abandoned, boarded-up theater and he had no idea how he got in there. His life changed after that, and he became very spiritual, with a strong interest in taking care of Mother Earth.

So many people contact me to help them understand what's happened to them, which beings they are having contact with, what is their mission, and how to come into their power. My guides always tell me the first thing to do is to get people out of fear and into their heart, to remind them how to live in the Christ Consciousness, and the rest will fall into place. The hybrids and the starseeds are equally important, but their missions are a little different.

Indications someone may be a hybrid

A hybrid usually has an unusual blood type, and often physical differences. The mother usually has difficulty with the pregnancy. Often, hybrids have uncommon allergies, food cravings and health issues. Their organs may be a little different, or their eyes different in appearance, some having slits for pupils, or their skin is thicker or a different texture, and some even notice a different body odor. But people may also see them shapeshift or their eyes changing appearance.

Sculptures

I began making the sculptures in 2003, but didn't offer them for sale until 2005. The first few were from memories of being with a Zeta-human hybrid baby and human-looking beings from the Galactic Federation and the Sirian Warriors of Light. Then I began to go into trances, making beings I had no recollection of, such as the Andromedan race called the Buddic tribe of Andromeda, as well as a variety of Zeta races and the Salamander beings. By the second year, I began hearing telepathic voices directing me on how to make their features. By the third year, I was experiencing new benevolent beings that would either physically appear to me, or I would see them in the etheric realm, or sometimes in my third eye as if I was seeing them on a computer monitor. These beings were the Blue Arcturians, the Blue Lady from the Pleiades, the Mantis beings, Zuma Zeta, Ka-Tsa-Hyan, and the Tall White Zetas. A few years later, after being taken to various council meetings, I began making sculptures of the Masters, such as Sananda, Archangel Michael, Ashtar and Melchizedek of the Great White Brotherhood.

I had no idea that these sculptures had soul aspects channeled through me into them until three years later when I was talking at an experiencer meeting and several people began sharing their experiences with their sculptures. Most people reported their sculptures talking telepathically to them or moving their eyes or mouths. Some saw their sculpture shapeshift into a full-size being, then found themselves in a higher dimension, face to face with the beings. There was a guy in England who had gotten a Sirian Warrior of Light sculpture from me. After his first time meditating with it, he called me, shaken, and said, "I wasn't prepared to suddenly go into another dimension, so as I could feel it happening to me, I jumped up and put it in my bathroom, making sure the door was closed so it couldn't get out!"

While talking with him, his mother, who passed away in 1990, began communicating with me. She said she was on a starship and was waiting to see him again, and when he got the courage to meditate with the sculpture again he would be taken to the ship to meet with her. He had always felt guilty because she died in his arms, and he couldn't do anything to save her. She was no ordinary mother; she had incredible powers and he didn't like the way she could blow circuits and computers just by coming too close to them. So when he gave up his fear he went to the ship and had an incredible experience.

People have also used the sculptures for calling in ships and communicating. The soul of the sculpture, a particular being, has also been known to heal people or teach them how to heal themselves and others. They also activate the starseed's DNA, and help them remember their powers. I had one young man in Sweden send me a voicemail explaining how his girlfriend's Tall White Zeta sculpture taught him how to leave his body and enter the body of a deceased young man who needed to be healed and brought back to life. I've made thousands of sculptures and am always humbled to hear the experiences of so many starseeds with their sculpture(s). I am always thinking of new sculptures that need to be made, but as long as I can physically continue to make these precious beings, I will. This is what I'm here to do. I'm here to help any way that I can, but it is up to the starseed to let me know when they want my help.

Are you encouraged by guides?

I've had a deep male voice speaking telepathically in my head since I was in my late teens. It was not until I was in my early 50s that I was allowed to remember meeting with what I feel are my guides. One exception is the brown wrinkled ET with gold eyes that had slits, and that was the first one to materialize in front of me when I was 46 years old. In 2007, when I almost died from a flu virus attacking my heart, I found myself in the etheric realm sitting at a table on a white marbled platform surrounded by bright white light. These beings were of a variety of races, but most were human-looking. I remember recognizing them and weeping out of pure joy and love as I thanked them for coming to meet with me. The following night I tried again to go to the Council of my guides, but instead met just one person who looked very much like the religious Jesus Christ. I was upset, and I started to walk away from him, saying, "No, I'm not about to become religious." I was stopped as a male voice said, "Neither is he, for he is about unconditional love and working with the Light of Source. You know him as Sananda." Perhaps this is why I had the uncanny ability to draw him in pastels perfectly when I was 20 years old, as if I had known him personally. At that point, Sananda turned toward me and humbly bowed his head, saying to me, "I am no greater and no lesser than you." He then took my hand and we sat facing one another as we meditated together. Since this time, I have come to understand that my higher self is one of the Masters in the Great White Brotherhood.

Do you have special abilities?

I'm clairvoyant and can communicate telepathically. I have seen inside an unhealthy body to determine what was wrong, and have healed animals. I was telekinetic, able to move objects with my mind, until a serious accident caused some brain damage. I do know that as my DNA is activating I'm discovering more abilities.

What protocols govern ET interaction with humans?

We starseeds are here at this time to assist humanity by being examples, but not to do the work *for* them. Humans are in need of understanding their true connection to Source and the many star people, and learning how to activate their own powers as well as how to stand in their power against those of the dark side.

There are many programs and beliefs that have gotten spread around that are disinformation, and when starseeds are waking up they need to know how to discern truth. One misconception is about NESARA (National Economic Security and Reformation Act), where people were told that everyone would be given the same large amount of money so everyone would be equal. This is a way of making people believe they have no work to do and that we will all automatically be equal. Where's the lesson in that? This Ascension is not about monetary things, but about the soul learning lessons, giving up greed, prejudice, fear and judgment and seeing the Source/God in each and every being. To repeat: it's about getting out of the head and living in the heart. My guides once told me that my heart is the umbilical cord to the Source, and I'm not about to cut that cord.

How do you define 'Frequencies?'

All things are electrical energy, so frequency is movement of energy that can be felt or heard. The higher a pitch/sound is, the faster the movement; the lower the sound, the slower the movement.

What is your understanding of Ascension?

Ascension is when the soul has learned all the lessons from the thousands of lifetimes in the third dimension and has moved into the heart for resolution.

Humanity is in the middle of the Ascension process right now, of experiencing All That Is. It is in the third dimension, which they say is the hardest to get through, like being in high school. There are so many different ways you can go at being a human; you can be greedy or powerful, you can be poor or have a disease, or be disease free. So you have many opportunities to get through the third dimension; you have thousands of lifetimes, and that is what it takes to ascend to the next level, which is the fifth dimension.

The fourth dimension is where the soul looks back at the lessons from that lifetime, then they have to let go and be reborn until they've learnt it all. It is all in the fourth dimension that you get the demonic beings that love to harass humans. But it's the fifth dimension that humanity is moving into, and that is the dimension of integration, of acceptance and learning what it is to love unconditionally. And after you experience that, that is where you get your master's degree. You are already in school, learning to be a master, and then your soul's purpose is to help others understand their lessons and move forward.

On the motherships we have the most incredible celebrations when we've completed the mission of Ascension. We get to party down. It's not about being drunk and all that, it's about getting to dress up, meet one another and share, in like a huge ballroom. We get to do what makes us happy. Even those we had a hard time with, or didn't agree with in the way they assisted humans, we get to party with them without judgment. It's like the awards, looking at what we've accomplished.

Miguel: Do we have a choice to ascend? Is it part of the metabolism of existence in some way, or just a preference on behalf of a group of like-minded beings, which they then impose on other less developed beings, like cosmic missionaries?

The choice is in the humans' soul. There are those who enjoy being of the dark, for example. They like taking slaves, being greedy, and that keeps them trapped in a lower dimension, and that's their choice. When they get tired of it, which happens eventually, they can move forward. And when they get to the next level, it's like a big breakthrough, and they get to really enjoy it. But because of all the choices and temptations, that's why it has taken six different New Earths for many of the souls to ascend. And the archangels of the Light are saying enough is enough.

In this lifetime they finally created a fifth-dimensional Earth that will be perfect. Everyone lives equally, among all different races, and enjoys health and old age. The Masters will help those who have ascended. But if everything is perfect, how soon will it be that you need a challenge? Because it is the struggles that give us accomplishment. The fifth dimension will be like R&R, where we reap what we've sowed and live in pure ecstasy. But then there will come a time when, maybe after thousands of years, we'll want to be Masters and help those of lower dimensions reach where we are.

Earth agreed to be a school for third-dimensional humans. At the end of each cycle she cleanses herself, shakes off all the fleas and becomes this pristine planet. And then maybe the next school will learn faster, and not do what they did on Mars.

The Creator can create anything. It only allows the destruction as part of the lesson, but has the ability to create the most beautiful worlds. And therefore, it doesn't have to keep the destruction. Mars continues to be Mars in the third dimension, because in higher dimensions, Mars is flourishing, it is pristine. We are seeing it the way it appears because it is a representation of what will happen if we don't change our ways.

At some point you will have the experience of what it is to be the Creator, and you'll understand the need for this, because in reality if we were to go back, we would see we have created the physical world. Because it doesn't exist, it is a hologram, allowing us to experience. It is for Source, as it needed this in order to keep itself interested in continuing.

So it's nothing more or less than a cycle, and we can change that cycle; but we can't change it for others, only for ourselves. And when we understand that, we ascend to higher levels, because if we could take every soul and put them in a room and get them to understand what their greed and need for control is doing to the planet, they would change their ways. When I died I got to see the other side, all the pain and suffering this causes.

If you don't like what's happening in the world, then change the way you think and act, and you no longer have to live that way. The third dimension is all about acknowledging the change and becoming the change.

When the Masters get bored of helping humanity ascend, they want to go onto another challenge. Then you help the Masters teach others. So in order to help humanity we had to forget what we knew, in order to understand what inspires them, and understand the way they think, act and react.

At a point we become light beings, experience pure love, and no longer want the challenges, we just want to be, and experience nothing but love. And then, according to my understanding, each of us that has become light beings, when we become tired of that, and ready to become a Creator and create our own universe, we start over, and we are God, knowing all; it is a cycle.

As we're helping others to succeed, we're learning even more—I don't know where it ends. We would probably become nothingness if we came to the point where we no longer wanted to experience. It's all about the experience. If we no longer want to experience, then what are we? Can we really handle nothingness? Do we really want to handle just existence, and nothing else? I don't want to do that. Because I see what I have learned, I feel the achievement, I feel the gratitude in being able to experience. Perhaps in my next lifetime I will come to the same conclusion, or perhaps I will come to an even more powerful conclusion. So we can only trust in ourselves, trust in what we believe is our truth. We're not going to be satisfied if we give up our truth and just say, "You tell me what to believe, and I'll believe it." There is nothing to be learned by just letting other people do it for you.

When you look at it simply, you can say that it was the experience, and that may be your conclusion. You may look at your life and say, "How can I help others, what can I release that no longer serves me?" You want to be the highest you can be, like a plant opening its flower. You want to be the flower. But you must draw your own conclusion.

Have you had contact with the military or intelligence agencies?

When I was a toddler I remember being taken to underground medical facilities where I was tested for various abilities. But I flunked the test, by design of the Masters. I came forward in the late 1990s when I joined an experiencer group. But the best of my experiences were yet to come once I gave up fear of the unknown: those ET beings! That's when I had my first experience with a being materializing before me, after which I began having three to four visits per week. Eventually, I was targeted by the NSA and the 'men in black' as their satellites picked up the frequency of the ships, which they could see were coming regularly to my area. I soon became a target to take out or shut up. This is when the NSA began using remote viewers on numerous occasions to cause me to have a cardiac arrest, and on another occasion, they injected me in the back of the head with a serum that would cause an aneurysm. Yet in every case my star family either told me what to do, or they healed me. So we have to understand how to call on this protection.

Manifesting protection

Protection is one of the easiest abilities, but it is important to always believe in ourselves, our abilities. We do this simply by surrounding ourself with the Light of Source, and filling our hearts with unconditional love—first directing it to self, then to all others. The darker, more negative a person, the more it is important to share your love and Light with him or her. This puts protection around yourself while also increasing your power and diminishing the power of the dark over you. The more we use our love and Light, the more our DNA is activated.

How do you feel about the global hybrid community?

We hybrids are scattered throughout the world, working in all walks of life and affecting all those we come in contact with. It is all by design, and each of us chose where we need to be to help those people that need it the most. We are not here to create followers, but to teach others how to find their own truth. Each group of beings represented here on Earth have certain strengths and abilities which is why we integrate throughout the world. But there will be a time when the starseeds are finished assisting in this Ascension, and humanity will be forced to stand in their own power. After all, Ascension is all about humanity remembering how to live in their hearts and not their heads; it's about taking their power back through living in the Light with unconditional love.

What would you most like to discuss with other hybrids?

To identify what humanity needs most now, in order to be independent of us and complete their Ascension so we starseeds can return home. To discuss the most effective ways we can all work together in a timely manner.

What are the best and worst things about being a hybrid?

The best thing about being a hybrid is experiencing other abilities and understanding them. The worst is that we are often scrutinized and judged unfairly.

How can humanity best work with you?

The only effective way to work with humans is to first get them out of judgment and into their hearts.

How do you conceptualize 'God?'

A Creator entity of pure unconditional love and white Light that lives vicariously through its Source-selves (incarnated in various physical forms), without judgment and prejudices.

When my twin sister died at age 29, I went into a deep depression a month later, and stayed up most of the night reading the Bible to understand where she had gone. I felt deceived because I couldn't find an explicit answer in the Bible, so I begged God, even demanded by saying, "If God truly exists, then prove it and take me to be with my sister!"

That night I fell asleep out of sheer exhaustion, only to awaken in the middle of the night to a mysterious shadow that brought warmth in its presence. A voice came from it, saying, "You cannot leave now, but when it is your time I will be with all your loved ones to welcome you through the way. Fear not, for your time is near." This entity then enveloped me in the most divine love, as if I was a baby being held in a mother's arms. This is when I realized that God is truly my Creator, my father and my mother. Would it make sense, then, that our Creator, the Source, who is that soul spark of self we call our soul, would ever judge or punish us? No, for the Source is experiencing All That Is through every being it created. The Source loves its Source-selves unconditionally. This is another reason why we are told to first love ourselves unconditionally before we are capable of unconditionally loving others.

What is the most important lesson you've learned?

I was not able to read books by other people, I had to learn my own truth. When I was told to go public it was my star family that demanded it of me, in the late 1990s. I came forward in 1996 through a contactee group. I wanted to find out if there were other people like me. I was in my late 40s at the time, and I had heard on a radio station that there was going to be a MUFON group at a mall in central Phoenix. They were going to be interviewing people to find out how many people have contact with UFOs and aliens. MUFON used to do this. I was excited about talking about things I was usually told to shut up about.

When I first went to talk to Ruth Hover—who was the MUFON psychologist and hypnotherapist at the time—every time I approached her I would start crying uncontrollably, and I couldn't talk to her. I walked around the mall for about two hours until I finally got up the courage. I said, "I just want one of your cards, I'll call you sometime." And she could tell I'd been crying. There was just something in me that didn't want me to tell anyone who I was. And I realize now it had to do with the military implant which was put in the back of my head, which would cause me great pain if I started talking about it. She could see I was very disturbed, and insisted we go and sit down and talk about it. I told her that even as a child when I wanted to tell my parents ... my father was gone a lot because he was in Korea working on a top secret military project, and my mother was a very devout Christian. She always thought I had a great imagination and she suppressed anything to do with my abductions, and being taken to underground facilities and tested. When I was about three or four years old I'd tell her and she would say it was just a dream. So consequently I didn't open up until I was five years old and went to school. So it was extremely emotional for me to open up to Ruth, because I never had anyone who wanted to talk about it with me, and it was incredibly painful whenever I tried to talk about it. But when my willpower became stronger than the pain, I no longer had the pain. We probably talked for an hour, and I was very emotional because I'd had numerous pregnancies where the fetuses were taken when I was only a few months pregnant, so it was very painful remembering those things because at the time I didn't understand why this was happening. I was the victim instead of the victor, and saw everything from the victim's standpoint.

Afterwards, I felt a great relief as if a huge weight had been taken from my shoulders, from suppressing all these emotions, and all these experiences my whole life. She asked me to attend an experiencer group that she had just put together. She started this because there were so many people coming forward who'd had experiences beyond what even she understood. Because if you remember there were a lot of people coming forward in the 1980s writing books about their experiences, but there were no books that I knew of that were about being a hybrid, or why they were a hybrid, or why they had a special mission on Earth. So I started meeting people who had almost identical experiences of being on the ships and having hybrid children.

It was difficult to talk about my experiences at the beginning because I still saw myself as a victim, like they must be doing horrible things to me because they took my children. And secondly, the other problem was that I'd had a major accident in 1993 where I was struck by a car while I was crossing the street so I had difficulty talking, and my brain didn't function properly, so I couldn't speak complete sentences. I was more like on a fifth grade level. I had gone to the extreme of wanting my windows boarded up because again I felt like a victim. And everything they spoke about regarding alien contact was always so negative.

But within six months I was strong enough to demand conscious contact with the star people. After three weeks of begging, I found that the only way I could have conscious contact was to give up my anger and resentment relating to my experiences, and love them regardless, so that I could learn the truth. How can I define that truth?

When I first started having conscious contact, I experienced the unconditional love that I had been seeking all my life and had never found with humans. It was a love that was so powerful, so all-encompassing, that there is no other way to describe it. The being materialized beside my bed; he stood approximately five feet tall and had brown wrinkled skin, like elephant skin. And he had gold eyes, a very odd-shaped head that seemed to be large at the top, and dented in a little at the back, forming another little bump. The neck was very long and thin, as was his body. He had three fingers on each hand and three toes on each foot. At the end of his digits he had a suction cup. This was the first time that I consciously felt such extreme love that I felt like I was melting, it was so euphoric. And I asked him—I felt that it was a male—I said, "Can I hold your hand?" Because I wanted to know what they felt like. It was like the skin of a chimpanzee. It was almost rubbery, it's a different texture to human skin. When I held his hand my whole body vibrated with such intense love, and we exchanged love in our hearts. It lasted maybe five minutes. They can't be in a physical form for long because our frequency is so much lower than theirs that it becomes painful for them.

I did ask them about the missing pregnancies, but only years later, and by that time it didn't matter to me.

When I was younger I couldn't shut off my brain, it was always creating, even in my sleep. And all that was taken away from me when I had my accident, and I had to learn all over again. When I had the accident I only lost 10% of my brain, but what the doctors didn't realize is that my spine was tweaked and my brain wasn't getting enough oxygen. So my brain kept deteriorating until I was nearly a vegetable. I had to have physiotherapy to stretch my spine and allow oxygen to reach my brain properly. So I had to relearn many things; it was very challenging and humbling and there were times when I didn't want to live any more. People looked down on me instead of thinking, 'Wow, she's really gone through a lot and is really trying hard.' People would even say, thinking I couldn't understand, "Well, she's retarded."

So when I think about that I also understand it is challenge of learning, of becoming. This is how the Source lives vicariously through us, experiencing the joy of accomplishment. So it can experience it over and over again. It's like people who climb mountains; they say that when they get to the top it feels amazing, but soon they have to find something new to challenge them. Because it's the excitement of the challenge. That's the reason why the Source made selves. And each aspect of our individual soul experiences something different. Wouldn't you want to know what it is to live on other worlds, to experience everything from being the largest to the smallest of beings? We get to do this in many lifetimes, and once we go back to the Source, to being a light being, the only thing that light workers do, is they watch over others, and it's like being a teacher, assisting each student.

When you give up your fear and resentment and see them as being other aspects of the creator, then you no longer fear them, and you have compassion and want to understand them, and what keeps them going.

Some people say they only want to deal with the light, and that if God was so perfect, why would he create the devil? They want to separate God from the darkest of all, but we also have to understand that if we can have a dark side, would not the creator Source also have a dark side? What would be the point of judging, because judgment only keeps us from the experience. And when we get to that point of being able to embrace without judgment, that's the highest place you want to be. One lady, who only wants to experience the light, was appalled that I had experienced the dark. She was limiting herself through fear. Being willing to embrace the opposite doesn't mean you have to *become* the opposite in order to understand it. I once found myself outside, surrounded by five of the darkest beings that humans fear the most. I said jokingly, "Are you here to eat my face?" And the one being that was the speaker for all the others said, with an English accent, "Oh no, we're here to thank you. You see we can't wait for the Ascension to occur, because it takes the strongest of the light workers to hold the darkness long enough that the lessons are learned. And we're tired of being in that darkness, of holding that energy. But because we are very strong we agreed to do so."

It's all about the Ascension; every soul is working on their own Ascension. We are all God-selves experiencing All That Is, and when we stand in judgment we prevent ourselves from experiencing everything. For in reality, there is no such thing as death. It's only the release of the physical container, so that we can be born again to new lessons and adventures.

The Masters expected more of humanity's Ascension, that more of the humans would ascend, and they haven't. And there's a certain disappointment in it and confusion. And what have we—the starseeds that are here on Earth assisting them—not done correctly, that there are so many humans still living in greed, judgment and prejudice? Because they can't ascend while they're holding onto a material world that in reality doesn't even exist—it is only for our lessons. So to hear how many of the Masters were saddened it kind of reminds me of the day in 1997 when my guides told me the key to Ascension that I was to teach humanity. They told me that only one out of every seven humans on Earth will ascend, and I thought, 'Isn't that sad?' And there are so many people out there who are misled, thinking everyone will ascend, but they aren't ready, they have not given up their greed, or their need to be in control. There are some who are such victims, and so angry, that they just want to be in power and have their own slave race. Ascension is very difficult once you've become a human because now you have more choices—but not everyone wants to make the right choice.

If people could only see the beauty and perfection in our differences, that everything is a piece of art, and let go of wanting everything to be a certain way, they would see the beauty in every single being. They would feel the compassion, they would feel their heart, they would understand who they are and where they came from, and they would stop the judgment and prejudices.

My world changed when I had contact. You don't know what life is all about until you experience that feeling of being perfect, of perfect love. That's why when I meet the beings I don't mind what they are. I was told years ago by a herpetologist that you could hold the most poisonous snake if you hold it without fear. Snakes pick up your fear, because fear is a very powerful energy, it's very scattered and chaotic. We have a converted basement, and we had a guy renting it. Because we live in the desert a rattlesnake had gotten in there, and he was hosing it and yelling and just going crazy because he was so afraid of it. I told him to stop hosing it and go call the fire department, because they deal with snakes. And I looked at it and for the first time I saw it as being beautiful, and I sat down five feet from it and communicated with it telepathically. I told it how beautiful it was, how dainty and elegant in its movement. And I sent it so much love, and it raised up and its tongue was going like crazy, and it just looked at me and communicated love back. I was never afraid, and when I stood to leave it didn't attack me. The firemen were aghast, and my husband told them, "She's one of these New Age woo-woo people that thinks if you love something you're safe." One of the firemen told me angrily that many people die and lose limbs from the poison each year. I said that I saw her as beautiful and I didn't fear her, and the fireman said, "What makes you think that's a female?" And I said because her frequency was so feminine. And when they picked her up and looked closely they said she was a female, but it was just a lucky guess. But they didn't understand it wasn't luck, it was about being one with the rattlesnake and understanding that it meant me no harm; it was just being, it was living the only way it knew how, and when I gave it love, it gave it back. It's all about being, and we have to understand their survival.

In the early to mid-2000s I had an experience with three Ant People. They came into my bedroom at night, but my husband slept through the whole thing. I thought I was hallucinating. I didn't understand. They weren't talking telepathically to me. I went to the bathroom and splashed cold water on my face, came back in, let my eyes adjust to the darkness. And there were these three giant ant-like beings with big bug eyes standing beside my bed. I wanted to reach out and touch one, but I thought, 'If this thing is real, will it bite me, claw me?' So I told it telepathically that I was going to go to sleep, and if it had anything to ask me, that it could do so in my mind. So I got in bed, covered up my head and rolled over and went to sleep.

A few weeks later I went to Ruth Hover's group, and I got there early and so did a friend. And both of us had the very same experience, except that mine was with three ant beings, and hers was with one. Hers shook her awake in the night, and she said, "*What?!* What do you *want?*" And it said nothing. But she kept her lights on more than I did at night, so she could see it well enough to draw the next day. So when I did a sculpture of the being, she came over and critiqued it. I took the sculpture to a conference and a guy came up and said, "That's the Ant People!" He told me to google 'Ant People' and I would see that the Hopi Indians talk about them.

So after that I decided that I wanted to be brave enough to meet them, to go into their underground facility and understand more about them. And as I did that I got to see their dens in the inner Earth, and to understand why they have antennae, and what their purpose is in being on Earth. These beings again stood about five feet tall. All ants have antennae that pick up frequencies that tell them if something is safe or dangerous. The Ant People only come to the surface at the end of every Earth cycle, right before the Earth is cleansed and renewed, and it flips and shifts. They have a pattern of frequencies that they are to recognize. Every person has our own frequency, it's called the "soul identity" and carries a frequency that only belongs to that soul. And they are given certain frequency patterns that they are to seek out, and those people that need to be taken to inner Earth at the time of the Earth changes are taken down there. And they are fed and kept alive until all the Earth changes are done, and the Earth is once again capable of sustaining life. Then they bring them up and they start to repopulate the new Earth. It was so mind-blowing to learn that about them; it's better than reading any books, because when you get to experience it, it's beyond words.

Charmaine D'Rozario-Saytch

Caution: contains material that some may find disturbing.

Charmaine is a 27-year-old English woman living in Southern England. Her human ancestry is a mix of English, Italian, Indian and Jewish.

How did you learn you are a hybrid?

In hindsight I've had experiences since childhood, but being a child I didn't have full understanding of who was visiting me. I have had missing time, and marks I couldn't explain, some of which I tried to photograph but the pictures would not develop. As a child I wasn't aware of precisely what an alien was, but I was open to it. At that point I had no recollection of the experiences I was having. In adulthood I met a couple of friends who were very into crop circles, ETs and things like that, and they had a questionnaire that they would half-jokingly put to people who may have had abduction experiences. Apparently I ticked quite a lot of the boxes. Spending time with them we watched a lot of documentaries on these topics and discussed them at length. As time went on I found out about more and more people who'd had similar experiences, particularly missing time. I had quite a number of them, and the longest period was six hours. I just remember a bright light, but I have no memory after that. So it started to make me question what was happening.

From the hybrid side, as I started to remember the experiences of being visited and abducted it got me wondering: why specifically was this happening to me? My friends said that it often runs in families, and your parents and grandparents might have had experiences. So I thought that was one possibility, but I'd always felt different, since I can remember, and looking back, there were definitely different characteristics that other children and teenagers didn't have. These are discussed in the 'abilities' section below.

So I started to wonder: am I different in ways I don't yet understand?

The real confirmation about being a hybrid came from one particular visitation, around three or four years ago. I asked: is there any way that you can confirm that I am a hybrid? The response was that I was changed into my Reptilian form. So that was a complete confirmation! This is discussed in the regression transcript below. I have been visited by other species but am not certain of their official names and origins.

I had suspected that I was a hybrid, and had a feeling that I was a Reptilian. I always had a fascination with reptiles. I remember a period when, if I sat alone quietly and closed my eyes, I had someone or something that I used to speak to, some sort of being, an energy that was always with me. I saw Reptilian eyes, which were mostly yellow with black slits. Sometimes I could see the skin around the eyes, which was dark green in color. It was only when I got older that I realized that other children didn't have special friends like that.

Later on I discovered I could talk to snakes telepathically. On one occasion I was visiting a friend, and her flatmate had a pet snake which hadn't been fed for a couple of weeks and was wrapped in a ball. I said I would speak to him, and although the guy looked at me like I was nuts, he put the snake in my hands. I said, "It's nice to meet you, you're very beautiful, would you come out, because I'd like to see you." And he was fine. The owner was astonished because the snake never let anyone handle him. And as he was so hungry he should have bitten me. So that gave me the sense that I had a connection with reptiles.

What is your ET component?

At this point I only know for certain that they are Reptilian. I don't know what they call themselves, but it is one of the many things I have been asking telepathically. To my knowledge they haven't answered yet. It's possible I may not be remembering for certain reasons.

I have wondered about a Mantis connection. It's been a bit of a running joke with my mother and sister, particularly over the last couple of years, as I'm double-jointed and have very flexible arms, hands and fingers. I often do unusual things with my fingers, put them in positions that others do not or cannot do, make circular motions with my fingers on top of others. My mother and sister will say, "You're off doing your Mantis thing again."

How were you created?

I've been thinking about it, but at the moment I don't know. I have two siblings, and after mother had them she was told she couldn't have any more. And then I appeared. Whether there's anything to that, I don't know at this point, but I do hope to find out more.

What connection do you retain with your star family?

Whenever I'm visited by any species I communicate telepathically. I've met Reptilians, Greys, Mantises, the Galactic Federation, and another race that looked like typical Greys, but their skin was orangey-sandy in color and a little bit Reptilian in texture. I have no name for them, and have yet to find pictures of beings like them. They showed me their breeding program and how it works. Their eyes were really striking. Although they are typically big and slanted like the Greys, they were human-looking with enormous blue eyes.

The visitations have changed somewhat. As a child I never had anything negative, but when I got older I started having negative experiences and abductions, which include rape experiences. These are discussed in the 'hybrid children' section.

I'm fortunate in that I don't have the fear that many people do; I'm happy for them to visit and communicate. A lot of people are very frightened, but I've been very accepting. Even the rapes haven't upset me; I've felt quite detached from it, and that there is a sense of purpose about it, like it's all meant to be. I might not have full understanding of why these things have come into play, but I can imagine that this is the right time for them to be happening. Some people have been traumatized and can't get over it, can't talk to people about it; I am very fortunate to have a family that's caring and open-minded, very understanding, and a lot of people don't have that. How can you cope if you can't tell anyone?

Barbara: I have run a monthly experiencer support group in my home since 1994, and they're so relieved when someone accepts what they say and can help them understand it. And that person may be having experiences themselves. It is only for experiencers; participants must have at least one regression with me or someone I trust that does accurate work. I think that's a good prerequisite, as some people may have had other paranormal experiences, but they may be different to ET contact, and everyone in the group wants to feel that they share that. I have also run them at UFO conferences, like the International UFO Congress. In the mid-1990s I insisted that they had an experiencer support group, and they started that around 1995, and they are still having them there and at other conferences. These people can meet and talk with each other, and a leader who is experienced in running such groups. It's a big help because they feel less alone, and often less troubled by it, and realize that all these other people are normal, good, intelligent people like themselves.

I would like to start an experiencer support group in the UK. It's been so helpful to chat with others, like Cynthia, and be able to share and compare experiences, looking at similarities and differences. I would like to be able to offer a safe space for people to do that; it's really important that everyone's in the same boat, and understands that no one's going to be judged. They can share if they want to, or just sit and listen. I feel lucky to be involved in this project, and connecting with people like Cynthia, Matt and Juju; I feel like they're connections for life.

What do you understand to be the purpose of your creation?

I have been sent to Earth at this time for various reasons, some of which have not yet been revealed to me. I do know that part of my work is to bring information to humanity, that they are not alone. However this does not mean that all ET species are friendly and are here to help humanity. Many humans are already aware that there are other lifeforms coming here, but it is important that more do so. This is not a time to remain ignorant and ignore what is right in front of you. There are wonderful opportunities for all of us, to grow, to learn and to open up together, but each individual can choose either to go on the journey of discovery and enlightenment or to stay trapped, blind and cut off from their full potential.

I am here to bridge the divide, to help facilitate bringing the hybrids together with the experiencers and abductees. Further, to bring them together with the rest of humanity, even the skeptics!

Some of those that have had experiences are afraid and have been traumatized by their encounters. I want to show them that not all species nor hybrids are bad. I can use my gifts to help people, to assist them in their lives and on their personal journeys.

If we are to get through what is to come then it is vitally important that we work together and stop allowing ourselves to be manipulated, controlled and deliberately divided by controlling parties. My personal motto is, 'Everything is possible, nothing is impossible.' This relates not only to the universe, but also to the lives of individuals. People can be what they wish to be—you can make a difference and change things. If you can think it you can create it.

I am one facet in the crystal, we all play a part in this universe and each of us is important. People are sent to me to help them recover from something, to be healed or to be able to move on in life. I am extremely happy to be able to facilitate in this way and helping people is incredibly rewarding to me. I am a qualified Reiki Master so I teach healing as well as give it. I am also a nutritional advisor and Emotional Freedom Technique practitioner. These are great ways to help people get back on their path and return to living a healthy and happy life.

What do you understand to be the rationale for the hybrid program?

It is my belief that there are various reasons for the hybrid program, and these differ depending on species and whether or not there is involvement with the military.

I believe that one purpose for the creation of hybrids is to bridge the divide between the ETs and humans, taking positive attributes from each race for certain purposes, such as healing, higher intelligence, stronger spiritual connection and so forth.

By contrast, some are created by the military to use their abilities as weapons.

What do you know of the differences between Earth-based and non Earth-based hybrids?

Earth-based hybrids seem to have more emotional ability, and a strong desire to help others and the Earth. Non Earth-based hybrids appear to be more aware of the bigger picture if you will, from a galactic point of view.

Do you have your own hybrid children?

I have six hybrid children that I am aware of, from different fathers of different races. My eldest son came from one experience in particular, when I was staying over at the house of the person who introduced me to this subject area. Whenever I'm going to be visited, I wake up instinctively. I was sleeping on my left side, and when I awoke I knew that someone was going to come into the room; as soon as he did I knew it was a male Reptilian. I can always tell the sex of the being. I could track him walking along the bed, and knew it was going to be a rape situation. I was quite frightened, and I communicated telepathically that if this is going to be that kind of experience I don't want to remember it, and I blacked out. I woke up still lying on my left side and sighed with relief, thinking he'd gone, but then he put his arm around me. We communicated telepathically and he apologized; he said he was just following orders. After that first experience I missed two periods and had a strong feeling I was pregnant. I have had other experiences with him since, and when I asked him why he did that he said it was for breeding. Since then I have met our Reptilian son. What's funny is that his father and I have dark green skin, but his skin is more turquoise. I've seen him two or three times, but I don't have regular contact. I have other hybrid children and it's the same with them. It could be that we do meet more often and I'm not remembering. Three of them are on what seems to be a military base in the UK.

I have had six rape experiences with different ETs. One of them was a very ritualistic situation. I'm not sure if it was on Earth or on a ship. I would like to do further regressions to find out more as it certainly throws up a lot of questions. I was in a room, and a man in a black cloak with a hood came in. I got the impression he was part of a secret society of some kind. He invited me to join their group, but refused to tell me anything about it so I said no. The more I refused the more aggressive he became. I was then led to a room shaped like a half moon, with windows on one side and a raised platform with high backed chairs, in which another group sat. They all wore the same black cloaks with the hoods pulled up, but these were a mix of ETs and humans. I kept asking, "Why have I been brought here?" I got the telepathic sense it was for breeding. Then a black and red being was brought in, and was led to the platform to speak to the head people. I sensed they wanted something from him, and made a silent agreement—he was also asked to join. I knew some of what he was thinking, and got a sense of previous talks, that they had communicated agendas with each other but not with me.

Then everyone left, and I saw a doorway off to one side, through which my Reptilian son entered. I knew it was him though it was the first time we'd met.

I was then taken to another room which was circular. Again there were people in robes, and the black and red being was brought in, and I realized a ritual was about to take place. I was put on the floor, naked, then the main man in robes came over and with a silver blade cut the palms of myself and the being then pressed them together. Then a chicken was brought in, which was decapitated and the man poured its blood over both of us. And then the being raped me. Afterwards I was taken to a bedroom, which had an en suite bathroom. I showered, and was trying to process all this. I wondered about what was happening on various levels. It seemed obvious that it was about creating a child, which was later confirmed in a regression. When I went back to the bedroom my son was laying on the bed and looked asleep. I could see his tail flicking back and forth and for some reason this struck me as incredibly funny and I burst into hysterical laughter, which made him open his eyes and turn to me. He said something telepathically to the effect of, "I think you've lost the plot." I think it was just my way of coping. But it was comforting to have him there. I have no further memory after that moment.

With regard to the three children on the military base I have no memories of being impregnated, but I have one recollection of waking up in what felt like a military base, and seeing an English nurse in the room. I asked her where I was but she wouldn't tell me, so I asked if she could at least tell me why I was there, and she said, "All I can say is that they're taking something." I had suspected that I was pregnant, so that was a confirmation that I was, and that they intended to take the fetus. I recall a man came in, wearing a blue medical smock and mask. I was then drugged, but I briefly woke up to see a man walking away from me, and his gait suggested that he was carrying something in his arms. I was drugged again at this point and the next thing I recall was waking up in my bed at home.

The second time I was taken to that facility it was to meet the three children, but we were not left alone together, we were monitored at all times. I have no recollection of the fathers, or whether it was through rape or implantation. A lot has come out through regressions, but I hope that I will begin to remember more, or perhaps have more regression sessions, because I would like to find out more of what's happened there.

There was a younger boy, I would guess he was around four years old and he looked quite human. There were two girls with very pale skin and big black eyes. One of them had bright green hair, and the other had more reddish-orange hair. I would put them at maybe six to seven years old.

With my Reptilian son, he was taller than me, which was quite a shock. He was quite adult, very grown up, which didn't seem to work out mathematically. So I wonder if they have a different aging process. I would like to learn more about that.

He was about seven foot tall, very muscular, very much a man, turquoise in color with the full tail, a typical Reptilian. On the first occasion when I met him properly, we had a conversation which was really lovely, and he asked what it's like to be human, to be in that form. I asked if he could change, if that was his only form. He didn't know, so I asked if he'd like to try to change form, and he said he would. So he laid down and I put one hand on his head and one on his solar plexus, and began a visualization; I pictured him shifting into a human form and said that if he had a human form that he should change now. And for the first time he had that experience of shifting, and he immediately began to cry. I asked what's wrong, and he said it was a completely different feeling to be in that form, that there were so many emotions that he couldn't understand. He found that very difficult to accept and process, which I hadn't thought about prior to that, so I found that quite insightful and interesting. He then got up and walked around to see how it felt. I was picking up on his thoughts, and one thought was, 'Oh, I haven't got a tail now!' He was so used to his normal walk, that way of balancing, that it was quite disconcerting for him. He was like that for around 10-15 minutes.

He had dark brown hair and eyes like mine, he still had a muscular build, he was slender—what you'd call a good looking young man. I thought, 'Oh wow, you actually look quite a lot like me!' Which was nice. I feel a very strong connection with him, more than my other children. I think I've had more contacts with him, seen him more. I felt proud of him, which mothers will of course say about their children. I just felt very proud and happy.

Barbara: I've found that women who have met their Reptilian children often say they're so proud of them, more than do the mothers of hybrids of other ET races. One woman, whom I worked with doing regressions for a number of years, met her two Reptilian hybrid sons. She said over and over again that she was so proud of them. They themselves were adults, 34 and 36 years old, and she said they were so wonderful. They had long black hair, which started from the middle of the top of the head, and they had fairly human features. Their skin texture and tone was Reptilian more than human. She thinks they came and did road work with a human crew in front of her house, digging a hole in the street. When she drove past them they would look at her, and two of them, who wore sunglasses at all times, kept stopping work to stare at her. She has always wondered if they paid a quick visit in the guise of road workers.

My mother said she remembers seeing my Reptilian son, about two and a half years ago. She was on her way to the bathroom in the night, heading down the hallway, and when she passed the lounge she saw someone standing there. She saw a shape, about seven feet tall with the tail and claws. They exchanged a look, and she got the sense he was there to visit, that he'd just popped in to see grandma! She felt a family connection, she felt calm and safe. So she went back to bed and left him to it.

The three children that live on the military base are not Reptilian. I know I have a hybrid child with a Mantis. After a regression with Mary Rodwell I had an information download where I was shown an experience in a stone room with three Mantis beings. That was another rape scenario, by one of the beings. From what I can recall I've never seen that child. Again, I don't know if I'm having connections with them—being able to see the children, but not remember it.

When I visited the children that live on the base I got the sense that the fathers are not around, that it's military personnel only. They seem to be kept in a single room most of the time, and that's where they sleep and play. I would love to think that they're okay, but the sheer fact that they're kept on a military base, and their purpose is that the military want to see what they can do, what abilities they have, and use them for the military's advantage ... I do worry, but it's difficult because I don't know where that base is. Not that I'd get very far if I went there. I get a sense of being drugged, and will wake up there, and then the reverse on the way back. I'll wake up in my bed with no memory of the journey.

How do you reconcile the multiple aspects of your identity?

As a child, I was very different, I had a knowing ... there were two sides of me battling. Sometimes I would have regular human thoughts, and then there were other reactions and thoughts, from the other side, and I wondered, 'Where did that come from?' So I was very conflicted, I had no one to talk to, no understanding, but the more I looked into this stuff, watching documentaries etcetera, the more I felt I was on the right path. I didn't know what I'd discover, but it was the most joyous moment of my life when I found out, and realized I'm not mad. I truly knew who and what I am. I felt complete, whole, and for the first time in my life I had no inner conflict. I felt calm and at peace. The internal battle ceased.

Do you have physiological differences to humans?

I have shapeshifted twice that I am aware of, and both times I was made to shift, it wasn't something I chose to do. Both are described in the regression section.

Barbara: The wonderful thing about the subconscious mind is that it appears to record everything, even what we're not conscious for, which is wonderful if people want to know, then it comes out. If not it stays buried. So you can usually find out about what you want to.

Miguel: So you're suggesting that even if someone is knocked out, their consciousness may be recording everything, in the way that out-of-body and near-death experiences allow a person to witness a situation from an external perspective? There's something deliciously subversive about that.

I have four implants, located in my nose, arm, hip and leg. One is to prevent me shapeshifting. I think this is military hardware, and is used to make me change shape when they want me to. I don't understand the technology, but would be very interested to go into that. I want to know what is happening, how this works.

The one in the left nostril is for tracking. The third manipulates chemicals in my body, suppressing levels such as serotonin. By doing so they can affect my health in a negative way, which they have done. This information came out in one of the regressions with Mary Rodwell. Switching off the implants was achieved this year. However, the military succeeded in switching them back on. I physically felt the tracker in my nose moving as it was switched back on. I also experienced a high-pitched frequency and pain. I hear these frequencies every day and sometimes they are painful. I believe these to be part of the monitoring by the military, checking the implants and adjusting them if needed. I am pursuing ways to switch them off permanently and to help others locate theirs, to discover their purpose and deactivate them if they wish to. They have no right to do this. It's a violation of my body and my privacy. It raises a lot more questions than it answers.

Do you have a sense of mission?

I feel that I've been incarnated at this point to help hybrids, and to bring them together. Also to help experiencers in the process of accepting and dealing with that. I want to help bring them together with the hybrid community, and to help humanity to come together.

I'm also a Reiki healer, practicing four styles. I'm a nutritionist, and help people to understand about what they're putting into their bodies, and how it affects them, and why they become unwell and how to rectify that. At the moment I'm studying acupuncture, to help people to understand the meridians and energy flows, and how they can tap into that and shift the energy. So it's all about helping people to be healthy, to come together, to open up to be themselves, and be more aware.

Are you encouraged by guides?

Yes, I do feel that. Also I've had information downloads from the Galactic Federation which has mostly been over the last two years. They have sent strong messages to say: go forward, bring together those communities, and get the word out about hybrids being here on Earth, as well as ET species and agendas. There is a lot of negativity around alien visitations or abductions, and of course there are negative elements, but it's about getting the message across that not all are negative. And again, Reptilians have had a lot of bad press. As soon as you mention Reptilians to those that know something about the subject people say, "Oh, they're trying to take over the world, they work with the Illuminati, they're trying to destroy the planet." And as a Reptilian hybrid I disagree! I'm out to *save* the planet, to help humanity as much as possible. Some people may go online and believe everything they read, so if they're fed information that Reptilians are murderous, cruel and controlling ... if they believe that, you will likely get those negative reactions from them. So it's about educating people. You should always question. You should meet them. How can you make an informed choice without the experience? It's about getting over that hurdle, but it's a big one. I think there are different races of Reptilians, each with their own agendas. People can look it up, and if one race has a bad reputation, all similar races get tainted. It's like humans races, none are all good or all bad.

I had an interesting experience running a stall at this year's Glastonbury Symposium. I had many people asking lots of questions which is great and that's what it was all about: instigating sensible conversation! I did get asked if I was a hybrid and I said yes. Some people asked what species I was and I said that I am Reptilian. I am very pleased to say that the whole weekend was incredibly positive; I did not have any negative comments and it was so lovely that people took the time to speak with me. I am booked in to have a stall at next year's Symposium and an ad in their program again, so I very much hope that people will come along to the stall to meet me and chat.

I advertised the support group in the program, which would be a regular meeting in the South East where I live, where people can come together and share experiences, or just listen, with no pressure. I just want to offer a safe platform. And it may create opportunities for them to develop a social life with like-minded people who understand what they're going through. For me, at first, not only was it frightening, but no one understood, and I had no one to talk to. Speaking to Mary Rodwell last year, she told me that many children are having these experiences. And that's something I'm very passionate about, starting something specifically for children. They can come along with their parents or families and have that safe space where they can talk about it if they wish to, or draw pictures, and not feel they're being suppressed; often they're told not to talk about it, especially in school. I can't sit on the fence; it's so important for children to have the opportunity to express themselves. They are often asking themselves, 'Is this real, or am I going mad?' They've got to be helped and nurtured.

Do you have special abilities?

I have always been very aware of frequencies, being able to hear some that others cannot. I am psychic; I'm shown or told about things before they happen by guides/spirits/ETs. I can read people's thoughts and intentions. I have an intuitive sense of danger, for example places or situations to avoid. I am able to communicate telepathically not only with ETs but also animals. I am a healer, and people report that their ailments are improved or cured after a healing session with me. Many people have told me that I am a natural counselor and my voice can put them into a meditation, or a happy, relaxed state, or even induce sleep. I can sense other people's fear or danger even if they are a great distance away. I can see auras and into people's bodies, which is useful for seeing health issues. I can also clear blockages and energy fields.

People commonly share their worries with me; quite often things they have never told anyone else, and they report feeling a release from speaking to someone about their concerns without judgment.

I use these abilities if they are going to be beneficial to the person, healing or helping them move forward.

What protocols govern ET interaction with humans?

I see the Galactic Federation as a Galactic Council, but I do not have the sense that any species are bound to this, or that all individuals within a member species will agree and do as the rest of the species does. It is the same on Earth, there is good and bad in every group. Some species wish to help humanity by sharing knowledge and technology, others are working with certain human groups like the military and secret societies for negative purposes. Other species are working independently and negatively with regard to humans, but that does not mean that every member of that species agrees or complies. Some do not wish to carry out orders but have no choice.

How do you define 'Frequencies?'

Frequencies can be in sound form, energy frequencies, color frequencies, and natural frequencies such as that of the Earth. The military has researched how to manipulate frequencies to cause negative effects in individuals and groups, such as fear and ill health.

What is your understanding of Ascension?

Our souls have gone through many lives and forms, not all of them are necessarily on planet Earth nor in human form. Although the outer shell changes over each lifetime, grows old and ceases to function, the soul continues. With each reincarnation and experience the soul learns and evolves; we do not remember everything from our past incarnations, only what we are meant to at that time. When it's time for the shell to cease and the soul to go back home, the soul ascends from the current life to space. Information is compiled from that lifetime and compared with previous incarnations to plan what the journey and experiences will be in the next life, before the soul is reincarnated into the next form.

What role can hybrids play in the process?

Many! Hybrids can: help people open up to their true selves and achieve their full potential; help with health issues, to get people back on to their right paths; open up people's spirituality; assist in people decreasing, dealing with and releasing fear; help the planet to heal and renew; assist in changing the way people view the planet and its resources; help share what we can all do to prevent any more damage being done to the planet. The list is endless!

Are you aware of coming Earth changes?

I do feel that we are currently in a very troubling phase on this planet, although also an incredibly exciting one! Humanity is allowing itself to be manipulated, controlled and subdued and this is most certainly not to the benefit of humanity at large. Nothing is set in stone and the current path can be altered, but it will not be if everyone takes a lazy, disinterested or disempowered attitude. There is quite enough of that, so let us bring some lovely positivity in! It is the responsibility of us all, and not just for us now but for future generations. Every action has a reaction and even the smallest thought or positive action makes a difference. You can be a pebble that causes a ripple in the pond, or just be a pebble at the bottom of the pond, but either way the choice is yours!

What do you understand about the New Earth?

There are negative agendas, such as those of the New World Order. However, there is much positive energy and good intentions too. The Earth is going through a huge transition at the moment, and as those inhabiting the planet we can either help facilitate that change and indeed a change in us, or we can hinder it. Humanity is so divided and too busy fighting and arguing to see what is really going on and do something about it.

What is your take on the takeover thesis?

I don't believe in dwelling on the negative side, as negative energy is created by doing so. Instead we could create positivity with it. This side needs to come to the fore much more, and I feel it is part of my mission to help bring that message out.

Have you had contact with the military or intelligence agencies?

Yes I have, and most seems to be negative. I have had my phone tapped, been implanted with a tracker and had other kinds of surveillance and intimidation. When I was visiting some friends a Chinook helicopter hovered literally outside the window with the pilot looking right at me. I have had Chinooks hover so low over my home that things have been shaking and falling over. As mentioned above, a secret society asked me to join, wanting to use me for breeding.

I've been drugged and taken to military bases in the UK where three of my children are being kept. The military have taken me and forced me to change into my Reptilian form, as detailed in the regression transcript below. I do have a sense that there are more experiences that I do not have full recollection of, but I hope to remember these and to uncover more information through further regressions.

How do you feel about the global hybrid community?

Getting the hybrids together, with all their power and abilities, offers amazing possibilities in terms of what we could manifest. Wonderful things could happen, and we can overcome the negativity and ignorance around this subject. But you only have that opportunity if everyone is connected. This project is a catalyst for so many things as it's bringing people together—the sky's the limit.

What would you most like to discuss with other hybrids?

There are lots! How do they feel at this point in their life, with their mission and direction? Do they feel supported? I know for me it's made such a difference, connecting to other hybrids, building that network. I'm intrigued about similarities and differences. Speaking with Tatiana, there were many similarities from childhood onwards. I wonder how many similarities we have, how much does it vary between species, or is it a general thing in the hybrid community? I would very much like to help build a hybrid community.

What are the best and worst things about being a hybrid?

The worst thing for me was growing up knowing you were different, and not completely understanding why. Having no one to talk to about it, who was going through the same things and could relate. And the internal struggle, feeling like you were two beings.

The best thing was having confirmation, and knowing what I am, what my path is, my mission, and being able to help people—if it helps one person it would be worth it. Some people have thought I'm crazy to put myself in that position just for one person, but it's not about numbers. If you can just help a few it makes a difference; it's a wonderful feeling and it's why I'm here. Helping to get people onto their path, giving them a chance to talk about their experiences without feeling judged, and frightened. And knowing that they're talking to someone who understands because they've gone through the same things. Some people get stuck in the trauma, but others have moved on, and use it in a positive way.

How can humanity best work with you?

By meeting me, speaking with me, being open-minded and willing to learn. No progress can be made through judgment and ignorance. Not everyone has to like me, or any hybrid, but at least spend some time talking with us before you make your mind up!

How do you conceptualize God?

For me God is not a bearded old man in the sky. Those that watch over us are many, not just one. Universal energy is not just out in space, it is all around us and within us. We are all unique, special beings and capable of so much more then we realize; in that sense it could be said that we are all our own god or goddess.

What is the most important lesson you've learned?

To be open—open-minded and open-hearted; to share my knowledge, experiences and thoughts with others so they may learn from them and gain understanding. Even if negative things happen to you, it can help others by sharing your experiences with them. I believe negativity can always be changed into something positive.

Regression with Barbara Lamb, August 2015

I was seeking information on the two occasions I shapeshifted into my Reptilian form. One was on a military base and the other was in a cave with three Reptilian beings.

Barbara first took me back to the moment that I was taken by the military from my home in Sussex to a base in the UK.

I'm in bed at night and I can hear a helicopter outside. It's not unusual to hear helicopters around where I'm living. I can see four people in the room who feel distinctly male, and military. They have a stretcher with them and wear plain, dark suit jackets; they have a strange feel to the material. All four have short hair, one with very blue eyes who for some reason stands out, despite the room being dimly lit. I'm injected with something in my upper left arm; I begin to feel very heavy and soon I cannot move or speak.

There is a kind of body bag attached to the stretcher which I am placed in. It has a full-length zip which they close almost entirely, but leave a small section unzipped to aid my breathing. I feel myself being lifted up, then I'm taken out to the helicopter. Two of the men get into a black car nearby and the other two get onto the helicopter with me. We fly for some time. The men check on me occasionally to make sure I'm still unconscious but do not appear to speak to each other or the pilot. It's very cold.

Eventually we land and I'm carried out and down a slope. It's cold and smells damp. We go down a corridor in an underground facility and I can see bright lights overhead. They turn left into a small, dimly lit room, then take me out of the bag and put me on a bed. There is a small table by the bed and I can see stairs leading down.

The man with the blue eyes stays in the room with me and the other man leaves. The men have stayed completely silent. A man that I have not seen before comes into the room with a box and 'Blue-eyes' opens it. It holds a metallic, cylindrical implement about 10-12 inches long, which has two needles coming out of one end and a wire coming out of the other. I have a strong sense that it holds a liquid that they will inject me with.

Blue-eyes brings the device to the bed and inserts the two needles into my upper left arm; I can feel liquid pumping in. The sensation is very cold and it seems that the wire coming out the other end of the device is an electrical wire that trails out of the door. I have the sense that it is connected to something, but I cannot see what. As well as the cold feeling, my body also feels heavy and I find it hard to breathe. The men begin to talk and I hear a kind of electrical whirring noise. They are speaking about starting something and I have the sense that the liquid that has been injected into my body is to facilitate an electrical impulse inside my body.

An electrical current is now coming from the needles and running through my body, and the pulse intensity is increasing. The sensation becomes painful and the cold is replaced by heat, which increases and continues to be felt throughout my body. The sensation is unlike any other I have felt; I can feel my muscles contracting without me actively doing this. My bones feel as if they are stretching, I want to move but cannot, nor can I speak. My skin feels very tight, as if it's stretching. I can feel my muscles growing, my whole anatomy changing. My fingers feel as if they're getting longer. I feel my tail begin to emerge and grow, and my skin changes to scales.

Throughout the shift I am laying on my back and I feel a certain familiarity about the change although with an unfamiliar sense of it being forced, taking place quickly and painfully. I can feel my nails touching the bed sheet where they have grown longer. My long hair has gone, my eyes have changed, and I can feel the scales on my skin. I am now in full Reptilian form.

My mind begins to feel clearer, less groggy and drugged. My body becomes lighter and less effected by the drugs they have given me. I find that I am able to move somewhat so I begin to think how I can get full control of my body. Blue-eyes takes the cylindrical device away. It's getting easier to move. He continues to watch me, and I have a sense that there are cameras in the room and that others are also observing me. We do not speak.

I manage to sit up on the bed, and at this point he leaves and closes the door. I am alone but the cameras still feel as if they are watching me and I manage to move enough to sit on the side of the bed, with my feet on the floor. I stand up and see myself in my other form. It feels familiar and comfortable, and I feel good. I notice a full-length mirror to the left of the stairs and look at my reflection. I have dark green scales, yellow eyes with black slits, a muscular body, a tail and increased height and body mass.

I feel happy to be in my Reptilian form, but annoyed that the military has forced me to change shape and angry that they are observing me—they do not have a right to. I had not consented to them taking me and forcing me to change shape.

I walk to the top of the stairs and head down. I can see a lit, open door at the bottom. It seems set up, but I continue.

Beyond the door is an empty room with white walls, very clinical looking, and I consider what I may be walking into. There is a two-way mirror on the far wall, but I am able to see through it and observe three men in the room on the other side. One is standing, the other two are sitting, and they are all wearing suits and ties. They are not all from the same organization; one is from the military, he is an older chap, greying at the temples. The men realize that I am able to see them. I notice that the door that I have just walked through has now closed and locked.

They begin playing different sounds and frequencies through speakers built into the walls. They play them at different speeds and volumes, and observe my reactions. Some are very high pitched and are quite painful to listen to. I can physically feel sounds and frequencies emitting from the speakers as if they have an energy to them as well as sound. Some of them seem to cause an energetic shift in my body. I want to protect myself, so I visualize my aura expanding, shielding me. The men are trying to work out what is happening; they can see that I am no longer being affected and they don't know why.

I can now feel a pulsing in my palms, an energy, and I move my hands out on either side of my body and push the energy shield out further. I am absorbing the energy and frequencies around me and changing it all from something unwanted and harmful into something that is protecting me. I push the shield to the sides of the room, into the speakers and down the wires as I know that if I can affect the electric systems that will cut out the frequencies.

A man in a white lab coat has entered the control room; they seem to be talking about why the speakers are affected. They are trying to fix them and I find this quite amusing. My shield is pushing against the mirror and the glass begins to crack.

I become aware that I am able to scan their bodies. The man standing up has a heart condition he is unaware of. One of the chaps sitting down has kidney problems; he drinks coffee all day long so this is affecting his health, and he is unaware of his full health issues. He gets a lot of pain, feeling tired and groggy. I am intrigued by this ability to see into their bodies and detect health complaints, and I think about using this to help others.

The military chap who is also sitting down, I begin to concentrate on his lungs, and suddenly he is not breathing properly and he begins to wonder if I am causing this. The man standing continues to speak with the man in the lab coat; they are getting faults and abnormal readings and are trying to work out what is going on. I am amused as I know the cause of their electrical issues. They invited potential issues to arise as they kidnapped me and subjected me to procedures that I had not consented to. They are discussing the prospect of me being the cause of these problems and seem uncomfortable about this possibility. They arrogantly assume that any subject will remain helpless under their control; they are not accustomed to subjects not complying.

I hear the door click and know that it has been unlocked. I go through, back up the stairs, into the room with the bed and out through the door into the corridor. I can turn right to head above ground and out of the base, or I can turn left, going deeper into the base. I decide to turn left and explore the facility further.

It is a long corridor, with high and wide grey walls, bright lights overhead and at intervals there are doors on either side. Some of them have small panes of glass that you can see through and others do not. Some have small boxes for keycard entry, some have fingerprint or retinal scanners.

There are two large, red, metal double doors. I go through and into a lab of some kind. It is a large room and there is transparent plastic sheeting around the room creating a false wall. I can see a lot of lab equipment beyond the plastic sheeting. There are various jars of flesh and skin samples, and there are five lab workers present, four men and one woman. They have not yet noticed me. Two of them are sitting down and they are looking through microscopes. The woman is going from place to place, checking things and making notes. I can smell the chemicals they are using.

The woman then notices me and is shocked, alerting the others to my presence. One of the men tries to shield what he is doing. I push through the sheeting and approach him. Three of the men run out of the room but the man shielding his work stays where he is and so does the woman. It appears to be flesh samples in some sort of yellow-orange liquid. The samples are ET in origin; I get a strong sense that they want to replicate and build new cells with the properties found in the ET species. I look through his notes; they are wondering if they can overlay that manufactured flesh on a machine, along the lines of AI but something far more than that.

They also want to build cells and implant them into a female subject to see if they could create a fetus with the abilities of the ET or various ET species. They would initially test this on a female human subject, with the intention of then testing this on hybrids and ETs. They are attempting to create new life and selecting the species and characteristics for specific purposes. The beings would be a form of 'supersoldier' that would be of great benefit to their future plans as well as lucrative for hiring and selling to other organizations and countries. The beings would be greatly enhanced compared to human soldiers. They would have increased strength and resilience, a much higher pain threshold, greater healing abilities, psychic abilities and so forth. They see the potential of creating beings who can infiltrate someone's mind undetected, to manipulate their thinking and decision making.

They plan to create these beings in child form so that they seem very innocent and would not be suspected. They would look sufficiently human to integrate into society, to walk down the street and blend in, but they would have enhanced abilities and would be under the control of the military and any other organizations that shared in the program. The children could be used for certain missions as they would not be suspected. They will be able to unlock doors with their minds, go into someone's mind undetected and so on.

As I am learning about these intentions I am reminded about one of my daughters on a military base in the UK. I know that she can go into people's minds, and it occurs to me that whoever her father is, the mix of his and my DNA has created her and her abilities. One night when she visited me I woke up knowing that I was going to have a visitation. I saw her literally pass through my window and wall and hover by my bed. She was very pale, with overly large, slightly slanted, completely black eyes, and fiery red-orange hair which was wavy like mine. I could feel her enter my mind but I pushed her out. We were being monitored by something that felt military; they wanted to see how we interacted and if her abilities worked on me and if I would even be aware of them. She had been told beforehand to try to push her mind into mine and she was being tested as much as I was. They are training her and setting her certain tasks so that when she is older she can be used by them to carry out missions. I have visited her, her sister and brother (all my children) on the military base that they are being kept on in the UK. We were monitored at all times, they were relaxed and did not try to use any of their abilities on me. My son looks human with dark brown eyes and hair like me, the other daughter is pale-skinned as well with natural green hair. Both girls are very slender with overly large eyes. The girls are more detached, but the boy feels as if he has more human genetics and is more emotionally engaged. He is happy to sit and play with his wooden toys but the girls are not interested in playing or reading and tend to sit or stand very still. The girls feel no need for interaction, not even with me, whereas the boy does want interaction and physical contact. The girls would accept it but do not need it. The girls feel as if their minds are older and more advance than their bodies.

Back in the base, I can hear that people have entered the room. I turn and see six men in black uniforms. They are not threatening me directly but they want to get me under some sort of control and out of the lab, and prevent me from exploring any more of the base. They try to convince me to exit the lab, to get me into another room to "talk," which greatly amuses me. I am still in my Reptilian form and consider my options. I notice that one of the military men has what appears to be a gun of some kind but there is a cone on the end; I get the sense that it does not fire bullets. The main chap states that if I do not cooperate they will have to get me under control. I am annoyed by this as they have brought me here against my will, forced me to change shape, and now that it has not gone as they had planned they are threatening me. The gun is something to do with energy waves and I can sense a pulsing coming from it. I am extremely curious about the technology. He directs it at me and I feel my body reacting. My muscles are contracting; it feels like a vibration is going through the whole of my body and I'm changing back into human form. I feel nauseous, hot and cold. The main chap approaches and holds my upper arm in the pretense of helping to steady me, but making it very clear that they have me under control and that I will comply. Another puts a blanket around me and they lead me out.

We go back up the corridor and past the first room they took me into. We head up the slope and through double doors of thick black metal, emerging into the open. I can see a tall electric perimeter fence with one set of double gates, grassland, a wooded area nearby and the helicopter a short distance away. The entrance is built into a grassy mound, concealing it from a distance and from the air. I cannot see any buildings, street lamps or roads. This is one entrance to the base but not the only one. It is easy for them to land helicopters as there is plenty of open space and I feel that this base is somewhere in the UK. During the helicopter ride from my home in Sussex it felt as if it was approximately 40 minutes to an hour to get to the base, heading north.

They get me back onto the helicopter. I am conscious, have full movement and am sitting on one of the seats. I have a soldier either side of me and two in front of me. I have a sense that they are taking me home. They occasionally glance at each other or at me but no one speaks. I am still feeling nauseous and it is very cold on the helicopter, despite having the blanket around me. The helicopter eventually lands, and I am taken back indoors and into my room. I am quite relieved at this point and am looking forward to laying down, warming up and the nausea easing.

I am feeling very disturbed by what I saw in the lab. The possibilities of how they could use the beings they create are immense and very troubling. Also the fact that the beings would not have a choice in carrying out orders. Especially with the children, they would be trained and forced to carry out set tasks. I have a strong impulse to free them so that they would not have to live like this, to be controlled and made to do things against their will, and for the gain of others like the military.

I found it interesting to see some of what I was capable of in my other form; it has made me think of how I can help others through using these gifts positively. I have a strong desire to use my gifts for helping others, with their health and spirituality, to train people to help others. Further, to work with water and the oceans and animal life to help turn the negative aspects into positive energy.

Barbara enquired at this point if I could recall any other occasion when I had shapeshifted. I recalled being in a cave with three Reptilians. I had suspected that I was a Reptilian hybrid and had been actively asking that if I was correct in this, could I receive confirmation somehow.

I find myself in a cave, and with these Reptilian beings I feel calm, unafraid. They stand around me, put their hands on me and make me shapeshift into my Reptilian form. The process is painless and voluntary.

I feel this is the first time I have completely changed into my Reptilian form in this lifetime, and prior to this the changes had only been partial. It feels very natural. The beings feel familiar and comfortable to me and I have no concerns for my safety. Age-wise I feel that I am around 20. To be in my Reptilian form I feel a deep sense of contentment. For the first time in my life I feel complete; before that something had always been missing. I'd been battling with myself, but am now at peace. I am in my Reptilian form for approximately five hours, and I stay in the cave with the Reptilians, communicating telepathically. When eventually they say that it is time to change back and return to my human life, I feel sad but I understand. I have missions to carry out that are best facilitated in my human form.

This is mainly to help people understand the ETs in terms of who they are and why they are here at this time. I can help open up people's minds and spirituality—even the non believers—to see the bigger picture, and help humanity to unite. People would struggle to accept this as fully and openly if I was in my Reptilian form. It would be easier for people to approach and communicate with me as a human, and therefore easier for me to carry out my work on Earth. Also there are a lot of negative ideas regarding Reptilians so some people would jump to conclusions and not be willing to accept or listen, and just assume that I am going to harm them, when my missions on Earth are quite the opposite. Ignorance is rife on Earth but this can be improved. Many people believe what they are fed without having any experience and making up their own minds.

The three Reptilians put their hands on me once again and I feel myself change back to my human form. There is no pain, fear or anxiety. I feel weaker in my human form, my muscles are not as big or defined, and I miss my tail. Looking at the Reptilians from my human eyes, they now seem quite a bit taller then I am. I still feel very comfortable in their presence and a strong connection to them. They are caring and nurturing. Although I am back in my human form I can still communicate with them telepathically. I am able to do this with all the alien species that I have connected with.

Robert Frost-Fullington

Robert is a 35-year-old American man living in California. His human ancestry is a mix of German, English, Irish and Native American.

How did you learn you are a hybrid?

When I started researching the ET subject, I noted I had many similarities with other ET experiencers. As far as I can remember I started to have encounters at around age five when I received my implants under my tongue. Then between five and ten years old there were some random encounters. Between 13 and 16 I would wake up with odd marks on my body and blood spots on the pillow. It went flat in my late teens and 20s, until a big awakening at around 28, and now in my 30s I have a decent understanding about my identity and my place in the universe.

Full realization comes on slow, because at first you have to start questioning your experiences. It's subtle things here and there, like my wrist for example. I was born double-jointed in my wrists. People gave me the nickname 'The Mantis' growing up. When I got into martial arts I created my own Mantis style which I incorporated into my other styles, partly because my wrists were more flexible and I had to develop a method of punching that would work for me.

At 29 I was fully activated, which was 2009. It was a life-changing event where my wife and I were out in the yard one night, and we had a 45-minute encounter with this huge black triangular craft flying slowly and silently over the house. It was so low I could have hit it with a rock. That got me started on my journey and things just snowballed from there.

Then in 2011 I sought out Cynthia Crawford. Sharing my background and experiences with her, she thought I might be a hybrid, and it did make sense to me. It wasn't such a shock, as I kind of always knew and it just made sense. It was more like a relief, like a coming out of the closet, and it let me move forward. But that's just the initial feeling, then you start getting into the how and why, and whole dual existence. It's like an identity crisis, and you feel even more alienated.

What is your ET component?

My core consciousness comes from the Mantis, and I have some connections with the Sirians, Tall Whites and Reptilians. Physically I have Mantis and Reptilian DNA. There are many different Mantis species out there. They exist throughout time and on all dimensions simultaneously. Relative to humans, there are both negative and positive Mantis species. Some look more like a bug, with an exoskeleton, claws and wings. The ones I work with are extremely benevolent. They don't have a shell, they're soft, they have muscles and fat rolls, as well as teeth; they're more organic, less mechanical-looking. They're like a cross between a salamander, a praying mantis and a human. They have less of a hive mind and more a collective consciousness. They have a sort of symbiotic relationship with a small Grey-like race.

How were you created?

That's been elusive to me. My theory is that, like the cuckoo—which lays its eggs in the nests of other birds which then raise its chicks—I think the embryo is implanted into the womb, and the parents are unaware. My parents had no clue whatsoever. I think that when the human woman becomes pregnant, she's taken up onto a craft, and the beings will take the embryo and create a genetic overlay, and replace it. Or they might make an exact copy with the ET genes, and implant that instead. I know that I had a twin that died in the womb, and so have some other hybrids. It might be that the ET twin survives, or is the stronger of the twins.

Barbara: I have heard that sometimes the twin is thought to be absorbed into the uterus or the remaining twin, but is in fact taken to be raised on a ship by ETs. And the twin that grows up on Earth receives visits from the 'vanished' twin, even if this relationship is not conscious for the 'human' twin. It can be troubling to the surviving twin, having had that connection in the womb, to then lose that.

I've certainly had a longing my whole life; it's a really odd feeling. When I found out about this, around age five, I wondered if all that stuff that had happened in my childhood was the ghost or spirit of my twin following me around. I had weird things like stuff flying off the shelf.

This could go back multiple generations, right? Let's think in terms of music, with how this works. When we create it you get a vibration, it can be real pleasurable and flowing. When these beings make music, they create planets and solar systems. So we have to think of these guys as being able to do things beyond our experience. We have to think of this at a massive scale over time and space. These beings, like the Mantis, they're practically immortal, they're ancient. They say they are masters of this universe, since they've been around since pretty much the beginning. Over the eons, they may play a major role in creating the hybrids, getting various DNA strands together from different groups. This is a setup over multiple generations, to get the genetics perfect, then they do their little tweaks to make them compatible. The genetic manipulation is ongoing; the embryo is the base creation, then throughout your life they are working on you, adding and activating different DNA elements. The beginning of my creation could go way back; it may have started in the Native American side, back in the 1800s. They may have been abducting some of my ancestors, adding in Mantis DNA to have the mix I need. My mother would have had to have been abducted as well, though she is unaware of it.

I've heard that, since the hybrid program has been going for decades on Earth, it could be that I have DNA from older abductees and hybrids. With Jacquelin and I meeting on the ship, it's possible that some of her DNA was used in my embryo, for example. But it gets even wilder than that. I was told by a Sirian contact that I may have created *myself*. These beings don't really die, they can just choose to live another existence. As an ET you can set up your own reality to exist here, then live that creation. It may be parallel to our idea of us continuing as souls and choosing to incarnate.

What connection do you retain with your star family?

The Mantis beings are always with me. I've been told by people who can see energies that they can see ten Mantis beings around me all the time. I don't feel their presence that often as it's such a part of my field. For the most part they don't want to interfere with me, they want me to figure things out for myself, and they guide me in various ways. Sometimes it's not until days later that I realize I had an interaction or guidance, but I often pick up thoughts from them, like, "Do you really think this is helping you? Do you really think you should have that third beer?" I get guidance on diet, exercise and keeping my thoughts at a high vibration; every thought has to be a loving thought, all day, 100%.

Manifesting love

To practice keeping my thoughts loving, I have a technique. First, learn to love yourself, because if you can't love yourself there's no way this is going to work.

To do this I need to be in love all the time, so I had to ask myself: what *is* love, and how do I use it?

I go back to a time when I experienced that feeling of deep love, like being embraced by my mother, or my wedding day, whatever experience gave me a physical feeling of love. I focus on reliving that feeling, imagine it in my heart, and try to manifest it.

Once you can feel that filling your heart, with every breath in, feel it expand from your heart throughout your body.

Then try to maintain that in your interactions. At first it's artificial, but with practice it becomes habit, and with habit it becomes natural, and you become a more loving person.

I see humanity as unbalanced at this time, so I feel I have to maintain a state of extreme love and benevolence in order to energetically tip the scales.

In the beginning my awakening was extremely physical, like a shock and awe campaign—like being slapped awake. Then it cooled down and became more spiritual and psychic, and more about inner, personal development than their influence. And then there is more connectedness to their collective consciousness. I think they are so deep in my mind that I don't even notice it. In my research it was definitely all guided, like they'll make a certain word twinkle to make me click on it. I've begun to see things out of the corner of my eye, like little balls of light floating around; I'm seeing new things every day. It comes and goes in waves.

If I want to connect to them I just turn it on, and if I want some privacy I tell them to bugger off. But probably there is no such thing as private thoughts. It's taken some getting used to, learning to separate my thoughts from theirs. I'd wondered at times, 'Am I becoming schizophrenic?' But they showed me the difference, which was a comfort.

In a way I think they live vicariously through me—it's a way to experience human life. They download my experience through my Mantis DNA, like turning on the Rob channel. I would say it's a safe bet that any time someone interacts with me, they're interacting with the beings through me.

When you interact with them it's like a drop of water in an ocean of consciousness. And I made a conscious decision to jump into that ocean, I wanted to take it as far as I could. I think it was a predetermined choice that I made before I came in here. So it's a free will thing on a level that's really hard to understand. As an ego I can choose, but as a soul I already chose.

What do you understand to be the rationale for the hybrid program?

I believe it's multidimensional in nature. I'm thinking how to build this image for you. First off, we can start with frequency. There's this whole frequency thing going on, you know, with raising frequency, high and low frequencies. You can think of the planet and humanity as a whole as a collective with a specific frequency to it. And the idea is that the frequency here is a little low, to say the least, due to collective negativity, this nightmare scenario going on here that hurts humanity and the planet. So one of the purposes is that the ETs put their DNA into hybrids, who help anchor the higher frequencies, to raise the vibration in the human collective mind.

You can think of it as bowl of steel ball bearings, with all of them vibrating at say, 10,000 rpm. We're all vibrating together harmoniously, but then you take another bearing, which is vibrating at something ridiculous like 800 billion rpm—which would be the ETs—and you drop it into the pot. What happens? It'll explode. So instead you take small bearings with a gentler vibration and sprinkle them in, to raise the vibration slowly. Eventually it can get to a more desirable level. Then you can start branching off to the other reasons. But I believe that is the main purpose: gently raising the frequency of this planet. With me, my DNA is peppered, it's not 50/50 human-ET.

But why do we need to do this at all? My theory is that one reason for the hybrid program is contact. This super-high vibration can slowly introduce itself to the world. That's how first contact works on a vibrational level. It's like that image in the Sistine Chapel, of God reaching for the dude. I know it's a cliché, but it's like we're extending our hands; our frequency's grounded here on Earth, and the ETs have more of a heavenly frequency, if you will. We help to make this connection. And as we raise the vibration more and more, they can eventually come down and make direct contact with the rest of humanity. Shifting the vibration shifts the mindset.

Interacting with them can trigger different things. They can give us sightings and experiences that get us interested in ETs. But the majority of people on this planet, it's their free will choice not to believe that ETs exist. So ETs can't just come down and say, "Here we are." That's another part of the program—hybrids are helping to awaken minds, to raise awareness, so that disclosure can happen. The big D. We're accelerating that awakening process in humanity, we're the bridge between worlds. And by being the bridge we have multiple dimensional degrees of effect around the planet.

With the term 'frequency,' I think in a way it's misused. Everything is vibration; me and this chair, for example. Is there good and bad between high and low? No, I don't believe so. Vibrations are different, but they're all part of existence—good, bad, high and low; it's all relative to me. I do things some would consider to be a low vibration, such as watching TV, partying, and even eating meat, but I believe the important thing is that if you want to raise your vibration, you don't let them affect you. I'm sure some of it does get in there—I'm not impervious to programming.

I've hung out with gang bangers, bikers, etcetera. I see it like this: if the point of us is to raise the vibration, then dammit, get to the lowest part of the pool and raise the vibrations from there. Help everyone, not just the top. It's okay to be a light in a dark place, just don't let it affect you, stay within your power. We came in this 3D form to interact, and some of us are hybridized so that more of our ET consciousness can come into these bodies and we can interact with this reality. So let's interact!

We have a tough job, but we have many tools for getting it done. For me, when I was younger I didn't like what I saw in the world, the way humans treat this planet and everything living on it. I didn't see how I could fit into a society like this, but that was my goal. So I came up with a plan to achieve that goal: change society. Later on I acquired the tools, which was the information I got from contact experiences, dreams, visions and so on, as well as universal laws like the law of attraction. Applying that law helped me create a group of like-minded people. This book project is the implementation of all of that, and can lead to more people having awakenings, and more opportunities to connect and collaborate in changing society. It's also helped me to develop a community of people that I fit into.

Our frequency has an effect on those around us for a reason, so we can't just sit at a computer and be a keyboard warrior. Guys: we have to go out there and *do* it, we have to *make* it happen. We've been learning and talking about this stuff for years, and now it's time to do it. It's like we've gone through school, and now it's time to get a job.

Something huge is coming and it's going to be a ride for us too; we still live in this physical reality and it affects us, and I think some of 'us' forget that. Like people who say, "I don't believe in the chemtrail reality so it can't affect me." Bullshit. It's affecting you. We have to get out there and deal with it on this 3D level—it's not all love and cupcakes here. Look at the world around you—it's collapsing. I'm seeing things dying all around me. It's a serious situation. We have to get out there—I can't let Joe Blow die because I did the work and he didn't—that's insane. How can someone claim to be such a loving being and not care that Joe Blow is going to die? He wasn't given the opportunity to understand he had a choice. It's not his fault, he's part of the program.

Which gets into the whole moral question of why raise the vibration. I think the truth of it is that it was allowed to get so negative here because there's no good or bad, it's just an experience. But the negativity has gotten so bad that humanity literally killed our planet. It's time to act, to step out of the negativity, that's been played out already. Forget all this transitioning to the fifth dimension and all that hoopla, it's just a new expression of life on this planet.

The ETs have shown me that there's a major transition event coming, but what is it? I'm trying to work out the physics behind it. First of all, right now at the center of the Milky Way there's a supermassive black hole in the neighborhood of 25,000 light-years from us, and it's named Sagittarius A. A galactic superwave event leaving the galactic center would take 25,000 years to reach us. Astronomers recently discovered a dust cloud approaching the center of the black hole, and it's going to wake it up. We've never been able to observe our black hole feeding in recorded history. But you see it happening in other galaxies, with their black holes feeding, sending out streams of charged particles like a laser. These things are huge gravitationally, they literally hold galaxies together, so when they are awake they have an effect on the entire galaxy. The last time our black hole awoke it sent a 50,000 light-year x-ray blast into space.

But there's more to it. As we're orbiting the sun, the sun is orbiting the galaxy. Our position in the galaxy and in the universe is constantly changing. Our solar system is moving into a more energetic section of our galaxy at the same time we get hit with this energetic wave. This wave has a frequency to it, which supposedly makes everything spontaneously evolve, it triggers DNA, but at the galactic level. Other planets in solar systems closer to the galactic center have already gone through the transition, so a lot of them are now helping us to get our vibration high enough on planet Earth so that when the superwave hits, we avoid having a bumpy ride, we get a smoother transition. Because this is a ship, and if we fail, we could all sink.

So I believe the hybrids' main tasks are to help raise the vibration and to bridge the gap to ET. Then ET helps train us for this event, so we get a smooth transition. I've no idea what's on the other side but I feel it's going to be awesome, it's going to be a cool light show, which will awaken everyone's minds, and I think it's going to be really positive. I think everyone is going to snap out of these programs, this negativity. I feel everyone will have a chance to choose. This has been planned over eons, to let the negativity play out—it's time. Will we make the transition smooth, are we pushing hard enough, doing our work, or are we just doing the keyboard warrior thing? If so, what's the point of having a human form? I could have been chilling over in Mantis land, meditating and sending love to help people out that way. But nope, I chose to live a human experience, to incarnate and be part of the process, to get in the muck and experience the ending throes of this old world and see it all blossom into positive experience, not just for a few, but for everyone.

A lot of us get so detached that all we can explain is the ethereal, and be so knowledgeable on the ethereal, but the point of being a part of this is to help connect the ethereal and the physical, because Ascension is a physical thing. We need to pull it down and ground it. You can't touch the ethereal, it's like grabbing smoke. I try to see the science behind these frequency things.

Do you have your own hybrid children?

I've had the beings ask me for my DNA before. I was on board a ship and met these beings with this 'children of the damned' look to them. They have a bowl haircut kind of thing, blonde hair, blue eyes. Real tall, real good-looking and polite. I remember how the ship looked inside, it was kind of *Star Trekky* in a way but real bright white. One of them came to me and said, "Hello, may I please have some DNA?" and I remember thinking, 'Mmmm ... sure.' And then its face changed. It was smiling, with orange-yellow eyes with a slit more like Reptilian eyes, and lime green skin. I didn't get a negative feeling from them, this was seemingly a benevolent being. Did they take it? What did they do with it? I don't know, that's all I can remember.

I've had marks on my body where DNA has obviously been removed, little triangles cut out of my flesh, injection points and other stuff. It wouldn't surprise me if I had children up there, but I haven't met any at this point, or seen any evidence of their existence. I did have a prostate problem out of nowhere, with bloody semen for about two months, and I did wonder if some of the beings had removed my semen in some way. Some of the beings are not too nice, unfortunately. They really need to work on their bedside manner.

How do you reconcile the multiple aspects of your identity?

It's not easy because officially, I don't exist. What is the government's official position on UFOs and ETs? They, and the general population, deny it. This creates what I call 'the separation effect.' It goes like this: I start telling people I saw a UFO and they say, "Oh, awesome." I show them a picture—same response. Some will say it's a government thing, not ET. When I tell them I met an alien they're like, "*What?*" Even in the UFO community—let alone in regular society—they say, "There's no *way* you met an ET." Then you go into "I'm a hybrid," and the belief just drops lower and lower. And the more intense the experience, the more people tune out. So you start feeling this separation, you go into what I call 'the non-existence zone.' This is what I am, a hybrid, but as far as the majority of people are concerned, I don't exist.

Do you have physiological differences to humans?

Physically, I've always had these double-jointed wrists, which meant I had to find my own style of punching when doing martial arts, because my wrists would just fold over. And some people have commented that I move oddly in general.

But what's really changed is my mind and the way I perceive things. It was explained to me—by a pretty advanced hybrid—that I had to have this DNA upgrade, or the information that I receive would have fried the synapses in my brain. Another part of it is that I may have been altered so I can travel on the ships physically without being harmed.

Do you have a sense of mission?

I would say it's a multifaceted mission. I don't have a complete understanding yet, but I've often been told by people that they feel I'm going to do something huge, something important, but they don't know what it is. I'm still trying to figure that out myself.

There are a lot of things we do to help out some individuals, but I can't talk about all of that. Anything we keep secret it's to protect people. I've had the black helicopters following me, the intimidation. You have to be careful with that stuff as you don't want to endanger other people. What *can* I say? Let's put it this way: a lot of us have overlapping missions. It's like, say your life mission is to taste broccoli—and I just happen to be a broccoli farmer—together we can help one another fulfil our individual missions. Figuratively, I'm helping someone eat broccoli.

Bringing this awareness to humanity is one facet, being something of an ambassador. I can help ground these beings, and when they're ready to introduce themselves to humanity I'm like a buffer zone, I walk between the two worlds, interacting with both.

Part of it is incarnating as a human being, coming from another race and experiencing life as a human at this time. That part of the mission is for the beings as well. The Mantis beings have a collective consciousness, so they don't know what it is to have a sense of a separate consciousness. Humans believe we're all individual and we're not connected to anything. So some beings come here just to experience the illusion of separation. That helps them understand humans better.

I'm also helping people who are learning about their own ET experiences, just like others who laid the groundwork in the past for me. Those who went through this the first time, all the ridicule, getting this information out—going through the mud in some cases—I couldn't do what I'm doing without them, and now it's my turn to add my piece, to do what I can to expand the understanding about these beings. With my generation, all this information is at our fingertips through the internet, so I can share other people's experiences vividly, and that makes me accelerate. And the next generation is going to be flung even further. We're accelerating each other and we're taking humanity with us, in a way. I act as an accelerator for some people, and as a cushion for others.

I often think that I went through such an extreme awaking to allow me to help others. I was scared shitless at first. I went from, '*Maybe* ETs are real,' to 'Oh my God, ETs *are* real,' to 'Holy shit, ETs are interacting with *me!*' to 'Holy shit, *I'm* part ET!'

And it just keeps going. At first it was a lot of fear. That's why I think they didn't let me know too much too young—they wanted to let me figure this out gradually. Every time I think I know what's going on I meet another hybrid that's further down the road than me and I think, 'Man, I've been acting like a jerk this whole time.' They just blow me away with their level of understanding.

I'm also trying to figure out a way to make a living that is more in alignment with all this. I build devices out of crystals, magnets and metals, things that can help amplify consciousness, so I'm thinking about starting to do that professionally.

Do you have special abilities?

I started to have crazy visualizations after my activation. As well as the 3D devices, I began to see, then create, 2D geometric designs. I make them on computer in black and white. Some contain ET glyphs, and at a conference I showed one to a woman and she went into a trance that no one could get her out of. When she came out of it later she said that she got stuck staring at it, then found herself on board a ship!

As I said, I haven't figured out all of my mission yet, but I feel I have all these visualizations for a reason. I have designs for energy devices, star gates and so on, but no way to fund them yet. I want to get my workshop set up and start building the smaller stuff first, including jewelry, and this can fund the larger stuff. I could also build them by commission.

Holographic healing technique

Healing is part of my mission, and I've developed a holographic healing technique. You can apply this to any part of your body that needs attention.

You first get into a meditative state, breathing steady, in through the nose, out through the mouth, relaxing your body and mind.

Then you begin to visualize. Say you want to heal a cancerous liver, to remove the tumor. First, visualize a perfect holographic image of a liver. Study biology if you have to, so you can best visualize it, so you can go to the cellular level, see the DNA strands spiraling, the cells, all healthy and perfect. Then zoom out and see the blood vessels, bile ducts, the gall bladder, then the meat of the liver, until you've created it.

Now imagine experiencing it, visualize having this perfect liver in front of you, then take that and connect it up; see each cell merging, all the veins, until your healthy liver is in place.

There is enormous power in visualization. I can use all of my body, so there must be a way for your mind to control your own immune system, to promote regeneration, rejuvenation; this is a way to do that. Do it and have other people doing it with intention, a group of minds connecting and simultaneously working on it. Energetically it works, then the body catches up. The healing takes time; we have to reprogram ourselves.

I use another healing technique. I initiate communication with the Mantis beings, and visualize them, in their cloaks. They have a stance, a presence, and I focus on that. Then I see energy coming out of them, and that goes into the body, helping the affected areas.

When it comes to having direct contact with the beings, I have a technique for that too.

Contact protocol

To be consciously meditating is the contact state. There is a feeling to it, and if you can maintain that while awake, that's contact consciousness. I also call it 'singularity consciousness.'

I base this system on the law of equal exchange. It takes a lot of energy for the visitors to get here, so if we request a meeting with them, we need to do the best that we can, with the resources available to us, to match that energy. I call this my 'contact gas tank.' The concept is simple: fill up the tank to have contact. It raises your vibration and lets you spend energy for the intention of positive contact. One very important thing: the energy you put into this is the energy you get out.

How to fill the contact gas tank:

1. Do not purposely harm a single living thing. Take the bugs and spiders outside the house. Water a weed growing out of the cracks in the concrete. Be consciously appreciative to all life you come in contact with. (Thank you for this experience little spider, but you live outside.) By doing this, the visitors will see that you respect and appreciate all contact with life on your world. This means you have the ability to respect and appreciate life from other worlds.

2. Be mindful of your thoughts. Try to look at the positive in everything, even things you don't like. For example, a friend just painted their wall the ugliest color you have ever seen, yet you still tell your friend, "It looks great buddy," because you don't want to hurt their feelings. Train yourself to not have that first negative thought; instead try to think, 'I'm happy my friend enjoys this.' The visitors are extremely telepathic—they hear everything you are thinking. Imagine how people around you would act if they can hear what you are thinking. So start training yourself now.

3. Perform at least one act of kindness to a stranger every day. The visitors can see how you treat others.

4. Love—the most powerful emotion in the universe. Love yourself, throughout the day for as long as you can maintain it. With every breath you take, feel love in your heart. Feel it throughout your body. When you're out and about, feel love for everyone you see. Stop for a moment and breathe in love, connect with all living things, and connect to their existence. Love—anything else is fear.

Some of these tasks may not seem to have any relevance to contacting beings from another world, but they do. It seems that when I follow these steps the best that I can, I tend to get a more interactive experience.

Expect first contact with the species you resonate with the most. It will initially happen in your sleep, when you are half conscious. They are so advanced that they know you better than you know yourself. If they sense fear they'll leave you alone.

To initiate it, let go of all expectations, fears and concerns. It's a physical feeling, and you'll know when it feels like the time is right. Eventually you'll have the urge to say, "I'm ready."

NB. To all the tech people out there, do not go into this to learn of technology. These beings are not just more technically advanced than us, they are more spiritually advanced as well. From what I've learned, the benevolent beings couldn't care less about technology, they are most interested in mentoring us in matters of spirituality. Be patient, the information on technology will come. They need to know you're responsible enough to experience their technology before they give it to you.

That's what I want to teach to a group, because if we can master contact consciousness as a group, we'll have a group contact. But I've found out that it's like herding cats.

When you achieve contact it will probably be one of the most beautiful experiences you can imagine. It can be like finding a piece of yourself that you've been missing. There is an overwhelming sense of awe to it. Their presence is just awe, but it's extremely gentle and they honor you. You'll feel extreme gratitude because they appreciate you so deeply. Just three or four seconds with them feels like eternity. It's an intense, emotional experience, and just accept it for what it is: a beautiful experience. It can connect things inside you that are still beyond our understanding. And you will find it changes you; it's incomprehensibly inspirational.

But you must recognize the law of attraction will be at work, that if you're in a negative space you may attract negative beings. Contact is a reflection of yourself—you get what you give.

What protocols govern ET interaction with humans?

There is a set of rules there, a 'prime directive' if you will. You also have different beings at different levels that can interact in different ways. For the most part we are on our own, they want us to solve our own problems.

Then there's the anthill thing—which is related to the 'zoo theory'—on why they don't interact. Imagine you as a person trying to help an ant colony that got stepped on, and the ants are going crazy. Every time you pick up a rock to try and help they go nuts, and you just make their situation worse. Imagine a ship the size of Jupiter manifests out in our solar system, or a million ships over a mile wide—and they could do that—people would go nuts. The only way you could help them out is to live among them, and help them to understand. The hybrids do that. The image of a seven foot tall Mantis being is horrifying to most people, but for me it's a feeling like being with your mom or dad, and you haven't seen them for fifty years. I can be a human, and help people to understand these beings and what they're all about. I can say, "Hey guys, don't worry about the giants picking up the rocks, they're here to help us."

I think people who are prone to being problematic may fly off their rocker. There will be a lot of disillusionment. What happens when so many people find that everything that they thought they knew was bullshit? The main problem will be what comes after finding out their governments have been lying to them about ETs since the 1940s. What else have they been lying about? Guess what, for the last 70 years you've been sprayed with toxic chemicals, creating a cancer epidemic. Oh, and we haven't needed gasoline for 40 years. It just goes on and on.

My process of awakening started with, okay, ETs are real, but now what? How long have they been here? What are they doing here? Who else knows about this? And I just kept going from there, and you end up asking, "Holy shit, are the people running this planet *completely* insane?" I think this same awakening process will happen to many. Then once enough people have opened their minds, the beings will mentor us. I don't see disclosure coming from the government, because it's the same as them admitting that they've been screwing us over for decades. I think the disclosure is going to come from the beings, and us saying, "Hey, don't worry about it." I don't think I'd trust it if the government led disclosure. If they said, "Hey, here's ET," I'd think, 'Well, what ET's this? One you created, or a real one?' Because I do know that that's going on.

Barbara: We are the disclosure at this point. Look at all the books and conferences in so many parts of the world. This is already going on, despite what any government person says about it.

No government can stop these beings doing what they're here to do. And I have a feeling they're going to do it. They have to. I think we're at a point with the state of the planet, that they're going to have to step in or we're going to lose this planet. And people have to realize that there's a choice to accept and understand this reality and take responsibility for our actions and inactions. I don't think it's fair that people just have to go on without knowing that. With some, the programming is too deep, and I think there has to be a mass sighting to awaken people's minds. Otherwise we're just going to keep on doing what we're doing, and killing this planet. If I have children, I don't see me having grandchildren. I don't see this planet will be able to support two more generations, to be honest with you. The Pacific Ocean is done. We have sea lions washing up dead in huge numbers. They're apex predators, and if they're dying, it means that the food chain is broken. We just had a news report saying they are having to put aerators in the bay because the sardines are dying through lack of oxygen. And that means that the plankton are dying, because they create the oxygen. We have tons of baitfish washing up dead because they have nothing to eat. Even the starfish are dying off. If a creature that's survived for 450 *million* years is dying, you know there's something wrong with the oceans. Then you have Fukushima, and all the micro-plastics ... ugh, we just spit on this world.

So what would it take to wake people up? We can offer our information, but maybe it would take a mass sighting, or maybe the black hole at the center of our galaxy waking up, to really jolt some minds. If you're looking at the Milky Way and you see its center light up and send out energy blasts in a beam 50,000 light-years long, that will wake your mind up for sure. You'd realize you're not so big!

But I have a feeling something is coming. It seems to be about things unfolding. I think they're going to show themselves, and I think it's going to be soon. I just hope that the world can hold together for a bit longer. We will see.

What is your take on the takeover thesis?

Maybe it could have gone that way, maybe there was a plan for that. Or maybe that idea was a plant to make people afraid of the hybrid subject, to keep it quiet, so the real hybrid program would stay hidden and in fear.

There's definitely a negative side out there, and it's not pretty. I had an experience with the negative side when I was 11 years old. My parents took off and I was home alone. I had a toy ambulance, the kind you push down and the lights and sirens would go off. I heard it going off upstairs so I went up to check it out, then the door slammed shut and I was thrown into the air then down onto my bed. There was this invisible force pressing down on me, choking me out, and this nightmare sound of monstrous breathing right on top of me and I blacked out. That was my first physical encounter with a negative being.

I have a feeling that they've abducted me a few times; I recall flying out of my house, going up into space on more than one occasion.

As for me, in my one-room apartment, I'm not taking over jack shit. I couldn't take over a McDonalds. I went in there today and it took me a half hour just to get a cup of coffee.

Manifesting protection

I've learnt how to protect myself better now, using spiritual protection. You'd be surprised how much this visualization stuff works. The body has an energetic field of influence. The brain can manipulate it—it works with imagination. With inner visualization you can manifest energetically in an instant, and physical things can work their way to you.

When you feel it you tap into the universal love attraction. Through visualization you can create barriers around yourself, set them with intention.

These negative entities don't exist here, they're not really phased into this dimension, so they're really sensitive to your thoughts and what you create with your energetic field. So if you imagine you're creating a ball of loving light around you, only things of the same energy can get inside. It really works, and it's important to protect yourself from these entities. It's not all kumbaya and hugs and kisses.

So yes, this negative stuff is going on, but I'm not close to it. Most of my experiences are extremely benevolent. To be honest I'd like to see a hybrid takeover—I think the world would be running pretty awesome. I think I'd make one hell of a President. I'd only have one law: don't be an asshole.

Have you had contact with the military or intelligence agencies?

I've been taken by beings, not humans. There was a period of time when they were trying to get me to work with them, instead of the group I'm working with. In around 2011-12 I was taken to an underground base, belonging to what I call 'the dark ones that hide in the light.' They look like tall, white Nordic types. They have long, golden blonde hair and blue eyes. I've seen them wearing blue jumpsuits with a weird insignia. They seemed nice and polite but they gave me an uneasy feeling—something just didn't feel right. They took me to what was clearly an underground facility, with the stereotypical overhead lights going down the tunnel.

I had a liaison with me, like a tour guide, but something felt off. We reached this weird geometric chamber and the guide said, "Here's your Ascension chamber." It was some kind of learning chamber. I thought, 'Okay, that sounds neat, but something doesn't feel right.' Then a being walked by and I saw his face change, like a hologram, and it was a brown-scaled reptile behind the hologram, with a nasty feel to him.

So the tour continued and we got to these cloning chambers filled with blue liquid. There were beings inside, like Greys. In the next room, he said, "Here are the controllers." They were a race that I felt had been conquered, and they looked atrophied, like Mantis beings, but the skin was wrinkled, all shriveled up. He said that this is where the channeled messages come from. These beings were plugged into machines; they looked kind of dead, like they were merged with the computers. They send channeled messages, but the difference is that they do a full possession of the person, and say things like, "I am Archangel Michael," or "I am Ashtar, of the Ashtar Command." They use a lot of the names that are popular within the field, just totally falsifying information for whatever reason. And I told them, "I've seen enough, I'm outta here," and the next thing I know I'm waking up at home.

They tried to get me again, within a month of the first, and showed me an image of myself with brain cancer, and they said, "You're going to die, but if you fight for us we'll heal you." I said, "*Hell* no," and I haven't seen them since. And it blows my mind to hear myself saying these things, because before all this started I would've said, "That guy's crazy!"

How do you feel about the global hybrid community?

I love the others within the community. I feel more comfortable around them, I can be myself. When we get together we accelerate each other. If it was up to me I would like to build a community together so I could be with them all the time and see what we could achieve.

What would you most like to discuss with other hybrids?

For one, how do they deal with the 'separation effect' I talked about?

I'd ask how they deal with the dynamics in relationships. How do their partners deal with it? My wife and I have shared so much;

seen so much together. She's real supportive, we do everything together. She has her own connections to various races of beings. So I'm curious if they have the same connection with their partners as I have.

I'd also ask: where does your information come from? Mine comes from my mind and heart; the beings do guide me along, point me in the right direction, but they never tell me anything directly. I'm dubious about beings that go around giving information a little too freely.

I'd like to do a conference for hybrids and starseeds who are just awakening, but I would do it totally different. I would get right into interacting with the crowd, rather than having long presentations. When I was awakening I had this huge problem, and I've been thinking about a solution to that problem. There's this burning, gnawing thing that says, 'I want to get involved and be a part of this.' The way the current structure is, it's impossible for me to become a part of this. It's taken years. In 2009 I awoke, and I didn't get involved until around 2011. People go years without getting help, or getting involved. I've always wanted to create something for young starseeds and hybrids to get involved, where these kids can just get up and talk about it, and we can get a discussion going, sharing our experiences. There are people out there with much crazier stories than mine, and they need to be heard. I would be at conferences listening to Q&As and knowing I had the answers! But with the current structure I have to sit and listen. I would like to see that change.

What is the best and worst thing about being a hybrid?

The best thing is that we get to experience awesome things which most people don't even know is real. That's beyond worth it. My top experience was our 2009 sighting of the craft, a triangle the size of a house. It was so profound and amazing. I've seen things that officially don't exist, like a black hole coming out a flying pyramid that oozed plasma. I got to see that shit. And I get an awesome view of the potential of humanity, of what it can be.

But the downside is that what I'm experiencing isn't considered real. That causes some major issues, that I didn't even know existed when I was younger. So thank God they waited until 2009 to wake me up, or my life would have been way harder. I was weird enough; I can't imagine adding that extra weirdness to me. It was already like, "Here's crazy Rob, the ET guy." The ridicule and the teasing was the worst part. It's like, "C'mon guys, I'm experiencing something real, don't joke about it." It definitely makes it harder to function properly in society without getting frustrated, irritated. Now that I know how it could be, and I see how it is, it's kind of disgusting. I feel so bad, hurt for everybody. But that's what we're here for, trying to help 'em out, right?

How can humanity best work with you?

The main way is to get people just to ask the question, "What *if* I'm telling the truth? What *if* I'm not crazy? What then?" That's all I want people to do.

The main problem is that the people don't understand the beings; they misunderstand to the extremes. On documentaries I see 'experts' giving their views on UFOs—who've never even *seen* a UFO or met the occupants—and I'm like, "Oh God, gimme a break." They're still stuck on human concepts like, 'you need x amount of fuel to go x speed' ... *jeez*.

How do you conceptualize God?

I like the way James Gilliland puts it. "A consciousness and energy that permeates all life, the one consciousness that encompasses all consciousness on all planes and dimensions throughout the multiverse. The Absolute."

I do have a visual of what it is, but not the words to describe it. I'm working on it.

What is the most important lesson you've learned?

The most important thing I've learned is how to be more human. I do have all these abilities and amazing experiences, but I still need to ground myself and experience this human existence. When I was first waking up I just let my humanity go, I saw it as a burden, that this humanity thing was ugly and I didn't want to deal with it. The hybrid thing helped me to escape, but then my human life started deteriorating. I became distant from my wife and friends and family. So I learned to be more loving and caring, to experience this reality fully, to enjoy being a human, and alive in this amazing time, when a species transitions from a type A to a type B civilization. So think how it is for a being who can experience anything it chooses, to come down and experience lack: I would imagine that would be amazing for that being, to experience these challenges.

I have days when I think, 'You know what? We're going to be okay.' Then other days I think, 'We're doomed! You people are a bunch of idiots!' And back to 'Maybe we'll be okay in the long run.' Since the beginning of the process, I was wanting it to hurry up all the time, to get it over with, but now I see it totally differently. I think, 'Please just hold off, I changed my mind, I'm finally getting this whole human experience.' I used to watch the markets, wanting them to crash, and if the Dow Jones dropped 300 points, I'd be like, "*Score!*" But now it's like, "Let things hold together, let me keep on doing good." Life's really been turning around lately, even close relationships that used to suck, and I'm seeing all this positivity. It would make sense that things would crash just as I'm on an upswing. But little things that used to bother me, now they don't. And getting in on this project has really helped me out a lot.

When you look at everyone's understanding of what's going on, you're going to get some overlaps, and some stuff that's way off, out of your understanding. In a way we're like pioneers of consciousness. The world's mostly been discovered, so this is like the new frontier, and what frontier is more elusive that our own spirituality? What *is* our consciousness? Learning about my own has been trial and error, experimenting with what concepts work for me and what don't. I'm my own experiment with consciousness, really.

Jujuolui Kuita

Jujuolui is a 43-year-old American woman living in Arizona. Her human ancestry is a mix of German, Irish, Scottish and Native American.

How did you learn you are a hybrid?

It's been a lifelong process of gaining clarity and answers, and I'm still getting answers every day. I knew when I was born that I was different. I would hear voices, get flashes, what I call 'flash memories,' where they would come and let me know things. This happened until I was six, when more things started happening, and they would speak to me through my implants.

I had an understanding that I came here with a mission and I was different. It's been a life-long, incremental process of learning exactly what that was. There were certain ages that were really valuable, like the age of five or six. Also in my 20s, and in my 30s was a huge one, and I haven't had any epiphanies since then. I think it's continual growing and learning at this point.

At age six, for a period of six months, my people came almost every night. I was petrified as I didn't know what it was and no one could explain it to me. My parents were Pentecostal Christians, and would have said it was the devil, so I didn't share it. The hallway was lit with yellow and white, and I couldn't understand how no one else could see that. My heart was racing, and right before they came through the door, I would black out. I thought I'd done that to myself, but later I learned that that's normal, so you don't see them. I also learned that that's the age when they insert the DNA. It had to be done that way because my parents did not contract to have ET contact.

When they came, I always thought it was in my room. On one occasion there was a black hole near the doorway. I thought I was really brave and ran to it to escape this whole thing, but I went down this pitch black hole and there were these big red eyes coming towards me and I thought, 'That was a stupid thing to do.' I ran back to my room and the same thing happened, I blacked out.

The only thing they allowed me to remember was the last visit. A being came through the doorway with a high-collared cape, like Dracula. I think that's what my mind allowed me to see, and I do have a lot of vampire experiences. He came in and sat down, and I felt he was my ship mate, like we're really close on the other side. His name is *Jer*-me [the J is pronounced similarly to the 'zh' sound in measure]. I don't really know how to spell it, but it's pronounced *Jer*-me. I can speak our language, but not spell all of it. Jer-me and I are the same type. He was talking to me the whole time, and he actually made me feel really calm. I knew I should have been freaking out and I remember thinking that wasn't normal. He proceeded to remove one of my eyes and did something with it. He then put it back in, and I got to watch the entire thing. There was no pain or fear, nothing.

When I was young I used to draw him, before I knew any of this stuff. I drew a bipedal Reptilian with a long tail. He looks muscular, athletic, very tall. I used to take the drawing to school, which was a bad decision. I'd figured it must be normal until then.

I drew a close-up of what we look like. We have a comb and a wattle, similar to a rooster. I'm still gaining some information about us; they tend to give me what's important. But with the eyes I get a kind of avocado, or yellow. I think they can change, because we're fifth-dimensional beings, I think it's how we view them at the time.

Barbara: I had a powerful experience of meeting a Reptilian male in my living room. He was tall and muscular, with an amazing energy. He told me he'd been specially bred as an ambassador. I held his hand for some time, and it felt wonderful. Then he just disappeared. Later I was regressed and learned more about the experience, which went on for a while longer than I'd recalled consciously.

When you touch them there's so much that happens, it's like a shock of energy passes to you, and that means a lot. People don't realize that that energy stays in you, and you change from then on.

When I understood what I was, it wasn't an 'Oh my God!' moment; it was confirmation, and I could move on. Things finally made sense. I knew I was true in my thoughts and feelings; I had a huge piece of the puzzle to confirm everything in my life. It created a foundation, and I've integrated it nicely. I know it's me, but I only discuss it with people who ask or would understand. And only if it's relevant.

What is your ET component?

We're the Fajan race of Reptilians [pronounced fah-zhan]. We're from a planet in the Andromeda galaxy called Faqui, which is pronounced 'fah-gwee.' We have other names we call ourselves. 'Fajayan' is our joint unit. We have an agreement with other races to patrol the galaxy together. It's for guidance, for neighboring planets and galaxies that request help of any kind. A lot of people refer to them as "universal police," but I don't like that name as it sounds too authoritarian, and that's not the intention at all. The intention is more for guidance and help, although we do wear armor, which I think is why a lot of people associate us with police.

Fajayan has a *proud* feeling to it, I think because that service is really something; it's a hard job, it's stressful, but it's about being of service. I'm not sure if I'm still a part of that while I'm here. I just know that that was my job before I came here. It's my direct past, I'm very connected with it.

When I became awakened and received all this information, my name was one of the things I received. Kuita [pronounced kyoo-ta] is the location on my planet where my extended family live, so I'm really Jujuolui of Kuita. Jujuolui is pronounced 'zho-zha-lee,' but I'm Juju for short.

I changed my name officially about a decade back. Because I'm a spiritual person I wanted the highest vibration, and my name has that for me. I changed it in 2006, and even have it on my passport, which I think is kinda cool.

There are physical differences in Reptilian forms. We have long tails, but I've seen some without, and that just looks painful to me. We choose our form as we're fifth-dimensional beings, and we've all agreed to be Reptilian. The tail is a huge part of your Reptilian being. I don't know how to explain it, and I can't understand how Reptilians could not have a tail.

Our general form is athletic; we're emerald green in color, and green has always been my favorite color in this life, so I brought a lot of things into this lifetime. They tell me I'm still alive there, that I didn't have to die to come here, but I don't understand it and so can't explain it.

How were you created?

My parents didn't want any ET contact, but I am very connected to my mother; I share the same birthday with her. And my grandmother on her side, there's some connection, possibly a star connection. I'm not sure, but I feel that it is, because my sister is open to this field, and she has some star children. But her purpose in this life is not to delve into that like I did.

So when I came in, what the splinter of my soul did was—according to what I've been told—it grabbed some Pleiadian DNA to bring into the human form. And the reason was to use star essence energy to develop my body. Then after birth, my own people would return to manipulate it, and insert Reptilian DNA before the age of six. So I was a human with some essence of star energy, like a normal starseed might be, but then my star family would insert some DNA, activate some, and leave some unactivated.

Sometimes people will glimpse my crest or see my eyes change, so it's like it's always there, but superimposed on a different level of vibration. A couple of people have seen me shift full-body. Friends have seen it when I'm in high-energy places, like UFO conferences or MUFON meetings, where the energy shifts. During a MUFON meeting my eyes shifted while they were discussing negative Reptilians. My friend saw my eyes changing and began stuttering out loud, so I had to tell her to be quiet, as that's the *last* place I'd want to expose that. I know when it happens, as it feels like a pressure behind the eyes.

Barbara: A lady once sent me pictures showing her eyes changing, and she said it was triggered by high emotion. When she was singing in an opera people saw her eyes changing, and the skin around her eye changing to a Reptilian texture.

For me, it happens with high emotion, like love, or gratitude. It's triggered by high frequency, so being around lower vibrations it won't happen. Higher, positive vibration brings it out. That's a good indicator of what kind of being someone is. If their ET DNA exposes itself in anger, what does that tell you about their nature? It's not a judgment, but it may show you who they are and where they're at.

We're in what's called 'the Star Alliance' with many species. We had to establish our intent before incarnating, and there's a lot of detail that goes into that, like which alliances you're going to connect with once you're here. Who is going to protect you, look out for you, teach you, help you with your information, heal you? We have no part of the Ashtar Command, no family bond with them. We had to work with the Pleiadians to make this body, so we all work together, but I'm closer to the insectoid species, the Mantis and the Greys. I'm really attracted to them and they've helped me so much. And I know I have hybrid children with them.

One of my mates is an insectoid called Kart-zan, who has a male energy. It's funny because in this life I'm not 'straight,' but when it comes to the ETs it's a totally different thing. We see things very differently, we don't have the same taboos and limitations. It's about how your souls connect to each other. It's beyond the body, beyond the sex, the color, the species. It's really deep. It's about energy entwining and what your souls do together. It's like music. It's a connection of energies, a symphony; it has a synergistic effect, it creates beauty. It creates music that other beings can see, and it has real, tangible effects in the universe. If you could see the energies swirling, resonating together, it would look like a galaxy being created. And that's why if you're a star being connecting with other star beings you can create things around you because you're attracting those otherworldly things to you. Imagine looking down at the Earth from a ship and you can see energies being created. Ugly energies from war, or beautiful energies from connection. If you could see that beautiful swirl of energies, wouldn't you want to go down and be a part of it? Like a UFO conference—it's a whole different energy, and that's why it attracts so many star beings. It's like they want to swoop down and collect it and feel it for themselves. It's magical, it's like going to Oz.

I realized when I was 14 that I had to be careful with coming out to people. My parents never accepted me being gay. They live their life simply, and use denial a lot. I tried sharing with my mom as we're close; I told her I'm from the Andromeda galaxy, and that my name was Jujuolui, but she didn't take it well, so I kept the rest to myself. When I wrote my book, explaining my experiences, I told her not to read it. She doesn't need to know that. I would prefer she didn't. If she needed some answers then okay, but knowledge can be a poison if you're not ready. I've done TV, radio, documentaries, and in the beginning I was sending her the links to see if she was open to it. She looked because she loves me, but it's not good for her. I'll tell her if I'm being flown to LA for a movie shoot because it's exciting, but I won't go into detail. I do the same with friends and co-workers. I'm pretty private that way.

What connection do you retain with your star family?

It's funny because the Greys and insectoids treat me like family, because they know my people don't come here. They pick me up, take me places on ships. They treat me like one of their own. One time they took me on board, flying over San Francisco—I remember the bridge. They were teaching me how to fly from the sky and go into the water. I had a band around my head, and in my mind's eye I could see the one who was training me, telling me telepathically. I would splash in the ocean, and he shook his head, saying, "No, you're not traveling; you go from point A to B, there's no transition." You kind of 'blink' from place to place, it's all mental. I was in awe of his intelligence; because we were connected I could feel how intelligent he was, that he had to lower his vibration to communicate with me so I understood it. I know how to fly a ship because I'm a pilot, but blinking from point A to B was different. I don't know why I was being taught that. It could have been on a higher frequency, but at the time it was real, tangible, I could see him, hear him, sense him, and it felt 3D. At the time I was wondering whether or not anyone else could see us practicing this dive maneuver by the Golden Gate Bridge.

During this conversation I have my guides with me to give me extra information that I don't have, and what I'm getting is that they have force fields around the ships, which can displace water for a smooth entry. Truman had a 'shoot them down' policy, and they know that, so they have shields up. There could be a lot up there that are cloaked, and I'm always asking them to show themselves, and sometimes they'll guide you to look at a star and give you a real quick blip, but it's a risk as our government has devastating weapons. So it's nice just to get a blip or a streak. So I know they're there, but cloaked, or set at a higher vibration. Sometimes there will be a group of people, but only one person will see the UFO. I think that they can connect, and lift the vibration so individuals can see the ship. Or that human already has a high enough vibration, without being a hybrid.

Lesson from a Grey on sending love energy

I was on their ship and he passed me a small hybrid baby asking me to send her love for growth and balance. This was very challenging for me because I had just come out of a relationship with a Grey hybrid and my heart was feeling pain. The Grey knew this, but also trusted me to follow his instructions and help this baby that needed me! Wow! is all I can say to that.

As I held the baby, she felt lifeless. He told me to visualize pure love as the brightest white light I could imagine, and see that going from myself to her energy being. As I began, he stopped me. I could feel his gentleness and love for both me and the baby. He instructed me to look at the light I was sending, for it had 'streamers' of other colors attached to it. There was red, green and yellow as well, which would cause harm to the child. This was crucial to get under control, and he asked me to put aside my feelings of pain, jealousy and self-pity for now. I had to instead concentrate on pure love so I could help this baby.

He stopped me about five times before any other 'streamer' could reach the baby and affect her energy being. But I finally did it! I was amazed, and in awe of this lesson, and the faith this ET had in me to do the job, risking the baby's life. Shortly after that experience, my own star family strongly urged me to take up Reiki. I now use that very wise skill as a Reiki practitioner and I am eternally grateful to that ET. Thank you, wherever you are!

What do you understand to be the purpose of your creation?

I came here not specifically for humanity, but for Mother Earth and the animals. Humankind was a third priority. Mother Earth called us, told us she was ready to evolve, to move to a higher frequency, and she needs help to do that. I was in my ship when she put out her 911 call. It was very powerful and emotionally overwhelming. It was like a quantum beam of energy that she shot out into the universe. I get chills every time I tell the story. It was really beautiful. I fell to my knees in my ship after the wave went through us. I went back to my council to report this event. Our whole intention of living is based on good for all, not just one group. We consider the whole of the Andromeda galaxy to be part of our home. Everything we decide, we decide for the good of as many beings as we can. So they allowed me, which is such an honor—and I don't know why I was chosen—to bring my fifth-dimensional frequency to Earth, to be part of the mission. My soul comes from a fifth-dimensional place, carries that energy, and being a hybrid allows me to carry more of that frequency. Being a hybrid doesn't make us more special, whether you're a hybrid or not just depends on your mission. We understood that a lot of other ETs were coming here to help Mother Earth carry that higher vibration.

As far as agendas go, there are as many purposes as there are ET races. Missions can be similar, some exactly the same, but each is representing their people.

With me, the implants they put behind my eyes allow me to send back all experience, a kind of biofeedback. Everything I experience in this lifetime is sent back to them. So right now you're on camera on my homeworld. At nighttime I shift into my hybrid state to send data back. You don't use a Commodore 64 for today's purposes, you use the right equipment. You need a 5D form to send the information back, so I shift into that form. My ex saw me shift one night, full-body, and she said the only reason she didn't run screaming was because she could see my characteristics, and realized it was me. I had never shared my ET identity with her before, I'd learned to keep it private. That happened at 30. That was a huge shift for me, it confirmed everything in my life. As she watched, she saw me shift back. It lasted under a minute, so she saw the end of the process. My people chose her to see that because they believed she could handle it. The fact that I could finally speak about it was a beautiful gift to me. She actually went through a lot with me, in terms of contacts, strange lights in the room, doors shutting by themselves. She was able to understand it.

It's not my mission to teach humanity, but I offer who I am to the world, and I'm open to people if they want to know, but that's as far as I go. It's kind of sad as I'm the only one from my planet; it's a lonely existence, being separate from my home planet all my life. But there are many ETs here from all over, and I feel like they're my extended family. I tend to have more of an ET perspective than a human perspective. I always think how the ET feels. I can see things more easily through the ET perspective.

How do you reconcile the multiple aspects of your identity?

I focus on the ET part as that is where my mission and my priority is. The human part is just the DNA used to create these bodies. Some people came in here with a dual identity, where they can take human form here and ET form on the ships, and I can sense that that's their mission, that they came in knowing that. I think it's adorable how these ETs come here, set their life up, figure out how it will work best for them.

When I go up on the ships it makes me upset as I always see myself in human form. But I recognize they aren't human and I tell them so. I don't know why I do that, but then they smile and walk away, or show themselves to be ET. A lot of the time we're taken up in groups, and I don't connect with the group as I know they're human. I feel more ET so don't want to associate with this group of human strangers, I want to associate with the ETs. I had one lady come right up in my face, and she showed her Grey form, and I was drawn into her eye. It was amazing—it was the galaxy. I fell into her eye and went into space. It was one of most beautiful things I've experienced. I went right into her soul and saw the universe.

I've always felt somewhat socially anxious, uncomfortable in my skin. I've had to deal with depression, and go through that process. But coming out the other side you realize it's a gift. How else do we get rid of negative energies? Disease is a way of working negative energy out of our system; it helps lift the soul to do your project, it's like the shaman's death. We accumulate negativity, karma, and sometimes get knocked on our butts to learn.

Some years ago I lost a soul connection, and moved towns. Then the truck carrying all my possessions caught on fire and everything got destroyed. But I came back from that, it was like the phoenix rising; I started with a clean slate, and I needed that to fulfil my mission. It can be easy looking back, but at the time it's hell. At times I felt like just walking out and succumbing to the desert, which wouldn't take long, but I have a mission. That said, I'm still ready to leave any time!

While I'm here, I'll help and be of service and remain joyful. Being joyful and loving keeps our vibration high; staying healthy and happy amplifies your mission. When I did hypnotherapy with Barbara I learned that the most important thing for me is to stay happy, to help anchor the light, absorb the light.

Dolphins and whales are the biggest anchors on Earth for the light; the more anchors we have the more light energy Earth is infused with.

I believe dolphins are true, perfect ETs on Earth. I have these dreams—well they're not dreams but they happen at night. I'm on a boat at night and I sense these beings in the water. I just jump right in with them. I always know that the people on the boat around me don't understand, but I don't care. It's about my journey.

Do you have physiological differences to humans?

When I was a kid in school we'd see a skeleton dancing around, singing about how the skeleton is put together and all that, and I didn't resonate with it. I couldn't see how I could be like that inside.

I am not certain of the extent of my differences. When I was younger they did something to my eyesight. I had to get glasses in my teens, and one day I found that the glasses were blurry and I had 20/20 vision again. I think they're keeping it that way because of the implants. They want to keep the vision as clear as possible, like if your camera lens is dirty you want to clean it.

Do you have a sense of mission?

Even humans have a sense of mission, so for us when we get a vision or a voice, it's a reminder of what we already know we're here to do. When I was planning my book *We Are Among You Already*, I was reading a Kryon book—I love Kryon—and I got a voice come through telling me to call Cynthia. I said, "After this chapter," because my vibration was so high from reading this book that I didn't want to put it down until I was done. Then they yelled at me, and said, "No, call her *now!*" So I said, "*Alright* already!" and went to call her. So that's what they do, they remind us.

Barbara: When I had finished the book Alien Experiences *with my co-author Nadine Lalich, and we were at the proofreading stage, I was taken by these beautiful, tall, thin, almost transparent beings, and they had been so aware of us getting together and writing that book. And they were full of encouragement and commendation for having done that. So we didn't have that at the beginning—it seemed like a very Earth-level project—but when it was completed they let me know that they were so pleased, and that it's time to get this material out and let people know. Maybe they were influencing it all along without our being aware of it. And I think they even helped Nadine find me.*

Yes, I think that we all receive guidance, like when we're looking for a new job or a partner. Because it's so rough down here I think we get higher assistance from someone, whether it's spirit guides, power animals, angels, family that's passed on or our star family.

Are you encouraged by guides?

My star family is always with me. Also, I am close with a number of ETs that check on me and help me learn new things. I constantly have to ask myself if things I'm experiencing are my imagination, or if it's coming from my guides. What works for me is being aware of the time. The creative mind takes time to create something, whereas truth is instantaneous. If it's 'instant knowing' I run with it, but if it's taking three seconds to develop, it's my imagination.

When you expand in consciousness you can begin to distinguish where the information is coming from, whether it's your higher self, or ETs. Like distinguishing between dreams and actual events.

Do you have special abilities?

I have a very humble standpoint on that. I don't like to think I'm more special than anyone else. Jesus said we can all do these things. I believe we all have the ability to heal, to channel healing, to connect with animals, levitate, be psychic.

I am particularly open to spiritual growth and expanded consciousness. I have the ability to tap into my star family and receive information, but it's for my mission so I don't really see it as a special ability.

I am intuitive, I have some psychic ability. But it's like a muscle, it's something you have to strengthen, but I don't work on it. I did listen to my intuition as a cop—it would give me useful warnings.

One time when I was driving to college, my people gave me a really painful feeling in my gut. I got a kind of mental/verbal cue to get off the highway and turn around. I thought, 'That's crazy, I want to go to college.' But they told me they'd only take away the pain when I turned around. It kept getting worse until eventually I yelled out, "Okay, *fine!*" The second I did what they asked, the pain disappeared. I don't know what that was. I assume it was something my soul didn't want to go through, or maybe it would have changed me in some way that would not be beneficial to my mission.

I've always been strongly connected to animals. I don't know that I'd call that an ability, but I guess it depends on your definition. I definitely connect more with animal life than humans. I feel that connection, like when going out for walks with friends. They would like it because there would always be wild animals that would come in close. I think there's an attraction to similar energy that would draw that being over. I wouldn't do it intentionally, but it would normally happen as part of my experience. It feels very loving and peaceful. We would have wild birds on a branch fall asleep right next to us. It's about where you're at as a person. They're so much more connected, they mirror where you're at. If you're attracting peaceful encounters, it's showing you that you're peaceful and balanced. It's all energy-related. I was meditating on a hill in California and had a coyote come within ten feet before it recognized me; it didn't realize I was there, and it was surprised. It was like, 'Oh my God, what are *you?*' It backed off, but wasn't aggressive. It obviously didn't detect anything off, energetically.

What protocols govern ET interaction with humans?

There's a lot of speculation out there, but I want to stay with what I know. I feel very strongly that ETs will not allow nuclear war. It affects things too deeply, at the subatomic level, and it interacts with other dimensions that are nearby.

But I'm not sure we intervene at all. To intervene or manipulate is more of a lower vibration. The way I've been taught and see things, is that we bring an essence in that is of a higher vibration, use our expanded consciousness and apply loving, spiritual, grateful energies, and affect the overall energy of the planet. My mission is Earth's animals—which affects humans as well—but it's for the animals first.

Not all ETs here are intending to increase the energy, not all are for service to others; some are more in service to self, and you will feel the manipulation part of it, the desire to control. If you feel that, and see that behavior, that is intervention.

Some ETs here sense that starseeds and hybrids are having issues with some beings trying to prevent them speaking, raising consciousness; the phone tapping is done by the self-serving part.

There is a species of Reptilian here that's not in service to humanity. It doesn't mean it's evil, but it's not here for *us*. There's a big difference. People forget to question that. It's like a human stepping on an anthill by mistake—if you ask the ants if we're evil, what would they say?

How do you define 'Frequencies?'

It's like music. Think of your least favorite. Then imagine walking into a bar playing that music. What do you do? It could make you turn around and walk out. It could make you feel sick. It doesn't mean it's bad music, but to you it's discordant. It hits you at an uncomfortable level, it doesn't resonate with who you are. That's all frequency. Then think of the most beautiful music: you can stick the headphones on and it takes you places, it brings information, it makes your body feel really good. That's an example of frequency and how it affects you.

What is your understanding of Ascension?

Everyone has their own understanding, their own truth. We all have an innate desire to evolve. My understanding is that Mother Earth herself wishes to move forward and evolve, and so does the human soul group, which wants to shift collectively into a fifth-dimensional existence. There have been many cycles of destruction in the past, including Atlantis and Lemuria, and the Earth goes into a heightened state, as she did when she sent out that cosmic 911 call. She will evolve with or without humanity. As far as needing help, that's why all us ETs came. The animals are already with her. The only thing the animals need protection from is humans.

So the Ascension process is about lifting our vibration high enough to slide into this next phase of living. At that point, when that transition happens—and it's already happening—there will be a level when people could go back home. I always thought I'd die at 29, and when 2012 came I thought I'd be gone by then, but our contracts are fluid, they can grow and change with what's going on. It didn't happen like everyone thought it would, but it is still happening. We are inside Ascension right now. If you look at it from 0-100, 100 being where we slide into the fifth dimension, we're in between. We're on the path already. At certain points along that timeline, ETs know that they can go back home. I'm praying for the time when I can go back home—I was ready over ten years ago. I'm doing what I can here, but I would much rather be at home.

> **Raising your vibration**
>
> It all starts with thinking, expanding your consciousness. It's an energetic evolution. As people learn to be more loving, grateful, accepting, of service, aware of actions and thoughts and what that does to other people, that is expanding consciousness. That shifts everything, as you think in a higher form. Everyone combined shifts the whole community into thinking and living a different way. All animals and ETs have higher consciousness. So that higher thinking is here, it's available, all people have to do is tap into it, to see and accept change. Caring is higher consciousness, respecting other life forms. It's higher thinking. It's not religion but spirituality. You have to constantly be aware of your thoughts, because the law of attraction brings things to us, according to where our thoughts are. We're creating our reality every second by where our thoughts

are. The more loving people are, with higher consciousness and vibration, the sooner we can shift together.

The higher your vibrational frequency becomes, the closer you get to the highest, universal truth, but our personal truths are different, and we must respect that. I see 'universal truth' as the highest, most pure knowledge of Source energy, the Creator of All That Is. Each evolutionary step a soul takes towards Source energy, as an increase in one's vibration, opens us to this pure truth. We exist here in physical, third-dimensional form, which grants us very little access to pure truth—compared to those of higher dimensions—so each of us has our own. I believe it is every soul's wish to evolve toward universal truth at some point. There is nothing more exhilarating or more beautiful.

The best way I can be loving and help here, is to put my truth across as sincerely, clearly and honestly as I can, and hope that it helps, but with no desire to control, change people, or make money. It's solely based on being true to myself, and being of service. We can't control anyone but ourselves; we can only lead by influence.

If I can be the best of myself every day, the highest vibration of myself, by watching what I think and say, then I'm being true to myself, and I will attract other people like me, attract experiences that are of that same vibration. It's actually painful to me, to listen to the media, to watch the news, because of the negativity, the things that are focused on. I love documentaries about nature, I love *Ancient Aliens*, but as soon as that commercial comes on, I switch off. I don't want that to be a part of my experience. I'm very deliberate in what I absorb. It takes time to build up a vibrational level, and become a certain being that you want to be, so why would you want to compromise that? You still have to interact, but what matters is how you choose to experience that interaction, in terms of how you feel, what you think about it. You can choose how you see things, and allow others to do the same.

As the Buddhists say, if you don't like the way you feel about something, change the way you think about it. This is Earth, and you are entitled to feel any way you want to. And I choose to feel more evolved. I will always choose the higher vibration. A lot of people feel like a victim, but instead why not choose a more evolved path of thinking? For example, one time I was on the ship and I had an incision in my back as part of a medical procedure. I could smell the burning cauterized flesh. But I didn't take it as traumatizing. I didn't have fear. They healed me, and I was thankful for it. So I took from that experience that I was healed, instead of feeling like a victim who'd been stabbed in the back. When I came back into my body I had no scar, so I knew it was an ethereal procedure, and I took it as a positive experience. I think they helped heal my kidneys as I had problems before then, which cleared up after.

The reason so many ETs are here is to bring as much light and higher frequency to this planet as possible, because Earth wants to evolve, and with all this shadowy government stuff going on, with negativity, greed, power and control, creating hierarchies, that's very unevolved, 3D thinking. We're trying to move past that. When you realize the beauty of equality there's no need for that. I had a friend at the DEA who learned that frequency towers around the U.S. keep the frequencies capped, like putting a lid over you, preventing your thoughts from expanding. Cell towers send out frequencies that are messing with the natural balance of life. We're trying to break through all that. We don't need that type of technology as we're all telepathic. It's all about the money.

But the light and love does not oppose anything. Light doesn't oppose, it offers what it is. It's available. There's no fight or war in the light, those are products of lesser energies. Negativity is weak, and when you realize that, it no longer affects you. It's similar to a cold or a virus: if you're healthy enough, eating well, you don't get sick. Sickness is a lower vibration, so if you have a higher vibration it cannot affect you.

It's like proof. The need for proof of something is a low vibration. When you become more evolved, move to a higher spiritual vibration, you don't need proof. Your eyes open to how things really are, and you get proof, but that's when you don't need it. You just know. So going from 3D thinking to 5D thinking doesn't just happen with a snap, it's personal growth. But with all these starseeds and hybrids here, raising the vibration, it makes that transition a lot easier. It's like a huge ladder that fell down from the sky, and says, "Come on, this is available. And if it doesn't scare you, we'll help you move up the ladder."

If someone is opposing, they won't move to the fifth dimension, and that's okay. It's not a judgment, it just means that their soul has not yet learned what it wants to learn. We view that in a loving way and we support that. We don't expect everybody to be in the fifth dimension—that's not loving. We want to help those who want to go, those who are ready. It's offering that ability to move on, that's all it is. We have our hand extended to you. If you're ready, you take it, if you're not, we also support you in that.

Ascension is more about the universe than humanity, it's about the universe expanding. Evolution is going to happen regardless—it's already happening. Humans can choose for themselves—no one is controlling or judging them. If you've learned everything, and are ready to go to a higher dimension, you'll go that way. For some, their soul wants to learn more, it wants a better foundation before ascending. The human soul group is made up of many smaller soul groups, some of which might stay behind—they will have another opportunity. While the rest go to the fifth dimension, they will go to another 3D world and continue learning there.

What is your take on the takeover thesis?

If David Jacobs is using the term 'threat,' I think it's a matter of perception. The words you choose show you where you're at with something. The hybridization program is definitely happening, but why do we have to see it as a 'threat,' rather than more of a profound happening, that includes humanity helping another species? I like that take on it much better—that's what I choose to focus on. And a lot of us hybrids have been asked to be like donors, to have hybrid children with the ETs, to extend the species' existence. To me that's a very loving, spiritual experience, not a 'threat.' It just depends on how you want to see it I guess. I respect everyone's view, but I certainly won't support his book by buying it.

I'm glad you've had positive experiences with Reptilians, Barbara. I've tried to explain that to people, but I've had to be really careful what I say because it can make me a target. Because too many people think all Reptilian ETs are bad. The one you met, who was an ambassador to Earth, that would be really challenging. I would never want that job. I know the negative ones have their impact. I've run into them on the astral plane. I ran into the Queen of England and that was kind of scary. I said to her in passing, "You're one of them," and she nodded with a smirk. That gave me chills. It was silent and brief, but felt profoundly unloving. You *could* have a fear response to it. I could definitely see where people would get into the drama of it all, because so many want a doomsday. I feel bad that people don't realize they're attracting it. I prefer to focus on the positive aspects. We need to be aware that we attract what we give our attention to.

But some takeover agenda may be in place, some evidence may support that, but it's not going to happen for me as I'm not choosing that. For a lot of people that may come true because they feel strongly about it; they will self-manifest it because of that thought process and that energy.

My star family will not come here. Earth is off limits for them, mostly because of the negative Reptilians already part of Earth's history. Too many have come here and set off something with the negative ones. It's more like a political thing, so they're really careful who they send. I'm the only one from my planet, which is really lonely sometimes. That's why I appreciate what you're doing, in that one of the intentions is to unite more, and let each other know who's out there that we can connect with.

Have you had contact with the military or intelligence agencies?

I went into the army at 18, I went to Germany and all that. I have that background, but was not a part of anything like the 'Reptilian militia' that people talk about. I loved the physicality, the training. I was a sharpshooter, I scored 300/300 earning the 'hawkeye' rating. I was selected for advanced training.

For me it was about getting out of Indiana, learning about others, growing up, seeing what I could do as a person. It was a good challenge. But there were no ET experiences related to it. Jer-me still came to me multiple times but I thought he was my spirit guide; I didn't make the connection until later that he was Reptilian. He protected me from some of the guys. I was sweet and shy and some of them took it the wrong way. I didn't pick up on their intention, and got myself in one or two bad situations, but I was always protected. Not every starseed who serves in the military is a part of some nefarious agenda!

How do you feel about the global hybrid community?

I think it's very healthy to unite, as we're still learning about ourselves. I'm blessed as I was given the ability to know who I am, but a lot of starseeds don't have that awakening as it's not a part of their mission. But because it was part of my mission to awaken others I wrote a book to help with that.

As we connect we can trigger memories, be of support. Just to know others are out there who are experiencing the same thing, it's so healthy, it helps in processing something you don't understand. The more pieces of the picture we get, the clearer things become, and the more wholesome we can be. The more we speak and share, the more we understand what's going on, because we all experience things differently. To fit together my background, why I came in the way I did, why things were triggered at different ages, it helped to talk about why things happen. I learned that my parents didn't want any ET connections, so I had to respect their wishes as a soul and come in a certain way. How many people know that unless you hear someone speak about it? So we really help each other a lot, to grow, to get answers, to become more balanced. And the more balanced you are, the higher your vibration can be. It all goes back to trying to be the best person you can be, and shining your light.

In terms of detecting other hybrids, I'm not psychic enough to automatically tell who people are, but I sometimes get glimpses. Sometimes I can see or sense it. But I would never 'out' someone. I might see another Reptilian strongly, but I have to be careful what I say, as they may not need to know it. I'm a Reiki practitioner and when I do sessions, there's a lot of things that I see—because it's a very psychic thing—involving other dimensions, energies coming from all over, and I have to be very careful what I relay to that person, because if I tell them I can see a huge, lanky ET working on them, it might set them back on their path. I would feel horrible if I did that as my intention is always to support positive growth.

I used to teach in my ET class that when hybrids and starseeds get together their lights combine synchronistically and are really bright. It's like a symphony. If you're on a ship looking down at Earth with heightened vision, you can see all these lights getting together and it's really beautiful.

I've been on the ship with partners and shared telepathy as we're walking around. It deepens the relationship but makes it much more intense as well.

What would you most like to discuss with other hybrids?

Lots. Sharing experiences, seeing their level of memories, hearing their language, learning about their origin, how they awakened, what their mission is. Hybrids are at all levels of awareness, so it's challenging to find people who are awakened, who enjoy contact experiences, and the metaphysical stuff like abilities, or walking into crop circles. We could talk about beings they meet in dreams or on other levels; it might make a connection for me, trigger another memory.

What are the best and worst things about being a hybrid?

Connecting with humans is really hard. I feel energy interacting between every living thing, and being so open and aware, and knowing that few others feel and know that, that's a huge thing to feel different about. It's innate, and the people I deal with may not take it the same way. It's like we're speaking a different language. Being so different, where it's not understood, you have to be the better person and accept it. That's the hard part: dealing with differences when it's not supportive of who you are.

Barbara: This may be part of why you're here, to help teach others how to connect more deeply and widely. Humans have a need for connection that expresses itself in many ways. We tend to look for connection with one other person in particular, but you are representing the ability to connect with all living things. That's a wonderful thing to share, and you may help to awaken that in people.

The good part is the sense of mission, and purpose. And the sense of so much more out there beyond our individual selves, a much bigger picture, and that gives you a seed of hope. It's a profound spiritual experience to know that there are much better experiences, and more profound things going on; we're not stuck in this little 3D world, there really is so much more out there that's beautiful, connected.

When you awaken you learn so much through your own research, trying to understand your experiences, and you find your inner spirituality through that process, learning how things work and why. So your understanding increases all the time, and you learn you're a part of something much bigger, and that there are all these beings helping you. And you're meeting some of them here on Earth who are going through their own emotions and dramas, and you have to get through your own prejudices because they're your sisters and brothers, and you might not even get along here. Just because you're a starseed that doesn't mean you'll get along. Or you might know them from the ships but once you get down here it's a whole other game.

But it's all about levels of consciousness. For example, some can only think as far as their city. Others can think beyond that, expanding their thinking to their state, and others to their nation. Few expand their consciousness to the world, or the Earth as a whole, which is really amazing. Because I'm awakened to who I am—a being from Andromeda—my thinking extends to the universe. I have to think universally about the effects of different actions and processes. How far do the effects go? Does it affect the beings?

Because it's so hard to tap into the truth of things, we have to go with our instinct, our best guess. But it's kind of exciting that way, it's like a never-ending puzzle; it just keeps expanding in all directions and we get more pieces of this 3D puzzle. It's a journey of learning, including self-identity, where you are constantly shifting your beliefs as new pieces come in and make you see things differently.

So that's the best thing about being a hybrid: knowing that there is so much more. But it can be depressing at the same time, being kept here in such a tiny section of 3D living. It's both at the same time.

Manifesting protection

What they want me to show you Miguel, is that when you said you were opening up to wanting guidance in this journey, as you said those words your whole energy shifted, and you have just allowed higher guidance from other beings. Your conscious mind sent a signal, it opened up your aura to receive. So just know that by saying that, all these ETs that are around this project have gotten the okay to help you. But just be careful with that.

What I did before the session was to surround this as a sacred space, where nothing of a lower vibration can come between us or around us. I used the white and the golden light to make it the highest vibration that I can. So just be aware not to be too open to receiving everything. You're in control, so when you're ready, say that you want it from certain higher beings. Go with your instinct: is it good or bad? Some are not necessarily bad, they're neutral, they're just not concerned with you. It's good to listen to your visceral response.

Negative entities, which are lower vibrational beings, have trouble surviving around love vibrations, which are higher vibrations. So if you can stop yourself feeling fear, and feel love and light, you can be protected from them. And that goes for life in general. Whatever you do, do it from a high vibration, do it out of wanting knowledge, or good connections, or love and light. And you will receive those things, and keep lower vibrations out of your experience.

Cynthia Crawford also encourages abductees to summon love in their heart, and send it to the beings. If they are not good, they will

> leave. They can't take that. It changes your experience. If you hold yourself in light, you will see and feel that experience more clearly. If people feel fear and anxiety, if they feel victimized, they are lowering their vibration. And they are really bringing to themselves what they fear.

We're triggers for other people. What we set off is what they need to learn. Like animals tell you where you're at, it's the same with people. If something about you is triggering them, they may make comments about it, rather than taking it in as something to examine for themselves. So I just try to push that aside and not take it personally, but it's not easy. It takes practice to catch yourself and not be defensive, and choose how you respond.

Because I'm so introverted I think that sometimes the Reptilian has to come out to help me do my job. After some days I have to center myself before I come home, because I'm not sure if it would affect my dogs. You have to understand that you share energy with every living thing on this planet: people, plants and animals. So if you understand that connection and what energy does, it really hurts when you're dealing with humans who act with rejection, or prejudice or fear. That's damaging, and so I tend to pull my energy back, and don't connect so it doesn't hurt. When I give it I give it, but it's at my discretion.

When I meet a human who seems more evolved than most, I just have to tell them. They are the ones who are opening up, who are understanding what is real and that what's important is on the inside. Like my mom, I don't see her as a starseed at all, but when I was doing a Reiki session on her I had tears in my eyes because I could see so much golden light in her. It was beautiful, it really was her core energy—pure energy, like a sunset. I'm not prejudiced against humans, but I am hesitant and anxious around them, though there are a lot of evolved humans out there.

I'm more comfortable at UFO conferences, because the energy is very ET. You get all this awakened energy, and you can sense a lot of people are awakening, or have yet to be activated, but you can feel it all there. At the same time you do get people who want to be open-minded but are actually more prejudiced. Some come with the intention of seeing the weirdos, or some come looking for proof—and the speakers better *show* me proof—and they demand extraordinary evidence. When I was at my booth selling books with Cynthia, some would come to me and demand proof, and I was shocked, because my thinking is not there. My energy comes down,

I vibrate lower to try to get to where they're at, and I don't like that. There was one guy who I talked with at my booth and I spoke some of my language for him, then I heard later that he'd been mocking me to a friend. That kind of shocked me, because with me he was sincere, and later he was mocking it, which was totally off. It's not pleasant when you think you connect with somebody and you think it's real, then you find out later it wasn't sincere. That's what is so prevalent on Earth, all these different feelings and intentions and deceit. And that's the hardest thing for me to deal with, playing a game where they're nice to your face, then stab you in the back later.

How do you conceptualize 'God?'

I've read a lot of books on ETs, their concepts, but for me personally I've got to a place where I see God is in everything. Everything has a piece of the God energy; I try to respect all lifeforms as a piece of the divine. But I prefer the term 'Source energy' because 'God' has a kind of father connotation, which comes from cultural upbringing. I like the concept of 'no sex required,' something beyond physicality and duality. I think it's so much more than that, and we can't understand that with our 3D brain. I think there's some Source energy out there that's created everything; it all trickles down. How much of you is your original soul, and where are the other pieces at? You're a splinter, and it expands to this huge tree—the godhead or the Source energy, then the Archangels came down from that, then the angels, then what we call gods. Maybe they each took a universe to create, some created solar systems, or maybe some have dominion over a whole galaxy. I'm not really sure.

What about the Andromeda Galaxy where I'm from? The Native Americans believe we go back to the center of the galaxy, called the Hunab-Ku, and that the human soul group reincarnates from the Milky Way cycle as a human soul group on Earth. For us starseeds, do we go back to the center of our galaxy? It might be a whole different God. I certainly don't feel part of the human soul group.

When I think about Source energy, it all came from somewhere—we're all connected. If you look at the grand design, step all the way back, I think you can see all this trickling down, souls splitting off and having multiple lives. So when we meet a part of ourselves, is that what a soul mate is?

What is the most important lesson you've learned?

It's all about spirituality. It's about interconnectedness, being loving, accepting, holding yourself in the highest vibration, expanding your consciousness, growing.

Lyssa Royal wrote a book called *Visitors from Within*, which talks about the way contact experiences have been misinterpreted. People would be taken on ships and shown their worst fears, and they felt it was traumatizing, they felt attacked by the ETs, but she explains how it was actually a gift. They were being shown their fears so they could face them, move through them and become self-empowered, stronger and lighter.

Be assertive, be in your truth, in your power—not aggressive but assertive. To evolve, and become who you truly are, and love yourself—and that's vital, as you can't love anyone else if you don't love yourself—you learn that what really matters is your soul essence, and nothing can take that away.

So work it through, have courage, surround yourself with white and gold light, use healing, stand in your power. But most importantly it's what you think, where you hold your thoughts. Hold yourself in a higher vibration of love and gratitude, be deliberate in your thoughts and use them wisely, and you won't attract those negative, fearful things. Some may see injuries, and can feel sorry for themselves, but that's not standing in your power. You can look back later on at things that were negative at the time, and realize that actually they happened at the right time, because you may not have finished that project or met that person, for example. It's intentional living, choosing and being aware, keeping positive and becoming your authentic self.

Vanessa Lamorte

Vanessa is a 24-year-old American woman living in Nevada. Her human ancestry is Italian.

How did you learn you are a hybrid?

Throughout my life I had many instances that indicated to me that I was a little different. At age seven I would stare at the sky and think about how I could move the molecules in the sky, and I would dream of UFO visitations and not be scared because 'nice people' would exit the craft in my backyard and allow me to board. They truly were nice and looked humanoid. My earliest recollection of the star beings is when I was four and newly moved to Las Vegas from Chicago. Three Andromedans, two male and one female, would visit me by my bed around 3am and they would open my blinds and tell me to gaze at the moon. They were kind and never frightened me. Overall, I was always very aware of the paranormal and spirit realms. I would sense beings, see them and hear them too.

My understanding of myself as a hybrid accelerated in my adolescence. It started with dreaming around 16, then around 20 the astral projection started very strongly. Then around 21-22 the past life conscious recall stuff really came online, but it was gradual. I visited a friend in Northern California, and we talked about transcending the self and consciousness through astral projection and meditation etcetera. She and I were great mirrors and catalysts for each other. I've had a theory since I was about 15 that when we're dreaming we access a common pool of energy, so we tried meeting in a dream. We talked the next day and said we had seen each other, so we decided to write it down, then show each other. It was the same exact thing. We were fairies, or little people, sitting in a forest of Northern Californian redwoods, sitting at a mushroom table drinking tea. Very *Alice in Wonderland*.

In June 2013 I'd just graduated with my bachelor's degree. I was experiencing a lot of lucid dreams and astral projection. Then I went through a period of rejecting myself as a starseed, where I didn't know if I wanted to believe that about myself. I took time to own it. I identified with being a starseed, but the word 'hybrid' is new, just the last three months. It was easy to say, "I'm a starseed, I've had previous incarnations on other planets and systems." I know that in this life, this body, I have galactic DNA.

I'm human, but I believe humans *are* hybrids. I don't believe it's healthy to be so sucked into our cosmic selves that we negate our humanity. I live a balanced life, carrying out routine tasks like grocery shopping and working out. But I also have a lot of multidimensional experiences. I find myself bilocating, being simultaneously here and somewhere else, on ships sometimes, carrying out other tasks. When I'm in a very meditative state, or doing chores, I feel myself go, and the bilocation happens. That's how a lot of information comes in.

I'm very clairvoyant so I see beings coming in, but I have very strict energetic parameters around my home, so I only ask for beings of the highest, purest vibration. And that's because I had a lot of very scary experiences growing up. My house is very active with different beings: galactic, angelic, elementals—I've got the whole spectrum going here. I'm very cautious about the energies coming in and always ask them first, "Who are you, where are you from, what do you need?" Other times they're my guides, and I recognize them.

What ET races are you made up of?

In my work with other people I usually pick up on two or three galactic origins/imprints, but for myself I have seven that I resonate with and feel have contributed to my DNA: Sirians from Sirius B and Lyrans very strongly, then Andromedan, Pegasian and Camelopardian. Also a small amount of Zeta and Pleiadian. I understand they are benevolent and are part of the Galactic Federation of Light. They, as well as myself, are working toward the greater good of humanity on Earth and the benevolence of the entire universe.

I see the galactic efforts and agendas on a spectrum. It's like saying all Americans are good or bad. Those are generalizations.

My interactions have been with the Lyran-Sirian Council, The Andromedan and Camelopardian Council and various other groups. All of these beings are highly benevolent. Sirius was seeded or originally founded by Lyrans, so that's where my Lyran piece comes in.

There are four major races on Sirius. There are humanoids, who look almost completely human, but they have slightly different features, particularly the eyes. The Sirians have slightly larger, cat-shaped eyes, but are very humanoid. Then there are Sirian Elves, who look very much like the Elves from Lord of the Rings, so not like the Christmas elves. They're tall, about six to seven feet, slender or athletic build, with all hair colors, and varying shades of skin color, from pale white to more tanned. I haven't met any African-looking Sirians on Sirius B, but I have met Sirius A beings and Pleiadians who look African. The humanoids sometimes have pale skin, but most often have bluish-hued skin.

There are some Sirians who have the more 'Egyptian' heads, elongated skulls like Nefertiti. Otherwise they look pretty humanoid. But they're a sub-group. Some have bluish skin, some white, some gold. Their features are typically Lyran in origin, with larger, feline eyes.

The other two groups on Sirius B that I've interacted with are the Mer-people (like mermaids) and the aquatics or cetaceans. Sirius B's other name is 'Oceania,' and it's a very aquatic planet. I've met different Mer, some half-human half-fish, both men and women. Some look less pretty and glamorous, but they still have value and are powerful. They look more creaturely, so they have scales on their arms, and have more lantern fish-like facial features, and are more intense-looking, but are not malign. The aquatic creatures include dolphins, whales and many species of fish. And there are very interesting creatures that look like Dobby the House Elf from Harry Potter, kind of troll-like, about three to four feet in height. They have gills, webbed feet and hands etcetera. They are interdimensional/holographic in nature, not completely 3D.

A lot of the planet is water, some of which is very icy. It's almost arctic, where many of the Elves live. I've also traveled to another Elven kingdom in an icy valley between two mountains. It has a very large housing structure for the Elves, and from the top you can overlook the water, like an estuary. The waters run down to the ocean where you'd see the Mer. But there's no hierarchy, it's not like the Elves are overseeing the Mer.

When I go there, via a portal, one self is a Mer. And sometimes I'm more human, or Elvish. I understand that I have multiple parallel lives, and selves. Sirius is not 3D, you cannot go there in person, so I travel there in my light body. It is 5D and up. I am using the words 'dimension' or 'density' to mean a realm with a different harmonic structure. Some are strictly 5D, others are more multidimensional in terms of portals, and how they interact with time and space. So have I visited in my physical body? No. But I have been on ships with my physical body. Sometimes ships are 3D, sometimes not, and many can cloak.

How were you created?

I understand that I had a normal conception via my human parents, but at some point while I was in the womb, my mother was taken aboard a craft and my DNA was embedded with more galactic coding. She does not remember any of this. My parents are very accepting, which I love about them. The first time we talked about starseeds, my dad's reaction was, "Oh, I'm definitely an alien." And my mother too. So I feel they are hybrids, but their galactic energy is less potent than mine. I view being a hybrid as a spectrum. To a certain degree, all humans are hybrids.

I was raised Catholic and the starseed/hybrid lifestyle fit fine with everything. It seemed my family's views changed suddenly as we became less involved with the church. Everyone in my family seems to believe more in a universal love than a religion, and that includes life outside this planet.

My boyfriend Matt and I live together. He's a paramedic, and very grounded. When I told him, "Well, I'm not really human," he took it well. He's empathic, and becoming precognitive, but it's developing organically, he's not consciously cultivating it. He's probably getting a lot of energies in this house. When we met, I saw us in our light bodies—myself as a blue energy and he as gold—and I was sucked back into dreams I had as a kid, where I was floating in space with a gold energy, and we'd play. So when I met him I recognized him. We both felt very familiar to each other.

Barbara: It's great that he can expand and accept this.

He might seem skeptical when trying to understand my reality, but he asks great questions to get to the truth. Which helps me clarify the things I am integrating. At the beginning it was destabilizing; a lot of things ramped up around four years ago—at age 20—and he was there for that.

Was there a soul agreement?

On a soul level, I do believe so. Though there is no conscious recollection of any conversations surrounding this. I also feel I had many galactic DNA and energetic imprint contributors. My guides have discussed with me that my Earth parents are my parents. I have one guide in particular, a Pleiadian-Sirian woman named Anika who told me that she was my mother in my first incarnation on Earth, in Lemuria. I actually was able to watch my creation.

What connection do you retain with your star family?

As mentioned above, I have experienced Anika, my Pleiadian-Sirian mother/guide. I also know about Tuk, an Andromedan man; he was one of the three that I remember when I was four years old. He came back into my life only two months ago. Anika and Tuk are part of the Lyran-Sirian Council and live on our craft and various other places. The Pleiades system always feels very serene and loving to me. It feels like heaven and in many ways I feel they are related to the angelic realms. I find myself calling them 'galactic-angelics' because they feel like both.

At times when downloads come in, I can feel different beings around me, conversing with me and giving me the information. At other times I've felt open communication from myself to them; often my energy is going up into the ships, almost like a bilocation experience. Sometimes when driving I've felt myself in their space, with me, but not in my car.

I go consciously when I want to go. I've never been abducted or felt disoriented when meeting them; they'll come holographically into my space, and ask if I'm ready to go onto the ship to do work, or learn something. It's always an invitation, I'm never forced. I notice that if I recall being on the ship in dreamtime, I'll remember that something happened right before—I would feel energy move, or see one of the beings, then I'd fall asleep and go.

But sometimes I do say, "No thank you." Two nights ago I was asked to go on a specific mission with them, but said I was really tired, so no. I was asked to go on the ship, to help push love and light through planets and star systems, like a space healing, and I was like, "That seems like a lot of work and energy right now and I'm pretty tired." One of the beings, who calls himself George—he has a long light language name that I actually can't pronounce—came and asked me. He laughed, he was very okay with it. He's

Lyran, a bipedal humanoid cat being. From the shoulders down he looks human. He's about seven feet tall. He has a human-shaped skull, with a really cute cat-shaped face, with cat-like lips and nose, but I don't see whiskers. He's not as furry as a cat, it's more like light peach fuzz.

In my first conversation with the Lyran-Sirian Council, I was told that they had a big hand in colonizing Egypt, which is why the Sphinx was created. I've since come across the same story from other people's channeling and information, particularly *The Prism of Lyra* by Lyssa Royal and Keith Priest.

Do you have your own hybrid children?

I knew I had hybrid children before knowing I was a hybrid. In April 2013 I was studying for my finals and almost falling asleep, when my daughter came in and said she'd be born June 17th 2018. I thought, 'Oh my God, who's talking to me? This is the weirdest thing ever.' That's Sophia, whom I'm expecting on that date. She wants it to be true but I have lots of things I want to do before then. I know I have free will, and am pushing and pulling with that. I've had other interactions with her, and she comes in as a fairy. She comes in as a pink orb, but can create form and become more dense so I can see her. She has given me pertinent information on medication. She told me to get geranium oil to ease menstrual cramps, and it worked well. She also helped link me with the Pleiadians, so she's played a role in my own evolution.

Last summer more intel came online with hybrid children and 'hybrid baby daddies.' I know that their DNA and energetic imprints have contributed to my hybrid children. I accept them for that but don't feel romantically connected to them. The hybridization program is so different to the parental roles on Earth. I'm aware of two boys and two girls, and all are on board a craft, where a lot of the hybrid children are. They appear to me as toddlers, so they've already gone through the process of collecting different galactic codes. I call it the 'spinning process.' It is done by doctors who are beings which exist on Earth but have other souls which do this work on the ships. These four have a large amount of DNA from Centaurus.

The four key stages of hybridization

1. On various hybridization program craft, they begin with a seed from Source, a light body of pure gold plasma.
2. Then they go through 'spinning'—the galactic infusion. They take the DNA and energetic imprints from people's energy signatures, and it spins, creating a toroidal field.
3. The galactic conception is where all the imprints and DNA start to coagulate and begin transforming into an integrated baby. At this stage they are not completely physical though the templates for a cell mass are constructed. They will remain at this stage in the care of nurses and other professionals who give them love and keep them nurtured until they are ready to be incarnated.
4. They work in harmony with the Earth parents to begin the steps for incarnation. This would follow a normal conception, though the divine planning behind the conception has already been extensively worked through.

When I see children on the craft as toddlers, these are the higher-dimensional, holographic or etheric souls that are waiting to be incarnated. Time works differently here and while a child may look to be three or four years old on the craft, when they choose to incarnate they will start from the beginning.

Galactic imprints are light code-oriented, as opposed to the physical DNA component. There is an almost infinite number of codes that can come from various people, so it's not like one sperm and one egg here on Earth. But people on Earth contribute DNA via a soul agreement. That's where the discrepancy between abduction and conscious agreement gets blurred for some people. I believe there is always a soul agreement in this program. But there are other programs where things have happened against people's will.

The information I have received on this is from the Lyran-Sirian Council, as well as other beings on ships I've interacted with. I was told that this has been happening everywhere else, and Earth is catching up. So for centuries it's contributed to human evolution. This next wave of hybrid children on Earth has to create more unification as they have multiple energies and pockets of information to draw from. They have more awareness of their energies and origins, and can help people to understand the rest of the universe, leaving behind this egocentric sense of this one Earth and one source of life in the universe. That's one aspect.

The other aspect is bringing codes to Earth to help raise frequency in the Ascension process. The hybrid program is not all of it, but the hybrid kids will raise awareness of our multidimensional aspects. With their coding, their light energies working with the Earth, they're natural healers and can transmute energy for the surroundings.

Barbara: So they can do this without having to talk about it? Just being will infuse these energies, send out frequencies which help people? Do you do that, even when not teaching, you're emanating that?

Yes, exactly. Everyone works with the universal energy field, just in different ways. Hybrid children have specific frequencies that they deliver through their field to help facilitate shifts in their environment for a particular outcome. Many times this occurs unconsciously and operates at a soul level.

We're all hybrids, because we can awaken and work with that DNA. It's about: what is your will? The hybrids come in with more awareness of how this works to help the rest of us, to help others to awaken. Being in your humanity is enough; experiencing your bliss, being in your authenticity, *is* the mission. It's enough to do that. You're already doing a lot for the world when you're in your authenticity. When the hybrids incarnate, their *beingness* is enough to help humanity—being in their bliss—and that's a big part of the teaching.

So the rationale is that we're going to assist the evolution process, basically taking the galactic codes, the energies—as well as angelic and elemental—we're taking all of the heightened energies and infusing the DNA with them, so that the hybrid kids are coming in equipped to teach, and to bring change.

The program itself, the modalities through which this is taking place, can seem creepy. People are going physically onto ships and giving their DNA. The way this happens, I've seen myself and others laying on tables, and laser-like instruments hover over our bodies, and create non-incision surgery, where they release the sex cell, the eggs or sperm, or the energy imprint. I see them being extracted into the laser. When it's vaginal, there's a tube of light inserted into the vagina, and they extract both the egg and the energy imprint.

When I'm there I'm not tied down, I know when I'm going. It takes place first as a light body, then I materialize up there. I'm never abducted, I'm usually visited before I go. I see a being in my room, I check in with the energy, and we start to chat, either awake or in the next state of consciousness. They don't tell me I'm going, it's more like an invitation. I'm always very willing to contribute. I agree, then I fall asleep, and shift between states of consciousness, then I move through a specific portal, with the being next me, then we go through the portal onto the ship. I experience it astrally, but the light body materializes as a double, and they take the energy imprints. Some people are actually gone at night, and the physical egg is extracted, but I'm not. But I've felt myself in my bed, consciously, with a being in the room, and it takes 10-30 seconds, I feel the transmission of cells. I can clairvoyantly observe this.

Barbara: During these occasions is your boyfriend, as they say, 'switched off?'
Yes, always. I have nudged him, but they won't wake him up. He's not ready to experience that. He'll say, "I can only believe you." He doesn't think I'm wrong or crazy. He actually likes the idea of hybrid kids, after I explained it to him. That doesn't surprise me as he has galactic DNA. He will go through his own awakening process down the line. I hear him speak light language in his sleep. I want to push it along because I'm excited for him, but I know I have to hold back.

The hybrid kids get called demonic etcetera, but Mary Rodwell calls them *'Homo noeticus,'* the new humans, and I resonate with that.

Barbara: My sense is that it is a benevolent phenomenon, based on the many regressions I have done. The hybrid children are here to expand, upgrade, enlighten human consciousness, and open us up to the whole galactic community, so that eventually we may participate in that. Women may be frightened at first, but as it unfolds they see the wonder of it, the positive purpose. It's interesting for me, when working with a person, to see that evolution in consciousness happening as they discover more and more. You have more perspective, a more expanded view than most of those women, so it's very interesting.

I would agree, but if a participant is uncomfortable they can opt out by stating that they no longer wish to be a part of this initiative.

My boyfriend was laughing about it, the fact that I have multiple partners, or 'hybrid baby daddies.' He said, "You're kind of like a galactic ho." But that's how it is. These women go on board ships, get impregnated, carry the fetuses back on Earth, then give birth to them. Or sometimes the children 'test out' the Earth frequencies by being carried in the womb for some time. They may choose to leave and at different times and stages of the process they could be just an energy that enters and exists, or they could have been a physical fetus and the exiting would look like a miscarriage.

Barbara: In my work I have known many people who have that as a regular part of their lives, with various species.

I did see myself sleeping with another being in my own bed, but I think it was one of Matt's selves. He was working overnight so I was in bed by myself. When the being came into my bedroom I was checking in with it and I realized it was one of his parallel selves. I was also trying to check in with my ego, and ask if I'm being galactically promiscuous. I always check out things before allowing them into my belief system. Some would say that's rationalization, to be fair to psychology. But with this being, he was blue, about seven feet tall. He looked like the beings in *Avatar*, but had a very different facial structure, more human than cat-like. I feel the beings depicted in that movie are very Lyran-Arcturian.

He had black, dread-like braids, he was very built, with thicker eyebrows and a kind of Persian facial structure. He materialized for about 30 seconds; I could only see him with my third eye. His energy was very prominent, but not intimidating. He spoke telepathically in light language when identifying himself. When he came in I knew I was about to have intercourse with an Arcturian, and I knew that he was one of Matt's aspects because the vibrations felt the same. The sex happened quickly. It was very blissful, very human and very quick. It was similar to the way the process takes place on the ship, with the vaginal light tube extraction. The penis looked normal until it entered me, and then it became like a light tube. It felt orgasmic, like the extraction of eggs on the ship. It was like a supernova, a 5-10 second blast, then he was gone.

It all happened so fast that I had to take a deep breath and rework those pieces. I think it was an implantation, like on the ships when afterwards I have a tender abdomen. Even if I don't remember in the morning, I have that sensation and I have a knowing that something happened last night. And sometimes the uterus will actually feel full. But this was like an instant conception. I remember having the child inside me, but it wasn't physical, it was in the energy form, like that ball that will spin that I was talking about. The child was collecting the earthly codes/frequencies. It has to spend time in the womb collecting mine and Matt's frequencies, before continuing the process. I remember I had a healing after that, and a friend said my sacral chakra felt very active. I didn't tell her the experience as I didn't know how she'd take it. That fullness lasted three days, then it was gone. I've only carried a child like that before for a week, and it's delayed my period. So even the energy form affects my body physically. I'll have late or missing periods, thinking I'm pregnant, and take lots of tests which all come out negative.

Barbara: Did something remove that energy form?
Yes. On ships if I carry the child, I'll have another contact experience; sometimes the beings come in and put their hands on my body, and I feel it release. The next day I look less bloated, less pregnant. On the ships I go on the table and they use the laser. And they use different symbols, infused with light to release the galactic fetus. During that week-long Earth gestation, on around the fifth or sixth day I went up onto the ship and they used a specific golden symbol to release the child. I wasn't sad as I knew we'd meet again, but I was a little disappointed as I was enjoying the child's energy, which was golden.

Barbara: That symbol reminds me of Lakota symbols I saw at a conference many years ago. They had a whole album of what they called 'star symbols.'
I can feel myself working with the Native Americans through my transmissions. When the Pleiadians came online, I could see him in my mind's eye, and he said, "You may call me Pleiadian. Some might call me Lakota-Sioux." I haven't taken the time to research the Lakota-Sioux, but I know they use light languages.

Barbara: who is incarnating the kids you've carried?
I have two hybrid children with Nick, a friend of mine and Matt's. The day before we were due to go to a wedding, I had this weird dream about Nick. I saw him on a huge mothership which had an outdoor park, and he was there. I wondered why I was seeing him. Then last summer I was pulled up onto a ship, and was taken urgently to another area, and was asked to help console him as he was there, and kind of freaking out. I found him fully clothed on a table, and he was stunned. He asked what I was doing there, so I had to explain that this is the hybrid program, and he'd made a soul agreement to contribute his energy imprints. So I was kind of the disclosure for him. Then in late August it happened again, and I knew they'd taken sperm this time. Around that time I was starting to have telepathic things with him, and he was becoming more telepathic. I was picking up on his emotions and thoughts, but we were not interacting on Earth at all, though we are friends on Instagram. I would suddenly get insights on him, then see him post

to Instagram what I'd picked up on. I was wondering, 'Of all people, why *this* guy?' I wasn't fully understanding what was going on at the time. I was starting to think I should tell him about the hybrid program.

Then in September I was going to see Bashar in Sedona. Matt was supposed to come with me but he had to work. I went through so many friends before asking Nick, but he was somehow the only person available to go. So at this point there had been six months of telepathic messages and meetings in dream time, and I hadn't disclosed anything yet. I was told by my guides to say nothing. Within 24 hours of the Bashar trip, I experienced the child coming to me. He had blue eyes and black hair, and physically matched Nick. And he called him his dad. So I realized the connection with Nick: we have a cellular union which allows the telepathic connection. So when I see he's the only person that can go with me on this road trip, I realize it's no coincidence. So I start telling him about the hybrid program and he's very accepting of it. I didn't tell him about our child at the time though. The Bashar trip went well, considering I never hang out with him.

A few weeks passed, then I got guidance to tell him, so I asked him to meet me for lunch, and he was actually very cool with it. I told him just like I'm telling you: very grounded, nonchalantly, this is just what it is. I prefaced it with, "You can think I'm crazy or not, but this is what I'm experiencing, over this amount of time." He was so cool with it that that suggested a soul agreement, that on some level he already knew it. Though he said he didn't see anything in dream time, he had no conscious memory of any of this. I said I don't know who they will incarnate to, or if he'll see them, but he was very accepting. He's single, he wants kids eventually. Between September and now it's helped evolve him.

Was it weird? For sure. Matt wasn't uncomfortable, but wanted to know how it worked. As long as I wasn't sleeping with him down here, he didn't care. I said I wasn't sleeping with him up there either, it's a matter of contributing DNA. I do know that Matt has contributed DNA to that specific child also, and I don't know how many other beings have. It's up in air as to who they will incarnate to, but I was told by two different psychics that a boy with blue eyes and black hair wants to incarnate to me. I know that Matt and I would provide the physical aspect for the conception and the child could incarnate into those cells. But I'm not sure right now how it will all work.

With Sophia, Matt and I are the main parents, in terms of contributing the most DNA. She's mine. I have another girl and two boys, and two on the way.

With Nick we have a boy and a girl. I've had more interactions with his kids than with Matt's. The boy comes in a light body—I can see him clairvoyantly.

I had a YouTube video up about my experience with hybrid children, the program and the information I have channeled about it, and there was a *very* mixed response to it. It had the most views and was the most controversial. I've been called a demon by some, while others have thanked me tremendously for talking about it because it brought them some context for their experiences.

I know that the hybrid children will be innovating the way we live through technology and new healing practices. It is a very exciting time for humanity! A world where everyone can be their individual self and in their highest bliss. Whatever that looks like. Total acceptance. A world without judgment. I feel this could bridge everything and create peace.

How do you reconcile the multiple aspects of your identity?

I call myself a human. The hybrid part is implied and evident in my work. I would consider myself more ET, and I base that on my experiences and capabilities, as well as my connection to my galactic family, council and guides. As I mentioned above, I view it as a spectrum and see everyone as a type of hybrid rather than categorizing into two groups.

Do you have physiological differences to humans?

None that I am aware of at this point. I do have a very flat spot on top of my skull. So do my two sisters, who are also hybrids. As an infant, my mom would say that I had colic and was intolerant of everything. I think this was an indication that I was a hybrid and adjusting to Earth frequencies because there was no explanation for my fussiness and the doctors never could find anything wrong with me.

Do you have a sense of mission?

I feel my purpose for this Earth is to live in my humanity and to spread that light to help others experience this way of being. I feel a sense of mission and that includes educating others about the information I have remembered about my outer-worldly lives and current astral travels. A word that embodies my mission would be 'inspire.' I teach and instruct, conduct healings, etcetera. However, the mission is to inspire others to be in their fullest power and bliss.

I've thought about getting a regular job, as right now I make a living from my sessions. I'm in my niche right now, but I'm thinking about how to bring more light and information to more people. Would a regular job help that? Every time I think about it I get major resistance. I'm an Aquarius, and though I don't want to pin myself to that, I do work best with freedom. I want to do more radio and conferences, but I'm just sorting out stuff at the moment, trying to get clear on where I'm going.

Barbara: I have the sense that with all of the experience you are having, visiting with the Lyrans, receiving downloads, communicating, going on the ships, doing the light work, it seems very much like what you are here to do, and as you are still in your younger years, there will come a time when the sharing of that richness opens up more.

Thank you, I feel that way. I'm incubating, kind of like a fetus.

Are you encouraged by guides?

Yes. The Lyran-Sirian Council are my personal guides. I also have a few that are not on the Council, of my own races and others. They can move between dimensions and densities. Although most keep a holographic light body when we have interactions on Earth.

Do you have special abilities?

Currently, I work as a psychic and energy healer and that is my strong suit. I also call myself an 'ET contact specialist' because so much of what I do is galactically-oriented. I offer sessions that implement both my intuition and my psychology background. I enjoy helping others through their psyche to understand their cosmic selves, and all that that means to them. Lots of women come to me, wanting me to tune into their experience and explain it for them. At first I struggled to tell them they have hybrid kids and are part of the hybrid program because I was unsure of how they would integrate the information, but as a psychic and a professional in this work, my integrity means I will tell the truth about what I receive. Now people are coming to me specifically for that, they're looking for answers on hybrid kids. If they think they have them, most of the time they're right. I think everyone has that inner knowing. I tell them how to work with it themselves; it should be a personal, intimate unfolding.

I had early experiences with telekinesis and telepathy, and have also had experiences with bilocation, remote viewing and astral projection as an adult. I can work with these at will. I use them with integrity and encourage others through my teaching to develop their own abilities.

In astral travel the frequencies in your light body are shifting to accommodate different realms, dimensions, states of consciousness and being. Some of it's astral, but on the Earth plane I can move into different states of consciousness, in and out of body, through different modalities such as Reiki, sound healing, light language, using crystal singing bowls and walking in nature. All of these bring bliss, an altered state of energy and consciousness.

Light language is like speaking in tongues. It's a different frequency of consciousness and is all about opening the heart chakra. It's all accessed and interpreted through the heart space. Sometimes I channel my guides, and they speak in different cosmic or angelic languages, and sometimes it's my higher self, it's coming from my own soul. The seed sounds within the languages provide vibrational shifts. I feel how different sounds and pitches and tones create a different harmony within my own vessel, and that's what I mean by recalibration using light language.

Light language is a heart-centered communication system that is truly universal. There are different light languages, dialects if you will, that come from maybe Lyra or Sirius and other star systems. It's a way to talk directly with the heart space, without cognitive, logical language, because words get in the way sometimes. It has so many different uses, but is a way to communicate on a soul level, and bring other frequencies and energies into existence.

It's a bridge between language and telepathy as well. I've noticed in my sessions with people that their intuition has increased through light language, as they are retraining their brains to not think, and to communicate through feeling, rather than the compartmental, logical, categorizing left brain. It can be very ecstatic as far as feeling goes, but it's more about applying intuition, using abstract methods of interpreting your perceptions and communications. While telepathy can be useful, the information stays within these states of consciousness and doesn't flow into the Earth plane. Light language has an advantage here because it brings these frequencies into existence.

I taught an extensive three week course on light language online, going over the various modalities. I don't think I'll teach it again that way because I see the value in allowing people to organically unfold in their process. It's a very sacred process, very intimate.

I would say I downloaded my light language. Often people are exposed to it at a Pentecostal church or in other charismatic religious settings, as it is often activated through exposure. But for me it was activated through the collective of beings I work with—the Lyran-Sirian Council. It's a group of 26 beings from many different places, but most are from Lyra and Sirius, hence the name. They oscillate between those two places.

They came and talked with me and I found myself repeating these weird syllables, wondering what it was, but I initially pushed it away as it was a little weird. It would happen in quiet spaces, when driving or at home by myself, and this language would just bubble up inside; it was pleasant to listen to in myself, but freaky at the same time, and I had to get over that. It's a level of openness, where I say to myself I don't know anything, or need or want to know anything, but being okay with unknowing is where more knowing comes in.

What protocols govern ET interaction with humans?

In my understanding and experience, intervention only happens when it is in the highest and best interest of everyone involved, including the star beings. They will not intervene if it negates the will of others.

How do you define 'Frequencies?'

We all work with frequencies and vibrations every day. I hear particular frequencies that indicate ship communication, guide communication and implant updates/healings that take place in my body. My light language work also works with frequencies. Through sound and light codes we are able to shift frequencies into higher alignment to prevent disease and to clear the aura/energy field. More takes place in light language transmission sessions but that is the brief description.

What is your understanding of Ascension?

Ascension is a process of recalibration to align ourselves with Source so that we can become one with, or come into equilibrium with this energy, and experience eternal nirvana. We're trying to move towards an equilibrium between our vibration and what Source really is. I see it like a canal—a system of balancing levels.

In short we're digging up all the ancient wisdom and bringing it forth and innovating and creating from this space. All of the exceptional capabilities that Merlin, Jesus and many other ascended masters had, we're moving towards that which is an ultimate owning of our personal power. And that's a big movement of the hybrid kids.

It is coming because we are 'raising our frequencies,' or having more awareness of the rest of our multidimensionality. It is coming because we are becoming more universal and unifying. The hybrids can and will be a bridge and link to the process. They will teach their parents about their origins and the ways of being on these other planets. Their experiences and knowledge will teach us how to shift and change.

What is your take on the takeover thesis?

I understand some efforts by ETs with agendas not in our highest and best interest have taken place and they have involved hybridization. Though I do believe everyone's soul agrees to the particular conditions. So while it is seemingly negative, there is a higher order behind that and on some level there was an agreement.

If we are incarnating these genetically modified children, from an introspective point of view, are the parents going to reject the children, not love them? I don't see how that point of view works, because parents are going to love their children, they're going to work with it. We can't incarnate all these people to take over the world, because there's this huge love component between parent and child, and that vibration holds so much benevolence. I have to get that off my chest because it's very triggering for me to hear that. There's a personal vulnerability because of my involvement in it.

How do you feel about the global hybrid community?

We could share intuitive development, past life remembrance, embracing of our galactic/cosmic selves. Also awareness surrounding the efforts and agendas in the rest of the universe, and educating the parents of hybrid children. We could develop deeper awareness in a safe environment. People often don't feel safe discussing these topics and therefore never do.

What would you most like to discuss with other hybrids?

I would like to see the commonalities between those who identify this way, and share other planetary experiences and personal stories.

What are the best and worst things about being a hybrid?

The best thing is being able to be aware of my multidimensional, multifaceted nature and opening to my consciousness and the universe in this way. The worst is bridging the ignorance of others and working with their projections.

How can humanity best work with you?

By embracing themselves and dedicating themselves to living in their own authenticity.

How do you conceptualize 'God?'

I view God as Source. The supreme and purest energy source that all comes from. We are all forms of God.

What is the most important lesson you've learned?

My message and my most important lesson is to embrace multidimensionality. I've gone through so many experiences that just shatter frameworks and belief systems; there's no way to integrate them otherwise. That's my first and foremost objective. In embracing that, we're able to access deeper awareness, consciousness, information, and it's about being okay with not knowing, and in that not knowing, we will know.

That's similar to what I wrote in my thesis, about the mystery, and being okay with the mystery of life—wanting to know the mysteries, but being okay not knowing. It's such a paradox, like how do you live like that, function like that? It comes down to you being in your power in each and every moment, and being very clear with who you are and what feels in alignment with your highest good in each and every moment.

A lot of this is an undoing of structures, old paradigms. Because we're taught in school that we need to have the answers, we need to know, and there is wisdom in that, but I feel like that's not where we're going now. We're going down the rabbit hole as far as how we get answers, and there's so much value in that process. I shake my head all day long, like I know nothing.

I think it's a timely conversation right now, because we have this Venus retrograde, this Uranus retrograde, the celestial influences, and we have this blue moon—the second full moon in the month—and it's so timely for getting down to it, like it's time to figure out: what do you believe about yourself? You don't have to have the answers for everything else, but in your unknowingness, what *do* you know? Really getting clear on what you feel you do know.

The celestial stuff was a way to explain the chaos, the dark night of the soul stuff, because it was not comfortable. And so many others are doing it simultaneously. Much as I don't like to give power away to celestial energies, I see how they influence this, and I see how to work with it. And it doesn't have to be painful.

Barbara: it must be interesting to be you, Vanessa. You've grown up supposedly as a human, in the human system, with family, friends, school, and all the concepts that that entails, and yet here all along you've had other awareness, perspective, about all these other layers of reality, the other beings, the cosmos, other dimensions, which you would never hear about in school, and with friends and families, and then you've looked into other things, other modalities of understanding, and how amazing that it's all in you. A tremendous variety of knowing and perspective, and ways of knowing, including the light language. When you're speaking in that spontaneous way, are you cognizant of what that's meaning?

At first no, but it felt good and uplifting so I kept doing it. Now I'm cultivating more awareness through psychosomatic awareness. It's about tuning in, using the physical body as a meter, so then a whole string of visions will unfold. And that's what I do in my sessions for my clients. I go into the heart space and transmit the codes that are intended for the healing at that time, similar to how

Reiki or other energy healing modalities work. Then I relay to them the awarenesses I received through various chakra points and clairvoyant visions. For example, I may receive information in my heart space like a heaviness during a specific portion of the sessions, and that will indicate something that is going on in their personal life, like a break up or death in the family, or a sacral chakra awareness if someone just miscarried.

People say we're damaging the Earth, but I feel like the Earth has her own way of recalibrating herself, and it's happening through natural disaster. I don't agree with the way the Earth is being treated but I feel in the end she will be okay. We are worried about existing, and in the grand scheme of things, how important are humans, and the Earth? We're actually like parasites. With the hybrid program people talk about the kids coming to save the Earth, but they are actually here to save *us*, humanity, not the Earth. It's a reality that we have to look at: why are hybrid kids coming here? It's to find innovations to help heal what we have done, even to help get us off the planet, which may not be hospitable for humans to live any more. After the bees die, we have four years to live.

We have these races coming here, the Lyrans, Sirians, Pleiadians and many others all trying to get us to wake up to ourselves, and the hybrid kids are definitely going to help with that, but the reality is that more innovations may be needed to help move us to the moon or Mars, or wherever it may be. We have to take care of ourselves and understand what the mission is.

Barbara: My understanding for quite a long time has been that the hybrids are here to upgrade humanity, to help us to be more conscious, more aware of other dimensions, more accepting of other life forms in universe, and help us become more spiritually oriented. Is that different to what you're saying?

I feel that's in alignment, but it's a distinguishing, that the hybrids are here to save *us*, not the planet, and we will have to shift and evolve to get to our next step. And that's a harder pill to swallow, but I want to be fair to what I know. If people don't wake up things will go awry and a lot of people will die, and that's really grim. That's scary. I feel like that's why I'm in this work, but I'm also working on trans-galactic missions, innovating how everyone relates to each other on a very macro level. There are some serious things that we may be on a trajectory for, and the hybrid kids will teach us how to do it, how to build a spaceship that can get us to another ship, etcetera. Like the movie *Interstellar*, where they're going to explore beta planets, I feel that that work is already being done whether it is disclosed to us or not.

The bliss work, the consciousness part, is all important, and I'm not negating that, but the deeper mission is teaching us innovation, how to be in integrity with innovations and technology. There are others who already know how to get off this planet. They're already saying that in 20 years we could colonize Mars. People are probably already on Mars and we don't know about it. That's why I feel it's so important to preserve, cultivate and hear out the hybrids, so we can innovate with integrity.

Earth was an experiment. I feel this is the big elephant in the room that no one wants to talk about. Earth is like the Las Vegas of the universe, it looks great, but then you arrive and it's like, "Oh shit, there's some weird stuff going down here." Some ETs get here and they're like, "It's beautiful, but there's a ton of work to be done." Some ETs think we could just let the people on Earth die; I mean it's a really small big thing in the grand scheme of things.

The hybridization programs were put into effect to correct the mistakes and misdeeds that happened early on in the creation of humans. At that time various groups of galactic geneticists began experimenting and splicing together different types of beings for science, and just because they could. With the Anunnaki, humans were a beta stage being brought to Earth for testing. They treated their 'creations' like slaves because they felt they had ownership of us. Many early 'human' discoveries resulted from Anunnaki projects. In these projects, they also pillaged the Earth's resources, damaging the matrix of codons for much of the plants, trees and land. The matrix is the energetic, multidimensional container of frequencies and codes that create things. We could call this DNA, but this goes a little deeper into the fundamental energetic pieces. When we damage the programming at the matrix level, it creates a structural distortion. The Lemurian age and civilization helped to refine and correct much of this, but we are still working on the last efforts. They didn't recognize us as sovereign beings. In that, many lost their will as they were denied their full human rights. As you can see with the hybridization program, genetic corrections are being made to instil our full human potential and to teach others how we can correct this.

Consciousness-wise and vibrationally, we need our people to tip the scale to gain more integrity, to gain more leverage universally, for going to the next step. The people are so important. It's about working with what we know, and being in integrity with our existence, and moving to a more authentic place, individually, universally and globally. I guess I don't want to portray the hybrid program as all rainbows and butterflies. It is wonderful, but it's to correct awful things that went on in the past. Like the Anunnaki and the Lyrans, there were some very selfish efforts there, with creating people. I incarnated as a Lyran for a reason; because I was on the other side of genetics, I understand my own past lives with genetics, how we carelessly created beings for science and genetic splicing. The Lyrans are highly benevolent now, and are members of the Galactic Federation. The Anunnaki, the Reptilians, some of the Draconians, and there's other groups I don't know about ... it's that materialism, like if we *can* do it, let's do it. It's a loss of will and a loss of power—there should have been a lot more integrity. It's like that line in *Jurassic Park*: "Your scientists were so preoccupied with whether or not they *could*, that they didn't stop to think if they *should*."

The hybrid program is about ripping off the blinders, all of the denial, and getting into the reality of what it *is*. We, in other lives, did some stuff we weren't supposed to do. Our Earth is in an emergency situation. We're trying to unravel all of that and heal it, and in the end I think it all will be very beautiful and very fine. But we have to look at the elephant in the room, we have to be honest so we can move forward.

A lot of this is coming up, a lot of disclosure is happening, a lot of people are talking more in depth now. I see it pouring out of everybody, on YouTube, on Facebook, people just exploding with truth because we can't hold onto any more junk DNA, or the lies, because that's not where we're going. We need full access to our light bodies, our potential, and that takes looking at all the nasty, and getting it out, getting it worked through. It's happening on a microcosmic level, and also tapping in globally.

Jacquelin Smith

Jacquelin is a 65-year-old American woman living in Ohio. Her human ancestry is German, English and Swiss.

How did you learn you are a hybrid?

It's been a process for me. As a child I felt different, that I didn't fit in. My mother recognized this too. Humans just looked strange to me. I would cross out legs on pictures of humans, and sometimes wonder why they only have two legs. It took me years to understand why I felt this way.

Memories started to come through at around age 12, and continued to emerge consciously throughout my life, often spontaneously. I recall attending night school on a starship before the age of five and long after that. I've traveled in and out of dimensions since then. I remembered that I had been genetically enhanced by my star guardians. They blended their DNA with that of other star beings, and a hybrid man living on Earth. My star parents are Tall White Zeta hybrids. They also mixed in the DNA of a number of other star races as well.

I started fitting the pieces of my life together as time went on. When I was 14 years old I sat on my bed and yelled in my mind, 'I want a ship to come and take me away!' A huge silver saucer showed up and hovered in my backyard just above the trees. My human side was thinking, 'Oh my God, they've come to take me away!' Yet my star being side was happy to see them. The craft made right angles like a cross then shot straight up into the sky and disappeared. I ended up on the ship and they started preparing me to have hybrid children.

One day when I was in my 20s, a woman was teaching me how to meditate and my original star family, Quabar, cut in and communicated, "We want you to know that your origin is with us." I've learned that Quabar is my core star being frequency but the Tall White Zetas are my star parents in this life.

What is you ET component?

I carry seven key star being frequencies. I carry others, but they are not in the forefront of my soul selves. I carry the Mantis, Tall White Zeta hybrid, Arcturian-Zeta hybrid, Quabar, a dolphin-like race, a bit of Reptilian (not the humanoid-looking ones) and a celestial/star race which humans don't have a name for. There are more if you include past lives as various star beings. I carry them multidimensionally in my frequency and can easily communicate with them and other races.

During Thanksgiving 2013 I had fourteen days straight of being on ships, having out-of-body experiences, moving back and forth in time, as well as having an aspect of me returning to my soul while a higher frequency aspect of myself came in and integrated with me. This is because we are walking through the Ascension process.

After this period my handwriting, signature and some other things changed. The bank called me and said, "We're checking up because this doesn't look like your signature." So I had integrated some of my multidimensional aspects of 'self.' My whole life has been full of these kinds of experiences.

I'd like to share some of the traits of the races I've mentioned. The Mantis are fun, loving and playful. There is a beautiful innocence about them. They're highly evolved healers. They're an ancient race and I've been in the dimension where they reside. The dimension is one of love, light and joy. When I visit that dimension I see neon rainbows everywhere.

My original star family is an ascended etheric group consciousness called Quabar who describe their origin as, "The seventh universe outwards from Earth." I call Quabar 'my soul's key frequency.' They're of a very high frequency, and don't have names in human terms. Quabar's consciousness is around me often, as is that of the Tall White Zetas. Quabar love to make fun—but not unkind—comments about humans. They throw out puns. I've written them down because I have started to write a book about ET humor. I'll say to my star family, "I know I'm a real drag sometimes, but *you* try being here on the Earth plane." And they reply, "If we had eyes to roll, we'd be rolling them." They make me laugh, and I love their dry humor.

These races, and others which I communicate with, love to laugh. They're joyful. The races I'm interested in communicating with express joy and love; I'm not interested in those that are overly serious or of lower frequency. But all the star beings I have relationships with love to laugh; they're funny, and they're amazing beings. I've been communicating with Quabar in a fully conscious way since 1982. They are love, light and joy, and I'm blissed out whenever they're around me. I love them, and I love all of my star being families. I'm able to communicate with all these races and speak their languages of light. I receive symbols from each race and they show me how to write them down and how to use them in positive ways, for healing, clearing and so on.

I saw an Arcturian-Zeta hybrid in my backyard during the Thanksgiving experiences. He was behind a tree and then came out but he hopped back and I said, "Please come out, I love you." He let me see him briefly then hopped behind the tree again—he was very shy.

Many people consider all Zetas or all Tall Whites the same, but they have their personalities as we do. Even though they might be a hive mind, a group consciousness, it doesn't mean they're all the same. Star beings have their own features too, which I can distinguish. I recognize my Tall White Zeta parents on the ship.

On the starship as a child I had an Arcturian-Zeta nanny whom I love deeply. I call him 'Sandman.' My parents always told us the Sandman would come and help us sleep. This allowed me to have a positive connection with him and other star beings.

Tall White Zetas can look similar to Zetas except that they have white shimmering skin rather than grey. They are loving and have positive intentions for Earth and humanity. Sandman is about four and a half feet tall with beautiful blue skin. His presence is innocent and childlike in the most positive sense.

How were you created?

When my mother was pregnant she was taken onto a ship and the Tall White Zeta hybrids and others implanted the enhanced DNA, which was taken from a number of races, as well as a hybrid man on Earth. My parents' DNA was a part of the package as well. I watched all of this take place while I was still in spirit. I spent many nights on the ship as a child, so the Tall White Zetas were my parents there. Also on the ship were Mantis and Arcturian-Zeta hybrids and others. I was raised there in a way and learned a great deal from all of them about love and traveling with my consciousness. They took me on adventures, meeting many species of star beings whom I'd already known from other lives.

On a soul level, my parents consented to this plan. However, they were not aware of any of this on a conscious level. Contact with star beings has been a part of my Earth family for many generations. Somewhere along the line, my family decided to be a part of interacting with star beings. The star beings blocked my parents' memories of being on ships by using implants. They also blocked my memories for a while because it was too much information for a child to handle. I was always considered the odd child in the family. My parents were aware of some of my psychic abilities. My mom would say, "Gee, I wonder where you got all these gifts and talents, nobody else in our family can do those things." My mother read my first book on animal communication and said she was amazed. She became more accepting in later years.

What connection do you retain with your star family?

I communicate with my star families on a regular basis. I will often reach out to them for support, love and information. And they will often contact me telepathically to share information or to let me know that they are present. I've developed a relationship with Quabar, with two Tall White Zetas called Zazu and Ametha, and with the Arcturian-Zeta I call Sandman. I am very connected to my Mantis family and dolphin family as well. I'm grateful to be connected with them as well as other star beings. These beings are able to literally view the world through my eyes.

What do you understand to be the purpose of your creation?

I am a bridge. I help star beings connect with humanity, and vice versa. The star beings have told me that just having my frequency on Earth assists with Ascension. They told me that I don't have to have a 'path,' because there *is* no path. Sharing my gifts helps to raise humankind's consciousness and frequencies in a way which opens the heart. I enjoy sharing the message that we are all One. And that all living beings are of equal value regardless of their form, and this includes those who have no form. Earth is a being and is evolving just as humanity and other species are evolving.

I've been teaching people how to telepathically communicate with animals and star beings for many years. In my second book,

Star Origins and Wisdom of Animals, they reveal and share information about their star origins. Essentially I'm a messenger, and the message is: we are all One, and love is everything.

What do you understand to be the rationale for the hybrid program?

Having hybrids present on Earth helps to raise humankind's frequency so that humans can evolve and embrace their cosmic family, and embrace themselves as star beings. The hybrids are bridges in this way. With major paradigm shifts taking place, humanity is evolving into 'the new human.' This means humankind's DNA is changing in ways which is allowing them to expand in consciousness. They are being activated by the higher frequencies and becoming aware that they have natural skills and talents which they haven't tapped into before because they weren't ready to handle them. This gives humanity an opportunity to develop their natural psychic abilities such as clairvoyance and clairaudience. More people will be experiencing bilocation, teleportation, and learning how to heal themselves and others without having to deal with space/time constraints. Many hybrids are already in touch with these abilities and are using them to be of assistance to others.

What do you know of the differences between Earth-based and non Earth-based hybrids?

The hybrids on Earth are working to support humanity in their evolutionary process as well as Earth. The hybrids who are in other star systems and realms are also building bridges between various species throughout the cosmos. This includes Earth.

Do you have your own hybrid children?

I have over 40 hybrid children. With the updated hybridization techniques the star beings now use, a woman doesn't have to carry every child, they only need her DNA, say from a strand of hair. I had three hybrid children a few years ago, and I said, "You know guys, I think this needs to stop now, for where I'm at in my life." And I feel that they are respecting that because I really needed that to end for me. But if they want to use DNA from my hair, for example, that's fine with me. When it was happening at 16 or 17 I wasn't aware they were taking my eggs, and that's probably a good thing.

I took care of some of my children on the ship and it was very hard to leave them. The beings told me that I have a daughter who's living in Russia, and that one of my sons couldn't be successfully integrated on Earth, so they took him to another place where he is doing his work. He's an engineer who is creating wonderful new technologies and trying to bridge humanity with our cosmic kin.

I know that I volunteered to be a part of the program just as my hybrid children have. It's all good, it's just emotional. I can talk with them whenever, I just have to send out an invitation and they begin communicating with me. They come as a group and speak to me with one voice.

My star being families raised my children. I'm here on Earth fulfilling my mission as a hybrid. I speak at conferences, teach workshops, and do private consultations with individuals about their lives, their Star Origins, and I assist some with processing their experiences with star beings. My entire life has been focused on sharing the message that love is everything and we are all One.

How do you reconcile the multiple aspects of your identity?

It's been a journey for me. I'm fine with it now, but earlier on I was not so fine, and I felt like I didn't fit in anywhere. I have always felt much more star being than human, but I'm happy to say that in the last 15 years or so, because I work with people all the time, I've come to embrace the human part of me in a better way. To accept and deal with my human aspect has been the greatest challenge for me, because I'm so ET. But today, I'm comfortable with who I am, and I'm dedicated to my mission. Since I carry seven key star frequencies it's been a process of integrating a huge amount of experience and information. I've done a lot of processing with past lives, and know I've had many more lifetimes as a star being than a human.

It's really a matter of trying to figure out how this world works. It's limited in so many ways. For example, why is there only male and female? In other star systems there are other choices. But I said to the Council of Elders, "If I have to come back to Earth, let me choose to be female. With the divine feminine coming in with the Ascension, I can fulfil my purpose better if I am female."

I am in touch with the star being aspects of myself, and with other star beings. I communicate with them every day; even when

I'm just walking around the house doing something I'll speak star languages. It's uplifting to do this because it's a much higher frequency, and hybrids are here to raise the frequencies. When I listen to the different light languages that flow through me, each one has a specific rhythm and flow to it.

The Mantis, like many races, communicate using frequency. When the messages come through me they're not words, and because of the limitation of our vocal cords they can't be exact. Mantis beings speak with a very high frequency, with clicking. Arcturian-Zeta hybrids speak with guttural sounds.

Some people have seen me shapeshift, and have seen my eyes change. Within those fourteen days of experiences with star beings, I had over three days of missing time where I was physically gone. I shapeshifted into a number of my star being selves on the mothership which was pretty wild, a lot of fun. I did that with the Blue Arcturian-Zetas, the Tall Whites and the Mantis. I've come to embrace all aspects of myself through the years, but it's an ongoing process.

Do you have a sense of mission?

As a hybrid I feel I hit the ground running in terms of starting my mission. At six years old I was off in other dimensions, communicating with ETs, and with humans and animals who had crossed over. I was in and out of many realms in a very conscious way. I've had two near-death experiences, one at six and one in my 20s. Those experiences allowed me to expand quickly in my life.

I've been told I was created to be an ambassador here, representing a number of races.

I'm a communicator, and I love to teach and share messages with people. I feel that my role is basically to be a messenger, to teach and talk about experiences with others, and to listen to their experiences. One of the messages is about helping humanity to understand how incredible Mother Earth is, and how important all other beings are: the star beings, the animals, the trees, the waters.

Actually, all of them are star beings. On other planets they don't even have a category for animals because they are considered as beings of equal importance. That's been a part of my message for over 36 years in teaching workshops. Humanity really needs to understand that they are not the most important race in the universe, or on Earth. I enjoy teaching people how to communicate with animals and star beings, which is a big part of my mission.

An important part of the message is that there are no 'good' or 'bad' star beings. Every being plays their role in the larger cosmic picture. Good and bad doesn't exist, that's a human perspective. Sometimes those of lower frequency offer the opportunity for us to experience contrast. We get to choose the frequency with which we resonate.

Are you encouraged by guides?

My guides are a mix of star beings, angels and other intelligent, universal beings. I have a great team of light workers—as we all do—that I call in for my work with people and animals. I consider their guidance, but most of all I listen to my heart and my soul to be clear on who I am and what I want to do. A long time ago I asked Quabar what my mission is, and they said, "You can do whatever you want to." And I asked them, "Am I on my path?" They replied, "There *is* no path, the only path is love." They said that just my frequency being on Earth is enough. We're all here with our frequencies to assist Earth and humanity through the Ascension process.

Do you have special abilities?

I have a wide range of psychic abilities and use them for a variety of purposes. I am telepathic, empathic, clairvoyant, clairaudient and clairsentient.

I was blessed with the ability to look through a body and scan it to see what's going on.

I have the privilege to be an animal communicator. I have been doing this work professionally for 36 years but have done it naturally all my life. I was one of the first animal communicators in the country which was very exciting, and today I work with people globally.

Healing work with animals and humans seems to come naturally for me. 'Soul recovery' is a specialty work I do with animals and people. It's a process of bringing back aspects of energy that have fractured out during some kind of trauma the animal or person has experienced. It helps them to regain their wholeness.

I track lost animals worldwide. I can pick up an animal's vibration by talking to the animal's person and/or looking at a photo of the animal. I am then able to psychically follow their energy signature and communicate with them about where they are physically.

It's fun for me to communicate with spirits on the other side—those who have crossed over, both animal and human—and to help those left behind to be at peace.

It's also a pleasure to work as a psychic, and a hypnotherapist, and to assist experiencers.

I teach classes and speak at conferences about star beings, sharing my experience as a hybrid. Most people are curious and many relate to something I've said in my talk, which allows them to awaken to who they are as a starseed and/or hybrid.

All of these abilities are natural for me and fun.

As a matter of personal interest I enjoy exploring consciousness and quantum physics. I have done plenty of reading, but my real learning has been firsthand with Quabar and others. My consciousness goes with them into space to see how these things are formed and how they function.

At times I have to be careful what I do with my feelings, as I can affect computers and blow out light bulbs depending on my mood. This can happen in heightened states like anger or elation. Some years ago, while feeling particularly happy, I was in a grocery store and cans started flying off the shelves. I was thinking, 'Oh my God I gotta get out of here!' That was weird, a bit scary for me. So I tried to shut that down.

As a child, when I was on the ship at night, the star beings taught me how to move objects using telekinesis. I've had to learn how to ground myself and control those energies.

They also taught me how to work with the power and energy of symbols. I enjoy receiving symbols from various star cultures—they flow through as I sit and simply write. Sometimes I know their meanings and other times I don't.

I have a practical emphasis in my work, giving the message that we're all one, and helping to awaken others on how to live from the heart. Those are my key messages. My main focus is on being the most loving being I know how to be.

I enjoy teaching 'Are You a Starseed?' classes. I help people get in touch with their star self by communicating with their star families. Some people want a Star Origin Reading which helps them connect with their star family initially. In the reading, their star families show up and start talking with me. I ask for the person's very first soul expression. I go all the way back to the beginning to connect them with that original incarnation. I refer to this as their soul sticking a toe in the water of the universe to have some kind of initial experience. I share it with them and give them the frequencies or tone mantras to speak, which brings their star family to them in a bigger way. I've done Star Origin Readings for many healers, and they tell me that afterwards they can sense their star families around them, who begin helping them in a deeper way with their healing work, which is just so cool and wonderful. All of that is great fun for me and them.

Miguel: I would love to do a Star Origin session with you. I would love to know if I have any of the beings connected with me.

I can tell you what I feel around you now ... [gets paper and pencil] ... okay, I see a whole team of light workers around you, to support you in what you're doing, in your missions here. I'm seeing the Archangels, they're just so beautiful and soft, and their energy is loving, but they are also very strong. So I'm feeling them ... definitely a lot of feminine energy around you. The Mantis beings are also showing up. I see some dolphin-like beings; they're not dolphins, they're the original beings long before dolphins on Earth existed. And this is interesting, okay, I'm seeing beings from Andromeda. I remember last time we talked, I suggested that you ask the Andromedan healers to work with you, so I'm seeing some of them around you as well, and Zetas. And I see—and I include these beings in the ET realm, whom I really love—fairy-like beings. So you have a wide range of beings around you which is really cool, and they're all here to support and help you, and you can always ask the Mantis beings for healing too, because they are incredible, ancient healers. That's what I'm seeing at this moment.

Miguel: Thank you. That's amazing. How does one go about calling them in?

Calling in your guides

Just state your intention. I say, "I welcome all those of love and light to assist me, to support me in mind, body, spirit and soul, in all that I am doing on Earth."

And say it from the *heart*, because they can feel the heart intention, which is more important than what is being said. By going into the heart and really feeling and meaning that, they know it, because it's a clear and high frequency.

I'm excited—I think you're going to have so many things opening up for you, you're not even going to believe it. It's going to be fun. You're already being visited. You're receiving a lot of support whether you're aware of it or not. I just love it, it's beautiful.

What protocols govern ET interaction with humans?

Through lots of communication from the star beings, I understand they can only intervene to a point. They are helping balance the Earth's energies, and they've intervened at military installations, knocking out the power. Their intention is to give us these messages—that we humans keep disregarding—to do away with war, with warlike behavior and thinking. If everyone on Earth would agree to do that, everything could change in a second.

They tell me that we are responsible for ourselves, that humanity has to find its way and grow. The star beings cannot directly intervene so thus we have the hybrid program, which is integrating star being energy here on Earth to create a new race. A new race in the sense that we remember who we really are, that we are divine love. That's the core of it.

Hybrids are here to slowly integrate the higher consciousness energy in order to raise the frequency to help humanity evolve, to become conscious and to remember that we are love. We are all One, always interconnected, we can't separate ourselves from them: they are us, we are them. Whether there's a being who's of low or high frequency, it's all *us*.

In the end, it's about the creator learning about itself. That's what it comes down to. It's like we're in a play in order to learn and grow through experience. There is no real opposition in this; there are no *sides*, because whoever we think of as another side is still *us*.

As we are raised into higher frequencies, that perceived duality disappears and there is only love, peace and joy. The 'New Earth' is love, peace and joy; we can be in those higher frequencies if we choose to—anybody can. But those who have a different agenda, they're just playing a role for the sake of duality here on Earth, because we all agreed to this. On Earth, it's an experience of learning, it's an experience of contrast, of the light and the dark. I think of it as a spectrum; we can think of shadow and light, which is a part of us all. Those who choose to focus on the darker side of the spectrum, their soul has chosen to play that role for the sake of duality, for contrast, and also as a push, in a similar way that a pearl is created through friction. I see those of lower frequency creating friction to help everyone become or remember who they really are. We are all co-creating this process.

How do you define 'Frequencies?'

Frequencies are the vibrational range of energy expressing itself, whether it be in physical or nonphysical form. This is how I define frequency in my second book when discussing star beings, who simply express various vibrations—as we all do. When they speak their own languages or share symbols with me, the vibration of who they are flows through.

Dimensions are different frequencies or vibrations, that's all they are. Quabar showed this to me; I travel with them through my consciousness, and at times I travel with my astral body. They show me the dimensions and other stars systems firsthand. They have shown me how dimensions are layered like an onion, and that there is no such thing as time and space, that's all illusion. Humans have created the illusion of time and space, so it's easy to get boxed in with that limited way of thinking. Time and space is important to humans because it gives them a construct for living in density. This is irrelevant to star beings because they are living in the now. These are the only words I have to explain this.

There are many different vibrational rates of tones and harmonics. If a person can attune themselves to let's say a fairly high frequency, their consciousness can be on Alpha Centauri in a second. So, if someone centers and grounds in joy and love, and then sets their intention to be in another star system, they can go. These are simply states of being, energetic states, which everyone has the ability to experience. A person can go where they desire, but if they believe that they are limited to certain dimensions or the Earth, then it's more challenging for them to experience those other frequencies which can help raise consciousness. These frequencies exist within us, they're within and without, as above so below. I call it traveling with my consciousness, but there's no time and space, it's all right here, right now. It's a state of being.

Quabar has taught me about this firsthand over many years. One could say I take a ride with them into these various frequencies. I feel like I'm on an amusement park ride. It's always fun. Of course, there are no words for these experiences. One time, I rode on a wave with them into what looked like deep space where they showed me the frequencies of Earth, the fundamental vibrational expression of Earth. The vibrations looked like endless ribbons of symbols, which created the physical form of the planet.

The Earth's density is a low frequency compared to the star being frequencies that I've had the privilege of experiencing. I love Earth, it's a beautiful, amazing planet, but it's very challenging to live in these densities. Some days I think, 'Oh my god, I need to take a trip to another star system.' That's what makes being on Earth doable for me. I can lay down on my bed, go home for a while and forget the Monday morning crap.

What is your understanding of Ascension?

Ascension is a process of growing and evolving as a soul. Humanity is gradually ascending into a higher degree of consciousness and remembering that living from the heart and loving is everything. It's also about being authentic in who we are. Every soul chooses their own pace with their Ascension process.

The soul is living many lifetimes at once, dealing with different challenges in order to learn what maybe wasn't learned in another lifetime. When we talk about this you have to involve what we call past lives, even though everything's going on simultaneously. Looking at the bigger framework, we're integrating past lives and future lives to come into a soul balance. The soul balances itself between the different spectrums of frequency. We may be here, dealing karmically with this world, still learning something our soul wants to learn, while at the same time living other lives in other star systems, or perhaps in another dimension where we are etheric, bathing in love, light and joy. All of us are integrating our multidimensional selves to regain our wholeness. This is part of what Ascension is about—returning to love and light. This allows our consciousness to expand and say, "Now I remember the truth of who I am: I'm not this body, I'm not this personality. I'm a beautiful light of creation, I'm divine love."

We're here to purify, to remember to not get attached to this world because this world is an illusion. What's important to remember is that we are love and light. Every soul is working out their karma, relating to choices they've made throughout many lifetimes. We're here to experience.

I'm not sure there's a simple answer. Again, it's not about the mind understanding it all, it's about what the heart feels and knows. The heart is very wise. What does your heart say? What does your soul say? The mind always wants to create a framework, the mind and ego always want to know the answers. They separate whereas the higher consciousness creates unity. Part of the great mystery is that we're never going to comprehend the whole picture—none of us will ever see the entire picture from the limited human point of view.

There are more UFO sightings taking place these days, and when they are coming in I'm feeling higher star being presence around. The star beings shared with me that when they come in with their ships they're emitting frequencies through a spectrum of beams, and these higher frequencies will trigger activations in more people. I communicated with star beings who are in Superstition Mountain in Arizona; they said that some races are leaving, while new ones are coming in to continue to raise the frequencies. The heavier presence of star beings is being felt by many of us at this time, and I believe it is slowly setting things up for that potential of unity. All of this has amazing potential for both humanity and the star beings.

Also, our chakra systems and DNA are being activated by the higher energies flowing onto and into Earth, which can bring us into a place of awakening as well as inner balance. This process raises a person's frequency and expands their consciousness. It also clears away old beliefs and patterns.

What can help everyone to move through Ascension with greater ease is to focus on things that bring us joy, which is a high frequency. Walking in nature can ground and uplift us, connecting us to Earth and ourselves. Of course, having a good support system of friends and star beings can also give us support. We can send love and healing thoughts and images to the Earth, ourselves, and all life forms. We can bless the sky, the trees and the stones as we stroll through the woods. We can radiate love to the stars. We can pray, meditate, tone, sing, dance, play and laugh along with everything else that celebrates life. Creative expression and beauty lifts our souls. Writing, gardening, and playing with animal companions and children contributes to global healing. Most of all, living from the heart raises our frequencies and allows us to see that we are One in love.

How do you feel about the global hybrid community?

We will continue to integrate hybrids into the cultures on Earth. The star beings know where to place each one; they know the appropriate climate, the intention, and we are all strategically placed. Sometimes things work out and sometimes they don't, but the star beings tell me that they're fairly pleased with the way things are going. For me it could never be fast enough, but for humanity, and for the human mind, the evolutionary process has to go at a suitable pace. But it is happening, and new bridges and frequencies are shifting things into the new paradigm, allowing humanity to evolve. It has to be done slowly because humans are not yet open to embracing their family from other star systems. The ego's fear of change and being out of control gets in the way. Compared to ten years ago, many more people are awake and aware. I'm now seeing big leaps happening all over the world, which is very exciting to me. My thought is, 'Lets just do it!' But it can't be done that way because it would blow minds. So it is being done in a loving, gentle way.

We're all here for a purpose, we all chose to be in these forms. And let's have fun while we're here! Some of the younger starseeds and hybrids are having a really hard time, they're feeling scared. They don't understand their nature. And they're angry at humanity. I hear them say, "Why am I here with these stupid humans?"

Barbara: Do you see the hybrid community as offering emotional and practical support?
Yes. I feel it can offer awakening starseeds support and comfort. It can help them understand who they are and what's happening to them so that they can release the fear. There are more organizations that support starseeds which is wonderful.

Also when an awakening starseed needs support, they can get that from a friend or their parents—if they are open to it—and I think that helps a great deal.

When I meet someone and I resonate with them, I love them whether they are hybrid or not. But when a hybrid connects with a hybrid, it's a different connection and understanding, which is also very supportive. With my hybrid friends, I can speak light language, talk about anything cosmic, and we appreciate it and have a good time. That doesn't mean I'm going to resonate with every hybrid because we all have our personalities.

I think in general the global community of hybrids is absolutely wonderful, but again, to me, the most important thing is love. It goes beyond labels, races, identities and abilities. Love, and understanding that we are all one, is the foundation of what we are here for. What's important is living from the heart. I'm not all about being a hybrid, I'm just doing what I feel I'm here to do. I don't view humans as lesser. I embrace, love and value all beings, whether plants, animals, humans, hybrids or star beings—I love them all.

Barbara: Do you think there is an actual hybrid community on Earth, any kind of organized way that hybrids can know each other?
I know online there is a community for those who have had hybrid children. I think it's wonderful to offer them support. There may be some organizations that support hybrids. Also, there may be differences of terminology, I'm not sure, because hybrids and starseeds know where they're from; they talk about where they're from and what they're here to do, so I see that as hybrid potentially. Or they're humans remembering their star origin. And that's really wonderful. I was lucky to find and connect with the people that I connect with and I'm very grateful for them. They are my star family and my family on Earth.

Miguel: What might hybrid skill-sharing consist of?
We all have our own skills and talents for our purpose here, and when we come together it's awesome because then we can share all the different talents and skills. This is amazing. Sometimes as hybrids we feel on the fringe; we can sometimes feel misunderstood, so when we connect it's joyful. The bottom line is: I choose to connect with people I resonate with whether they are hybrid or not. Yet I'm really grateful for my relationships with hybrids. I would be lonely if I didn't have them. I wouldn't do as well living on Earth.

Barbara: Is there a special joy and relief in discovering each other?
Definitely. When I met Robert Fullington for the first time we just looked at each other and both of us said, "Oh my God!" We knew that we'd been on ships together. We got to know each other a little better and that's when we spontaneously did the Mantis bow at the exact same time. It was ecstasy because you can't do that with a human who isn't in touch with their star origin. It's a soulful joy.

More and more hybrids are coming together. I don't like the separation of saying hybrid or human, but it's true that we've been genetically enhanced, and it does make us different in that way. But we're in a human container, so we also experience what it's like to be a human.

Miguel: Could hybrids increase their abilities and personal wellbeing through connection?

I think so, yes. when we're with other hybrids we're activating each other and whoever else is around. I've been told that I naturally emit an energy that uplifts and heals people; I don't always consciously think about doing that, although I may at times. I'm just having fun. So we do activate each other, but we could activate each other even more.

We can share with humanity the good that hybrids have to offer and this leads to the good that star beings have to offer. That's key, because it's not about us really, we agreed to do this in service. The bottom line is that we're bridges; this is how I've always seen myself. We are bridging our cosmic families with humanity, so that humans can realize that they are cosmic citizens and therefore evolve in a much quicker, more profound way.

I'm a practical person and I look at the practical side of everything; it's not about putting on a show, it's about sharing the talents and skills that we *all* have, on some level; it's just that the hybrids carry the higher frequency of DNA. But the bottom line is to bridge our cosmic family with humanity. It doesn't serve a purpose to just show off this skill or that skill, there needs to be a positive intention or focus to say, "We're sharing these abilities because you too are connected to the stars and have a star family; isn't it exciting that you can discover that connection?" I always come from that place with teaching and educating others about their star origins. This is about everyone learning, growing and expanding; it's about evolving, because my hope is that humanity is going to make it this time; humanity hasn't done so well in the past.

What are the best and worst things about being a hybrid?

It's been a life-long journey to understand what it's like to be hybrid. I have spent years wondering what it's about. I've floated in front of the Council of Elders a number of times saying that I want out of here, and they would say, "Look, you agreed to come here; you don't have to continue but we would love for you to continue, and there are fun things on Earth."

Yes, I'm grateful I've hung in here, but there have been some challenges with being a hybrid. The upside is, I enjoy being of service to others. That's fun for me, I enjoy sharing my experiences which can help support others who are just awakening to the fact that they're starseeds and/or hybrids. It's a privilege to be a part of something greater than myself.

The downside is that it can be a challenge to live in this world and be so empathic and telepathic. I wonder at times, 'Is this my feeling, or the other person's feeling, or is this from the collective consciousness?' It takes practice to sort those things out.

I spend a lot of time walking in nature intentionally, because nature is love—plants, trees and rivers are all love. I enjoy talking with people, but what keeps me sane is staying connected to the Earth.

I can walk down the street and hear a dog communicating, "I'm not happy with these people." And I have to say, "I send you love and light, but I'm sorry I can't physically come over there and help you." So those things are a challenge.

I'm grateful for the gifts I am able to share with others. Also, I enjoy being able to communicate with star beings because I enjoy their company, their communications, and I appreciate their humor. It's fun to share their messages with others about who they are, as well as Ascension and other things. My life is certainly never boring! There are many wonderful gifts that come with being a hybrid.

How can humanity best work with you?

Firstly by simply respecting and honoring who we are. Hybrids, like anyone else, have their own messages and opinions to share. It helps if we are not looked at as strange, but understood as being here for the purpose of awakening others and assisting the Earth.

It helps when people are supportive and are open to listening to our experiences as hybrids. My childhood wasn't a 'normal' childhood. I was on starships, flying in and out of dimensions astrally, and communicating with people, animals, and other beings on the other side. It is important that children with these experiences are heard and understood, not teased or shut down.

How do you conceptualize 'God?'

I have seven key star families and I've communicated with all of them about how they conceptualize God. The word they use is "One," meaning that everything that exists is a single, interconnected whole. Among the many planets and stars I've experienced and have come from, there's no such thing as worshipping a god. Star beings respect and connect with love, or the One. Another term we would use is 'Source,' and another is 'pure awareness.' I also refer to it as 'the All' in my books. One, Source, pure awareness and the All. These concepts also equate to energy, and ultimately to love.

Beings can use Source with intention to create whatever is desired. When I say beings I'm also including planets, stars and other systems.

Quabar said to me, "Even though we're more highly evolved, this doesn't mean we know everything. Our common connection is that we are all divine at the core."

We all are divine love, which is everything, the One and the All. The star beings I've communicated with—and I've communicated with many of them—don't box in 'what exists' because that creates distortions, as humanity has shown. The man in the sky with the beard is a 'boxed in' concept that humans have created about God. Religion may be helpful to some people on their path in this life, but for me it can be a detrimental way of thinking which involves control and guilt. With that comes misperceptions and distortions. Some feel religion has enslaved humanity for a very long time.

We're breaking free from that now; many old systems are crumbling, which is excellent. Humans are looking beyond old, limiting beliefs and paradigms which no longer serve a purpose. Star beings are around me right now, having a group discussion about this, which is fun. Humanity has gotten stuck in limiting beliefs and become enslaved; then of course it's easy for others of lower frequency to have an affect on them.

But the star beings with whom I communicate are about truth, and truth can't be boxed in. It's about looking beyond this illusion and connecting with divine love which is who we truly are. And in Oneness, the Creator is everywhere; if I touch a tree, the Creator's in that tree, and it's the same for everything. Everything is the One, is the All.

In the different star cultures I come from, they honor all living beings, that's their fundamental way of being. Love is truth, and the One is love.

What is the most important lesson you've learned?

To love myself and to live from my heart. By going into our hearts we can remember who we are. Our heads can lead us places that aren't the truth or that can throw us off track. Even people who are in communication with star beings are learning about this. It can get tricky because everyone has filters and we need to be clear about where our guidance or information is really coming from. I like keeping things simple. I talk about the heart, love and Oneness in the books that I've written with the star beings, including the one I'm currently writing about my life as a hybrid.

It's easier for animals to love unconditionally because they have retained their heart centers and intuitive abilities. The animals taught me how to love in a better way, and the star beings taught me how to love in a clearer way.

Humans focus on themselves, and believe they are superior to all other forms of life. The animals, who are also star beings, are playing a big part with the Ascension process, as is Earth and many other species. Humans think they're the only ones helping to raise the frequencies, but that is a myth. My second book is about the star being animals who shared information about what star systems they come from as well as information about Ascension. Many people tell me they resonate with that information, which is wonderful.

Not only is humanity going through Ascension, but so is the entire multiverse and everything in it. The star beings have shared this with me in depth. They're all moving through their own Ascension and evolutionary process too. They have said, "We're evolving too, we don't know everything." I like to share that because I think it's very relevant.

They have said, "What we would all love is for humanity to treat Earth better, to respect all species and to honor and respect the indigenous races who understand living in harmony with nature." Humans have forgotten how to do this. I teach many workshops based on the fact that we're all One. I wish humans could be kinder, and more tuned in and sensitive to all beings. That spider on the wall can look really scary, but it has a soul too, and is radiating Creator's light—it's Creator's child too and you don't have to kill it, you can put it in a cup, place it outside. It has been part of my mission to teach these things. I had a woman in a workshop who was terrified of spiders, she would scream and become hysterical at the sight of them. Three days after the workshop, she called me and what she said made me cry. She said, "I remembered everything you said, and I talked to the spider and told it, 'You're a light of God, and though I'm still scared of you, I'm not going to kill you.'" She found the courage to put the spider in a cup and put it outside. That might sound trivial but it's profound. It's important for humanity to appreciate all living beings, to appreciate nature, because we are One, and if we're not connected to nature we're not connected to ourselves.

The point of hybrids being here and connecting with humans and having hybrid children is important. We are in relationships with humans and if we have a child, it's one more hybrid on Earth. A whole new race is being birthed on Earth: the new human. We star beings came here to help create a new race.

Ascension is about living from our hearts not our heads, and remembering who we are and that love is everything. I can't say I'm loving 100% of the time because I have the human side, I've got the ego and the mind. But at our cores, it doesn't matter if we're human, hybrid, star being, fairy, or a tree—we are all divine love. That's the core of everything. We're lost without divine love. This is where humans can get off track, and I'm including myself, because the ego and the mind get caught in the drama of the illusion. Love is who we are and we're all beginning to remember that truth.

Love is the most powerful force there is. Above all else, I would say that loving the self is key to loving others. If we don't love ourselves, we can't love others, and that's when humans can fall into negative patterns and project this onto others.

Even though, as a hybrid, I talk about focusing on the high frequency of unconditional love as often as we can, we must also honor all aspects of who we are since we are in the human experience on Earth. And let us honor the light in every being. What's important is knowing who we are, why we're here, remaining aware, and being authentic in life. *That's* the higher frequency. And we're all meant to shine.

Matthew Thomas

Matt is a 28-year-old man English man living in Northern England. His human ancestry is a mix of British and Irish.

How did you learn you are a hybrid?

It's only been the last few months that I've been really aware of all this, but about six months ago I had a Grey come into my front room and since then I've been questioning things, looking up things, and that's how I came to meet Cynthia Crawford. It's been very gradual, but I'm at the beginning stages, trying to find my way, learn about myself.

It all started with the visitations from the Greys. The first time, it was unusual in that I didn't have any communication with him, I just got this feeling that there was someone in the room with me, moving past me, because I'm sensitive to energies. So I just relaxed myself, closed my eyes, then when I opened them, I could see him as he stood in my front room. He was about three feet tall or so, and he looked at me, and within about ten seconds he was gone. It was a shock, because it was like, "Oh my God there's an *alien* in my room!" It was quite an experience; it was like I was acknowledging I knew he was there, and he was acknowledging that I knew he was there. But I didn't know *why* he was there. I'd always believed, but it was different when he came to me. I'd always had a strong knowing that we're definitely not alone, that there's a lot more beyond this planet. I've always been intrigued by the stars. My friends might think I was nuts if I told them, but each to their own.

After seeing the Grey I saw him a couple more times after that. I then started doing my own research, and Cynthia opened a lot of doors when it comes to that. She told me her opinion, that I was a hybrid, that I was here for certain reasons. From that point things started clicking into place, including how I feel, not 'belonging.' I almost feel like I'm visiting this place, that I didn't originate here. My experiences growing up fell into place, like dreams where I'm taken astrally to this particular place. I only saw the inside. I was in a room with people dressed in white. They were testing me and at least ten other people. They were testing our visual skills and we were told to look at a screen. We were told if we didn't pass the test they'd kill us, trying to frighten us into taking this test. Since well into my early teens these things were happening. So more has started to fit into place recently. There's too much fitting into place for it not to be true. I was in disbelief for a while, I was denying everything, but I feel a knowing that this is what I am.

The only way I can put it is that I feel alien to most people. I'm just very different to anyone I know. And I find it hard to communicate with them, even on a basic level, like eye contact and general conversation. I just do not connect with most people. I have two or three friends I see but we never talk about this stuff. I get a negative reaction from most people. I think they sense that something's different, and it makes them back off. It *is* lonely, so it's been great having Cynthia there; she's an amazing person, she's comforting and welcoming, always happy to help. Now that I've been more open about it, speaking with yourselves and others, I can now talk to others easier.

My dad always felt he didn't fit in, that there was more to life than meets the eye. He's got quite a few of his own beliefs like this. But I didn't tell my dad about the Grey until about a month ago. It's quite a taboo subject. I was throwing bits at a time to him, to let him digest it. I'd talk about the Greys, hybrids, and ask what he thought about it. It was all very gradual. But bringing it up kind of opened up how he feels about this. We've had a mutual information trade. I've even told him I'm a hybrid now. He's reacted very well, he's very open-minded. I've even wondered if he could be a hybrid himself. It's just been really strange. I never thought I might be able talk to him about this, and not only do I discover I can talk to him, but I find out that he's got his own thing going on. He's only a 15-20 minute drive from me, and we meet up every Sunday. Since we've understood this, we share this, and it's all we talk about now. It's constant. He's constantly finding out more about himself. He hasn't talked to Cynthia, but he's starting to think about it. I've pointed him to her YouTube videos, and some of Barbara's. In the past two weeks he's been watching some of your stuff. I give him links, and he either watches it or it he doesn't. I've only just started talking spiritual stuff to him, so now that we're talking about this stuff, it's great for us both. He's 54 now, and he's been thinking about spiritual stuff the last few years, and watching David Icke and things like that. He likes to learn continually. He avoids TV, there's so much crap on there it's unreal. There's so much control; it affects your energy, the way you think about the world and that. When you're not aware you just suck it up. I'm very into fantasy films and that, but I choose what I watch carefully.

What is your ET component?

I feel like the Tall White Zetas are my main hybrid species, but I also feel I have an aspect of the Sirian Warriors, the blue race—they follow me around daily. That's who I seem to connect with. There could be more, I've so much more to learn, but that's what I've figured out so far.

With the Tall White Zetas, as soon as I was open to it, I started feeling them around me. Another time I was taken astrally, and was inside some place, maybe a ship, talking to three of them. Then I woke up in a strange way, like I wasn't asleep, laying flat on my back as though I'd just been placed there.

The Sirian connection is all early stages. I feel an aspect of them in me, I'm very drawn to them. I feel like they're around me and are wanting me to learn more about them. At the moment I'm limited in my abilities, though I have spontaneous telepathy and clairvoyance. I'll see things like the Grey; I can tune in and sort of do it that way, but my strongest side is feeling things around me, getting flashes—it's not intentional.

They'll let me know in other ways. For example, last night I was talking to them, just one-way, then the lights started flickering, which they never do. They also mess with my fire alarm. The other day I was talking to them, I was saying I felt like they were around, then saw my keys fly across room. It's like they're trying to communicate in others ways, to let me know they're here, that I'm on the right track. If I'm worried or confused they'll find a way to let me know, to confirm it to me. I also find I see numbers like 11:11, 20:20 etcetera when I'm on the right path, or for confirmation about something.

The other night I got up to go to the bathroom, and I could feel them in the house. It's more a feeling and a knowing at the moment, rather than seeing. I'm getting pretty good at knowing when they're there.

How were you created?

I suspect that when I was conceived something was added to me as a fetus, but that's just an inkling. I believe it was a soul contract between all parties. I definitely think it was predetermined. My mum was constantly in the hospital, needing extra scans and tests, and they thought I'd be disabled because of how much fluid was surrounding me. The doctors didn't know what was wrong. There were so many complications, so I suspect I was genetically adjusted as a fetus. At birth I had to be revived as I was unconscious. I had an operation the first month as my stomach tubes were attached the wrong way. After that I was in the hospital for weeks on drips. Eventually I started healing, but I was ill for the first five years of my life. I had bad childhood asthma, but that's improved. I also had whooping cough, and my lungs were very weak. Many times I stopped breathing. I'm in a lot better health now, but still very susceptible. I had liver problems recently. Again, they didn't understand it. Then all of a sudden it was just gone. So I do feel like there's someone protecting me. I'm certain of it. I heal without care, all of a sudden. Doctors just brush it off now. I'm so grateful, I feel very blessed and lucky.

What connection do you retain with your star family?

If they want me to know something specific, that's the way they do it: I just know things suddenly. They gave me an exercise to awaken my perception, my third eye. I was meditating, asking how could I improve my perception and abilities, and I had this exercise just appear in my head. It helped to open my third eye, increasing my own abilities, particularly heightening telepathy and visions.

Opening the third eye

I put myself in a void with my eyes closed, and imagine a big blue-purple light is stuck to my forehead, and gleaming outwards. When I inhale, I suck the light in through my third eye chakra to my pineal gland. When I exhale, I project it to the surface of my forehead and out to the atmosphere. It's like a vacuum I control with my breath.

Vision is different. Once when I was driving I saw patterns of sacred geometry overlaying the landscape, which told me I was reaching a new point, ascending to a higher level. But the visions

> are different every time; sometimes the image is in your face. But with the exercise, it was simultaneous. I suddenly felt energy coming out of my head, and the download was on top of it. It was like, "Here's the exercise, here's your light: work with it."

In terms of telepathy and communication I do hear the odd sentence, but I'm not tuned into it properly yet and during the day you've got so many thoughts in your head that you don't notice them. But I use meditation which quietens my mind, and then it is clearer.

Sometimes I think of a statement or question and if I get an immediate reply, I know *I* didn't think it.

I had a vision a year ago. I was outside looking at plants in a garden and I thought, 'Each of these things has got its own consciousness, and I can communicate with every plant.' Then straight away, overlapping that thought, I saw each plant's aura stretching out two inches. It was spontaneous. As soon as you put your attention on something, it gives attention to you, and a connection is made.

If my dog is ill and not showing it, I know he's ill. If he has an upset stomach I'll get sympathetic pains and start looking around me for what might be causing it. Then the dog might just throw up. So I still have a connection but not a communication one.

I've got a kind of energy empathy. I pick up so many different energies from being around people that I can't figure out what's coming from where. I feel squished by other people's energy. I have my own way of protecting myself, by surrounding myself with light, either as a sphere covering me or an energetic wall pulled over and in front of me. Even touching other people, like a hand on my shoulder, sends a shock though me. I thought it might be negative transmission, but it can't be that. I can't even hug my dad, or my brothers—people I'm close to—without feeling uncomfortable. I can hug my mum sometimes, but sometimes I pull away. Maybe it's the way I'm managing my own energy, I'm picking up too much. I have to ground and keep my energy pure and bright. After being around people I have to surround myself in light, and sit in that light for half an hour.

After you put me in touch with Jacquelin Smith, she and I were talking on Skype and bouncing off each other, then right after I had an amazing experience. I found myself being taken into a mothership, which was the first time I'd experienced that. There were hybrids everywhere, hundreds of them. Funnily enough I have a friend called Zeta, and she was there. We were walking around and I saw a lift, shaped like a flying saucer, but room-sized, and it could go in any direction. Then there was a part where there were four chambers, like showers, but more like sprays, and you moved though each chamber, like they were coating or sanitizing or cleaning you. I saw Zeta the next day, and she said, "You were in my dream last night. I was waiting for you and we were going to go somewhere."

I've been on a ship before, but didn't see a lot. I don't think it was a mothership. There were three Tall White Zetas talking, but I didn't understand them and couldn't remember what they said. When I opened my eyes, I was on my bed and I felt like I'd been placed there. I got up to go to the bathroom, and knew they were in my house. I could hear them moving about and feel them walking past me. It's not frightening to me, though it was quite shocking to me when I realized it was really happening. I don't seem to scare very easily, I feel used to it somehow. I have a knowing that I'm safe, that there's nothing to be afraid of. I do feel I'm one of them.

The only time I was frightened, I don't know if it was ET or some other negative beings. About a year ago, I was in bed when I started hearing a weird sound, like a drumming. It had a ritualistic feel to it. Then I started seeing eyes all around me, looking at me; they'd appear and disappear. They were more like animal eyes, but a demonic version. You could even say Reptilian, as they had a vertical slit. It felt like they were feeding off me, coming for my energy. It really freaked me out. I didn't know what they were, but I knew it wasn't good. I tried to not be afraid, and send them love. They came three nights in a row, and on the last night, I finally said, "Get out, I'm sick of it, you're not welcome here." I was in a more dominant frame of mind. And it worked, they left and haven't returned. It was such a relief, I felt like I was being tortured by them. All I could see was eyes. They had power over me as I was so afraid. I don't know if they were malevolent ET types. This was before my first contact with Greys, but for two or three years I'd been growing spiritually, trying to contact angels and guides. But that was my first in-your-face experience.

What do you understand to be the purpose of your creation?

Healing would be the main one, that's a big part of who I am. There is another aspect, which I'm currently trying to work out. I've had experiences in meditation where I feel there's a type of war that's coming. On one occasion, instead of doing a normal meditation, I sat there silently relaxing, then I was taken somewhere, like someone's home. They had an old-fashioned grindstone and a man was sharpening a sword. I asked him why he was doing that, and he said, "We're preparing you for war." But he didn't say what kind of war. I've had some other experiences like that, and I feel that something is coming and I have a part to play in it. There could be more aspects, I still have so much to learn.

In my regression with Barbara I was told by the Greys that there was a large mass of energy heading to Earth which was going to make big changes, and that I will help and guide people when this happens. They added that integrating hybrids, ETs and humans was part of my mission here. In this regression I was confronted by a Sirian Warrior of Light, who was evidently a figure of authority. He was very to the point when he told me that I need to believe in myself as they believe in me, and that I am a warrior. I got the feeling that he was also letting me know that I have their support in all I do.

What do you understand to be the rationale for the hybrid program?

I think there are a few things. I have a feeling they want to learn about our world and our consciousness. They exist in one consciousness, whereas our perception is that we're all very separate—even though we're all one really. We have a dualistic perception; they don't understand how that is and want to experience it. It's the opposite of humans, who want to experience oneness.

They are helping to develop humans as a whole, and they'll have a big impact. The more hybrids there are, the bigger the impact on the Earth's consciousness. We're raising human consciousness, raising the frequency. So it's experience, plus learning, plus helping us. It's very different to be a hybrid, and we're helping to incorporate something that's important to the process. The blending of us all is bringing a sort of union into place.

Do you have your own hybrid children?

I think it's a massive possibility, because about a year ago I woke up and had had a wet dream, which I'd never had before. I've since heard so many things that gave me the sense that it's a possibility that they'd taken sperm. It would be a brilliant thing if that's what had happened, but I may learn more about that later.

How do you reconcile the multiple aspects of your identity?

I feel like I'm one of them, rather than a human. It goes back to not fitting in. I'm happier now, but still feel I don't really belong. I have a longing to be back there, and I'm looking forward to going back one day. I get the feeling that once I've done what I'm supposed to do I can go back.

Do you have a sense of mission?

I feel I'm doing it, but have a lot of growing to do before I can get there. Healing is a big part of it. I'm good at it, it's something I came to do, but I still have a lot to learn.

In trying to find things out too fast, sometimes I trip over myself, I stumble. I need to let it happen. I have this excitement, this eager feeling. I know there are good things to come, but it's a bit frustrating as I want to be there now. I like to get things done, so slow processes can be difficult.

This past week I've been reminiscing about meeting new people through this book, and I keep finding I make a connection straight away that I don't get with most people. I find it difficult to bond with people in general, but this has been totally different, which is really comforting. I'm not used to it, but it's a good feeling to make those bonds with others. Usually you have people you get on with in general, but here I click with everyone. When I spoke to Tatiana for the first time we talked for nearly two hours; we clicked immediately. So I'm loving it, I feel a part of it. You have to keep it all in usually, but there's no restrictions to what I can say here, and I feel very at home.

Are you encouraged by guides?

My guides, angels and star family all help me to stay on course and help me to find out things that I need to know or be aware of.

Do you have special abilities?

I'm a healer, I have a website for Reiki remote healing. One aspect of my mission is to heal people and help them come into their power. I can teach them how to heal themselves and about finding their own paths. I feel very passionate about it. I'm still in the early days with that. I did free healings before, to build experience, but it's beginning to develop now. I'm sensitive to energy and have the ability to read people which happens without conscious thought. I can also remote view depending on my energy levels, which is where you project your consciousness to another time and/or place. I can see energy in the air and I can use clairvoyance when healing.

How do you define 'Frequencies?'

Frequencies are different levels of existence. They are what separates the physical from the metaphysical. They are the different layers of reality which are what we call dimensions. Everything vibrates at different frequencies.

What is your understanding of Ascension?

Ascension is evolution. It is growth. It is our experiences and lessons which have taken us to the next level of our being. Ascension is essentially our frequency existing on a higher level of consciousness.

Hybrids can help with the process of waking people up. We can help people come into their power and realize that we are all infinite beings with amazing abilities.

Are you aware of coming Earth changes?

I am aware of some changes which are coming to this planet. There are big changes which will happen here on Earth. Some good and some which we would class as bad but they are necessary for the evolution of humanity and Mother Earth. Part of my regression experience revolved around this concept. The Earth itself will be moving into a different vibration.

What is your take on the takeover thesis?

I don't feel they're a threat, the intention of it is all good. There are some not so good ET races already on Earth, in control. But I only know little bits, I have no view on that side of things. My experience says that the hybrids have positive intentions.

Some negative Reptilians give a bad name to all of them, but I'm sure there are some very nice ones out there. It's like saying all humans are good or bad, they're getting judged as a whole.

Have you had contact with the military or intelligence agencies?

Whether this was military or not I'm not sure, but I have experienced a type of intelligence and the influence they can have. About three or four months ago I experienced a form of mind control which was trying to influence me to commit suicide. At the time I was in a good place and there was no reason for me to feel like that. I knew that something wasn't right. What I did was bring my focus to the present moment and surround myself with bright white light and push out any negative energy that was currently in my auric field. From that point on I felt fine. White light can clear this form of control/energy away from you.

How do you feel about the global hybrid community?

I think it would be a really positive thing to come together. I think we could achieve so much. I would love to see a massive meeting or conference, with people from all over, where we can come up with a way to put ourselves across. It would be amazing. It's such a taboo subject; lots of people are not open-minded about it. I couldn't imagine what we could achieve together, but it would be great to see what we could do to help, to change the world. If we could do that I'd consider my mission was at least half done. That's what we're here for. Connections are being made now and we can get to a point where we have enough people to begin to achieve bigger things.

Between ourselves we can be supportive of each other. It's great to see people living successfully as hybrids. It's an amazing feeling to be able to speak to others, to have that support, share your experiences, and receive help if you're struggling. There's no cap on what you can say, no judgment; there's no such thing as crazy, it's just how it is. I'm so happy and grateful to be involved, it's opened so many doors. Meeting these people has made a massive difference.

I knew I'd be able to help Tatiana, who came to her own realization while I was talking to her. When there are things I've not understood, when people are talking to me I realize where I'm at, which helps me understand. I can do that for others; I want to help as many people as I can.

What would you most like to discuss with other hybrids?

Experiences are a biggie because sharing with each other opens up other realities. I'd like to ask what others think about how we can best help humanity to wake up and see what's going on. How can we help humanity to better themselves, and take back control of this planet? They would be the main things.

The whole thing's a trip anyway, but I'd like to talk about the main problems that we could sort out. If we could start making a massive difference on this planet, that would be everything that I want. Even small changes will have a great influence on things to come, a ripple effect.

But at this moment in time I'm still trying to find myself, so give it a bit of time, and if something like that conference happened I could have more to say along those lines of how we can wake up humanity, teach people how to heal and empower themselves, and reclaim what's been taken from us, so we can start living a real free will existence.

What are the best and worst things about being a hybrid?

The worst is definitely the whole growing up thing and having to deal with random things you don't understand. But at the moment, it's having to live alongside humans that don't get you. It's so hard for me to relate to people in even simple ways. I do get a bit fed up with this 3D reality, the restrictions, when I know there's so much more to it. It's still a battle to keep positive. Sometimes I shut things out because I'm feeling down. When I'm in this state it is much more difficult to receive information or guidance. It only seems to come through when I'm keeping my vibration higher. It's a lot easier to receive info when feeling positive.

The best thing is that it's given me a sense of belonging, in that I know I've chosen to come here, and I don't feel like I feel because I'm an oddball. It makes me feel better, it makes it easier to be here. I'm starting to feel that it's okay to be different, and that I'm happy to be different. But not everyone sees the self worth in that. A lot of people who aren't awake, it's like sheep, so to feel left out of that, I now understand why. I feel grateful I've woken up, and am realizing who I am, and it's not a bad thing that I'm different. I've felt so bad, to the point of suicidal in the past, I just didn't want to be here. I was a very angry child growing up. When you feel a certain way and don't understand why, it's torture. But I'm happy to be here now. This is a game-changer, completely. I have my moments, but I can't wait to help people and do what I want to do. What I feel I came to do. I definitely feel like I'm in my zone, that I can make that difference. There's so much that we can achieve. I feel I know my mission, and am happy with who I am and what I'm here to do. Over the past six or seven months, my vibration is in a better place most of the time. I'm not in that low, depressed, can't-handle-it vibration. Which is a massive relief. It's lifted me to a state of bliss, most of the time. And sharing experiences with hybrids, helping each other ... it feels great.

How can humanity best work with you?

The main thing for me is to be open-minded. We are all free to make our own decisions and have our own beliefs. Knowledge in a lot of cases is power, which is no good if it isn't heard. Just being open-minded to the possibilities without pre-judgment.

How do you conceptualize God?

Since childhood I never accepted it's one all-knowing being. My school threatened to throw me out when I said that in Religious Education class. My teacher flew off the handle, tried to get me kicked out. She said I didn't deserve to be there, that my place should be taken by other kids who believe in God. I've always seen God as the Source of All That Is, the energy that makes up everything. Now I'm in limbo, sort of back to struggling with: where does Source come from? Energy is part of everything, including thinking, but where does this energy come from? That's what baffles my head. Where does it end or begin? I'm trying to route it back but I try to stop thinking about it as it's a bit head-bashing. A lot of things are beyond our conception so I try to give it a back seat.

Barbara: Infinity is a hard or perhaps impossible concept for us to imagine.

Those sort of questions, I can't wait to get out of this body to see for myself; I feel so many limitations, it gets frustrating.

Barbara: I too look forward to when I can know the other aspects of this reality. I see it as a great adventure.

Cynthia said ETs have souls, and go back into the soul dimension after physical death, so we can get to know them, but most humans wouldn't encounter them as they wouldn't be looking.

What is the most important thing you've learned?

I can point to three things that helped in my awakening process.

Meditation is definitely number one. It can calm the 'monkey mind,' the internal dialogue that won't shut up, the rational 'protect me' part of your mind that shuts out things you don't like. It's only focused on the past or the future, so if you're in the now you're out of the monkey mind. You'll never find it talking about what's happening now—never anything useful. Meditation goes deeper, it trains your brain to pick up on subtle energies—you're almost training yourself to be more open. Everyone can transmit, but it's about learning how to use your antennae to receive better. It can also help with intuition and developing your moral sense. It can fine-tune things and make them more accessible.

Morals are a vital part of self-realization, which is essentially trying to become a better person. You have to take a good look at yourself and see your faults with honesty. For example, stop denying that you do something—when you *clearly* do. You have to ask things like: am I acting from my highest good, or preventing myself doing something I *should* be? The clarity you get from meditation helps facilitate this. It helped me to wake up to see that everything's part of everything. Once I got that my morals changed automatically. Part of it was conscious, but a lot slots into place because you have a different outlook. Once you change, you deal with things in a way that serves you—and other people—better.

Looking after your body in general is the third key thing. You have to look after the vehicle you're in while you're here. Unless you're doing that the rest of it isn't going to fall into place properly. The meditation and morality is nowhere near as clear if the vessel is impure. But remember that you are not your body. Don't let these bodies obscure the true light being that you are.

Part III – Crossing the Threshold

Part III is principally a thematic summary section with a degree of comparative analysis. Given the depth, variety and complexity of the material, it can be useful to read across the texts and identify the similarities and differences.

We found that some areas seemed to form the core of the subject, and these have been examined in their own chapters. These are: Methods of Creating Hybrids; Purpose (including: Frequency; Ascension; Bridges and Ambassadors; and Missions, Abilities and Services); Guides and Star Families; and The Heart.

In these extended chapters we have quoted the hybrids directly—and occasionally at length—as their explanations require their own flow and detail to capture their understanding. It also focuses and reinforces the commonalities between their experiences and perspectives.

The other material is summarized more briefly in a single chapter.

We finish with some provisional conclusions and reflections on our own experiences of working with this remarkable group of people.

Short Summaries of Part II

Backgrounds

We interviewed eight people, six female and two male, with ages ranging from mid-20s to mid-60s. Most are Caucasian, mainly a mix of Celtic and Anglo-Saxon with some Native American, Jewish and Hispanic blood. Five of the hybrids are resident in the United States and three in England.

What is your ET component?

It is difficult to be precise on the number of ET races represented as the hybrids do not always know their full makeup—and not all races have names as we know them. But there are at least 15 separate species that they know of: Andromedan; Anunnaki; Arcturian-Zeta hybrid; Camelopardian; a dolphin-like race; Lyran; Mantis (Kekoresh and others); Pegasian; Pleiadian; Pleiadian-Sirian; Quabar; Reptilian (Fajan and others); Sirian Warriors of Light (the blue race); Sirian from Sirius B; Tall White Zeta; and Zeta.

How did you learn you are a hybrid?

The majority said it has been a process of putting the pieces together over time. Each said that they always felt different from childhood. Some had mysterious health issues and some had paranormal experiences which they only later had a context for.

Their awakening took many forms. Cynthia was told by her father. Tatiana's own body told her through kinesiology, and Charmaine was shifted into her Reptilian form by a group of fellow Reptilians.

Many of them did their own research to further develop their understanding, including talking with other hybrids and starseeds, but at some point, all of them began to have conscious contact in various ways. Regression allowed more memories and experiences to come through, and some of them pointed out that their star family suppressed their memories until they were ready to handle the reality. Several expressed their positive sentiments on having their nature confirmed—a mixture of joy, relief, peace and completeness.

Do you have your own hybrid children?

Jacquelin, Vanessa, Charmaine and Cynthia discussed having a number of their own hybrid children, created by varying means, living in various places and existing in different states. Vanessa uniquely described being visited by the spirits of her children-to-be. She also detailed the method of creating hybrid children on the craft, involving the infusion of galactic codes. Charmaine recounted experiences of meeting some of her children in an underground military facility where they are held, apparently to study their nature and abilities with a view to weaponizing them.

There is enormous variety in their experiences with their hybrid children, and one cannot help but be moved by the strains on those maternal bonds. It was clear that the same bonds exist, whatever the nature of the mother or child.

How do you reconcile the multiple aspects of your identity?

There are some interesting contrasts in this area. Integrating human and ET aspects is one challenge; integrating multiple ET frequencies—and past lives as ETs—is another.

Once they have sufficiently awakened—and that itself is an ongoing process—they begin to focus on defining and fulfilling their mission. Some are very public, very engaged as a hybrid, and others do not present themselves in that way.

Robert talked about 'the separation effect' that occurs when explaining his nature to people. The further he takes them into it, the more they withdraw, and the more alienated he feels. And yet he, and Jacquelin, found that along the way they have also learned to live better as humans.

Although they all report feeling more integrated and balanced over time, several of them stated that they still look forward to completing their missions on this planet and returning home.

Do you have physiological differences to humans?

The hybrids commonly reported childhood health issues and frail systems. Cynthia has upgraded muscle density, but she also has more porous bones and an antigen that prevents her having blood transfusions. Robert and Charmaine both have double-jointed wrists, and Charmaine also has double-jointed fingers.

Robert said that the major shift for him has been his expanded mental faculties. He was told by another hybrid that he had been upgraded by the beings, as he realized his capacity for visualization had increased dramatically, allowing him to picture in detail the 2D and 3D 'consciousness-amplifying technologies' which he has begun creating.

Tatiana has found that, following visits from the Pleiadians, her hands have become unnaturally hot, which may be connected to healing abilities. In addition she has found her psychic and intuitive abilities have ramped up.

The hybrids exhibit a variety of psychic gifts, which are discussed in the chapter on Missions, Abilities and Services.

The most radical physiological differences are the shapeshifting abilities. Charmaine, Juju and Jacquelin all discussed experiences of either voluntary or involuntary shapeshifting into their ET form. Jacquelin was able to take the forms of several of her star being frequencies during her 2013 Thanksgiving experiences.

Juju said hers is involuntary. "For me, it happens with high emotion, like love, or gratitude. It's triggered by high frequency, so being around lower vibrations it won't happen. Higher, positive vibration brings it out." Juju was interviewed for the Reptilian episode of Jesse Ventura's TV show *Conspiracy Theory*, and at one point her eyes were seen to shift to Reptilian slits. She said that she can't control it. She feels a pressure behind her eyes and they change.

Barbara has also witnessed Cynthia's pupils shift to slits.

Charmaine said that she was shifted by a group of Reptilians the first time, but the second time she was physically forced to change by a combination of fluid injection and electrical pulses in an underground military facility. She was changed back by the use of a 'gun' that emitted a particular frequency.

What protocols govern ET interaction with humans?

On the face of it, there are contradictory answers to this question. Many hybrids say that the ETs have a policy of non-interference, but just the presence of hybrids here—with all that they bring—is its own kind of interference.

It seems that what they mean is that the races they are connected to rarely, if ever, intervene directly with the lives of humans. They pursue at least some of their goals through the hybrids.

Juju: "I'm not sure we intervene at all. To intervene or manipulate is more of a lower vibration."

Robert: "There is a set of rules there, a 'prime directive' if you will. You also have different beings at different levels that can interact in different ways. For the most part we are on our own, they want us to solve our own problems.

"Then there's the anthill thing—which is related to the 'zoo theory'—on why they don't interact. Imagine you as a person trying to help an ant colony that got stepped on, and the ants are going crazy. [...] Imagine a ship the size of Jupiter manifests out in our solar system, or a million ships over a mile wide—and they could do that—people would go nuts. The only way you could help them out is to live among them, and help them to understand. I can be a human, and help people to understand these beings and what they're all about. I can say, "Hey guys, don't worry about the giants picking up the rocks, they're here to help us.""

Cynthia: "We starseeds are here at this time to assist humanity by being examples, but not to do the work *for* them."

Jacquelin: "They tell me that we are responsible for ourselves, that humanity has to find its way and grow. The star beings cannot directly intervene so thus we have the hybrid program, which is integrating star being energy here on Earth to create a new race. [...] Hybrids are here to slowly integrate the higher consciousness energy in order to raise the frequency to help humanity evolve, to become conscious and to remember that we are love."

Some spoke of certain circumstances where more direct intervention was possible.

Vanessa: "In my understanding and experience, intervention only happens when it is in the highest and best interest of everyone involved including the star beings. They will not intervene if it negates the will of others."

Jacquelin: "I understand they can only intervene to a point. They are helping balance the Earth's energies, and they've intervened at some of the military installations, knocking out the power. Their intention is to give us these messages—that we humans keep disregarding—to do away with war, with warlike behavior and thinking."

Juju: "I feel very strongly that ETs will not allow nuclear war. It affects things too deeply, at the subatomic level, and it interacts with other dimensions that are nearby."

Robert: "There is nothing any government can do to stop these beings doing what they are here to do. And I have a feeling they're going to do it. They have to. I think we're at a point with the state of the planet, that they're going to have to step in or we're going to lose this planet. [...] I have a feeling something is coming. I think they're going to show themselves, and I think it's going to be soon."

These particular beings evidently have a complex relationship with both the hybrids and the rest of humanity. It seems they work through the hybrids and other contactees on a far-reaching mission to protect and enhance life on Earth. Several hybrids have said that major events are heading our way, and that they will play various roles in helping humanity deal with them. Some of this is discussed in the next section.

Earth changes and the New Earth

The Ascension chapter deals with many aspects of this, but additional views were shared.

Cynthia talked about her experience with the Ant People, who showed her their underground realm. Their antennae allow them to identify and locate certain individuals who they take to their world to wait out the Earth changes which "cleanse" the planet. These preserved humans then repopulate the renewed world. "Earth agreed to be a school for third-dimensional humans. At the end of each cycle she cleanses herself, shakes off all the fleas and becomes this pristine planet. And then maybe the next school will learn faster, and not do what they did on Mars."

Matt stated that he is aware of coming Earth changes, which are necessary stages in the planet's evolution. Again he sees this in terms of a vibrational shift.

Robert also referred to a "transition event" that is coming, an energetic shift that will effect all of life on Earth.

The term 'New Earth' was used by some of the hybrids. Jacquelin said, "As we are raised into higher frequencies, that perceived duality disappears and there is only love, peace and joy.

The New Earth is love, peace and joy; we can be in those higher frequencies if we choose to—anybody can."

She went on to discuss the roles of light and dark which people have chosen at the soul level to play out in their lives on Earth, in order to experience contrast.

Cynthia echoed this to some degree. "But because of all the choices and temptations, that's why it has taken six different New Earths for many of the souls to ascend."

She went on to suggest that the negativity has run its course. "The archangels of the light are saying enough is enough. In this lifetime they finally created a fifth-dimensional Earth, that will be perfect. Everyone lives equally, among all different races, and enjoys health and old age."

What is your take on the takeover thesis?

The comments on the 'takeover thesis,' commonly discussed in David Jacobs' work, were varied. Some are aware there is a parallel hybrid program underway which is in the 'service to self' column— as opposed to the 'service to others' work that they are a product of. Tatiana, Charmaine and Juju all stated that they don't give attention to the negative aspect, and some preferred not to discuss it at all—often referring to the law of attraction.

Juju talked about the choice of words. "I think it's a matter of perception. The words you choose show you where you're at with something. The hybridization program is definitely happening, but why do we have to see it as a 'threat,' rather than more of a profound happening, that includes humanity helping another species? I like that take on it much better; that's what I choose to focus on. And a lot of us hybrids have been asked to be like donors, to have hybrid children with the ETs, to extend the species' existence. To me that's a loving, spiritual experience, not a 'threat.'

"Not all ETs here are [...] for service to others; some are more in service to self, and you will feel the manipulation part of it, or wanting to control. If you feel that, and see that behavior, that is intervention. [...] There is a species of Reptilian here that's not in service to humanity. It doesn't mean it's evil, but it's not here for *us*. There's a big difference. People forget to question that. It's like a human stepping on an anthill by mistake—if you ask the ants if we're evil, what would they say?"

As someone closely involved with the hybrid children aspect, Vanessa has strong feelings on the 'threat' perspective. "If we are incarnating these genetically modified children, from an introspective point of view, are the parents going to reject the children, not love them? I don't see how that point of view works, because parents are going to love their children, they're going to work with it. We can't incarnate all these people to take over the world, because there's this huge love component between parent and child, and that vibration holds so much benevolence. I have to get that off my chest because it's very triggering for me to hear that. There's a personal vulnerability because of my involvement in it."

Many of the hybrids reported negative experiences with dark energies, but some suggested that it may be a matter of perspective, that there may still be a soul agreement to participate in that.

Robert has had invitations to support the efforts of self-serving beings. "So yes, this negative stuff is going on, but I'm not close to it. Most of my experiences are extremely benevolent. To be honest I'd like to see a hybrid takeover—I think the world would be running pretty awesome. I think I'd make one hell of a President. I'd only have one law: don't be an asshole. [...] As for me, in my one-room apartment, I'm not taking over jack shit. I couldn't take over a McDonalds. I went in there today and it took me a half hour just to get a cup of coffee."

Robert's response rather firmly grounds the discussion, and speaks with its own kind of eloquence to the point that, as discussed in the chapter on Hybrid Discourse in Ufology, it is apparent that there are at least two hybrid programs underway on this planet. Jacobs may be accurate in his conclusions concerning one aspect of the phenomenon, but the accounts shared in this book—and in Quiros' doctoral dissertation—indicate a very different agenda to that of a takeover of Earth. What level of overlap may exist—which would suggest either deception or misunderstanding—is unclear. As ever, reaching firm conclusions in this field remains the preserve of the supremely confident.

Have you had contact with the military or intelligence agencies?

The responses to this question were similarly uncomfortable for some of the hybrids, also relating to the law of attraction.

Charmaine shared the most detailed experiences, opened up through regression sessions. If we accept that hybrids exist—and have psychic ability and the capacity to shapeshift into powerful reptiles—then it stands to reason that the military and intelligence communities will be keen to weaponize these attributes for their advantage. Countless innovations that we live with daily were driven by the desire for improved attack, defense or intelligence.

Some of the hybrids talked about having star family protection from such covert agencies, and given the surveillance and intimidation that several report, they need it.

How do you feel about the global hybrid community?

On a much lighter note, we wanted to understand something of the relationship between the hybrids, and their sense of what the Earth's hybrid community could achieve together.

Tatiana: "It's a nice idea to have a community like that, to join everyone. The point for the beings is for us all to be together as one family."

Charmaine, Robert and Matt spoke about having a conference for awakening hybrids and starseeds, allowing them to come together, share and make sense of their experiences, and find support. Matt said of his contact with other hybrids, "There's no cap on what you can say, no judgment; there's no such thing as crazy, it's just how it is."

Jacquelin: "Some of the younger starseeds and hybrids are having a really hard time, they're feeling scared. They don't understand their nature. And they're angry at humanity. I hear them say, "Why am I here with these stupid humans?" [...] I feel [the hybrid community] can offer awakening starseeds support and comfort. It can help them understand who they are and what's happening to them so that they can release the fear. [...] When I met Robert Fullington for the first time we just looked at each other and both of us said, "Oh my God!" We knew that we'd been on ships together. We got to know each other a little better and that's when we spontaneously did the Mantis bow at the exact same time. It was ecstasy because you can't do that with a human who isn't in touch with their star origin. It's a soulful joy."

Juju: "I think it's very healthy to unite, as we're still learning about ourselves. I'm blessed as I was given the ability to know who I am, but a lot of starseeds don't have that awakening as it's not a part of their mission. But because it was part of my mission to awaken others I wrote a book to help with that. [...] We really help each other a lot, to grow, to get answers, to become more balanced. And the more balanced you are, the higher your vibration can be. It all goes back to trying to be the best person you can be, and shining your light."

Working out the public relations aspect of the hybrid story came up several times. Overcoming the ignorance, negative stereotyping and misinformation that has been spread is vital in bringing balance to the narrative and being more representative of the hybrid program and ET interaction on Earth.

Beyond that, there was a consensus that greater, wonderful things could be achieved by combining so much knowledge with the various abilities that they have.

Robert: "When we get together we accelerate each other. If it was up to me I would like to build a community together so I could be with them all the time and see what we could achieve."

Juju: "I used to teach in my ET class that when hybrids and starseeds get together their lights combine synchronistically and are really bright. It's like a symphony. If you're on a ship looking down at Earth with heightened vision, you can see all these lights getting together and it's really beautiful."

Cynthia: "We are not here to create followers, but to teach others how to find their own truth. [...] We hybrids are scattered throughout the world, working in all walks of life and affecting all those we come in contact with."

Jacquelin: "It doesn't serve a purpose to just show off this skill or that skill, there needs to be a positive intention or focus to say, "We're sharing these abilities because you too are connected to the stars and have a star family; isn't it exciting that you can discover that connection?" I always come from that place with teaching and educating others about their star origins. This is about everyone learning, growing and expanding; it's about evolving."

What would you most like to discuss with other hybrids?

The younger hybrids in particular were interested in comparing abilities and experiences in order to learn, and get more context for their own. Juju summed it up: "Sharing experiences, seeing their level of memories, hearing their language, learning about their origin, how they awakened, what their mission is."

Robert expressed curiosity about how others handled the hybrid aspect of their identity in their relationships, and also where they got their information. "Mine comes from my mind and heart; the beings do guide me along, point me in the right direction, but they never tell me anything directly. I'm dubious about beings that go around giving information a little too freely."

There was a big focus on what they can do to better help humanity evolve. Matt said, "I'd like to talk about the main problems that we could sort out. If we could start making a massive difference on this planet, that would be everything that I want. Even small changes will have a great influence on things to come, a ripple effect."

How can humanity best work with you?

The hybrids listed a number of requirements for what we might term a productive working relationship: being open-minded toward them; respecting and honoring them (in the way that humans expect from one another as a basic courtesy); meeting them in order to cultivate an informed opinion; listening to children who are having experiences and not shutting them down; working on themselves through, as Vanessa said, "embracing themselves and dedicating themselves to living in their own authenticity," and as Cynthia reiterated, "getting out of judgment and into their hearts."

Robert left the key question hanging for humanity to consider: "What *if* I'm telling the truth? What *if* I'm not crazy? What then?"

What are the best and worst things about being a hybrid?

There are many highs and lows in the lives of the hybrids. Peak experiences—the kind that change you forever—are a part of all their lives. They experience visions, visitations and vibrations that most people can barely imagine. Their worldview is expanded far beyond this world, yet here they are, living in cultures which often deny they *can* exist. They tend to experience an inner conflict prior to awakening to the reality of their hybrid nature, and difficulty in dealing with such a narrow cultural view of reality—and all that that entails. But they all spoke of their joy in carrying out their missions, and how special it can be to connect to and collaborate with other hybrids. Their connection to the star beings and worlds, galaxies and dimensions beyond our own gives them great joy and comfort.

Tatiana: "The conflict I always had inside me is no longer there. This has opened a new world to me. The best thing is knowing that I can help, that I have a natural mission and I'm going to do it. [...] As for the worst thing, I don't see anything particularly negative in it yet. But I have learned that when a hybrid baby is born it can be difficult for them, with allergies etcetera. Adjusting to living in a real body as a human on Earth is not easy."

Cynthia: "The best thing about being a hybrid is experiencing other abilities and understanding them. The worst is that we are often scrutinized and judged unfairly."

Charmaine: "The worst thing for me was growing up knowing you were different, and not completely understanding why. Having no one to talk to about it, who was going through the same things and could relate. And the internal struggle, feeling like you were two beings.

"The best thing was having confirmation, and knowing what I am, what my path is, my mission, and being able to help people—if it helps one person it would be worth it. Some people have thought I'm crazy to put myself in that position just for one person, but it's not about numbers. If you can just help a few it makes a difference; it's a wonderful feeling and it's why I'm here. Helping to get people onto their path, giving them a chance to talk about their experiences without feeling judged, and frightened. And knowing that they're talking to someone who understands because they've gone through the same things. Some people get stuck in the trauma, but others have moved on, and use it in a positive way."

Robert: "The best thing is that we get to experience awesome things which most people don't even know is real. That's beyond worth it. My top experience was our 2009 sighting of the craft, a triangle the size of a house. It was so profound and amazing. I've seen things that officially don't exist, like a black hole coming out a flying pyramid that oozed plasma. I got to see that shit. And I get an awesome view of the potential of humanity, of what it can be.

"But the downside is that what I'm experiencing isn't considered real. That causes some major issues, that I didn't even know existed when I was younger. So thank God they waited until 2009 to wake me up, or my life would have been way harder. I was weird enough. It was already like, "Here's crazy Rob, the ET guy." The ridicule and the teasing was the worst part. [...] It definitely makes it harder to function properly in society without getting frustrated, irritated. Now that I know how it could be, and I see how it is, it's kind of disgusting. I feel so bad, hurt for everybody. But that's what we're here for, trying to help 'em out, right?"

"It's not easy because officially, I don't exist. What is the government's official position on UFOs and ETs? They, and the general population, deny it. This creates what I call 'the separation effect.' It goes like this: I start telling people I saw a UFO and they say, "Oh, awesome." I show them a picture—same response. Some will say it's a government thing, not ET. When I tell them I met an alien they're like, "*What?*" Even in the UFO community—let alone in regular society—they say, "There's no *way* you met an ET." Then you go into "I'm a hybrid," and the belief just drops lower and lower. And the more intense the experience, the more people tune out. So you start feeling this separation, you go into what I call 'the non-existence zone.' This is what I am, a hybrid, but as far as the majority of people are concerned, I don't exist."

Juju: "The good part is the sense of mission, and purpose. And the sense of so much more out there beyond our individual selves, a much bigger picture, and that gives you a seed of hope. It's a profound spiritual experience to know that there are much better experiences, and more profound things going on; we're not stuck in this little 3D world, there really is so much more out there that's beautiful, connected."

"Because I'm awakened to who I am—a being from Andromeda—my thinking extends to the universe. I have to think universally about the effects of different actions and processes. How far do the effects go? Does it affect the beings? [...] So that's the best thing about being a hybrid, knowing that there is so much more. But it can be depressing at the same time, being kept here in such a tiny section of 3D living. It's both at the same time."

Vanessa: "The best thing is being able to be aware of my multidimensional, multifaceted nature and opening to my consciousness and the universe in this way. The worst is bridging the ignorance of others and working with their projections."

Jacquelin: "I'm grateful I've hung in here, but there have been some challenges with being hybrid. The upside is, I enjoy being of service to others. That's fun for me, I enjoy sharing my experiences which can help support others who are just awakening to the fact that they're starseeds and/or hybrids. It's a privilege to be a part of something greater than myself.

"The downside is that it can be a challenge to live in this world and be so empathic and telepathic. I wonder at times, 'Is this my feeling, or the other person's feeling, or is this from the collective consciousness?' It takes practice to sort those things out.

"I'm grateful for the gifts I am able to share with others. Also, I enjoy being able to communicate with star beings because I enjoy their company, their communications, and I appreciate their humor. It's fun to share their messages with others about who they are, as well as Ascension and other things. My life is certainly never boring! There are many wonderful gifts that come with being a hybrid."

Matt: "The worst is definitely the whole growing up thing and having to deal with random things you don't understand. But at the moment, it's having to live alongside humans that don't get you. It's so hard for me to relate to people in even simple ways. I do get a bit fed up with this 3D reality, the restrictions, when I know there's so much more to it. [...] Sometimes I shut things out because I'm feeling down. When I'm in this state it is much more difficult to receive information or guidance. It only seems to come through when I'm keeping my vibration higher. It's a lot easier to receive info when feeling positive.

"The best thing is that it's given me a sense of belonging, in that I know I've chosen to come here, and I don't feel like I feel because I'm an oddball. This is a game-changer, completely. I have my moments, but I can't wait to help people and do what I want to do. What I feel I came to do. I definitely feel like I'm in my zone, that I can make that difference. There's so much that we can achieve. I'm happier with myself, I feel the positives are outweighing the negatives. I feel I know my mission, and am happy with who I am and what I'm here to do. [...] It's lifted me to a state of bliss, most of the time. And sharing experiences with hybrids, helping each other ... it feels great."

How do you conceptualize 'God?'

With so much access to other dimensions and larger realities, it was irresistible to ask the hybrids to describe their conception of God. The most common term used was 'Source,' which was described very similarly from person to person.

Cynthia described Source as the original all-encompassing consciousness which then split itself into "Source-selves" in order to "know what it was to come from nothingness to become All That Is." Every being is an aspect of Source, through which Source lives and learns vicariously, "experiencing the joy of accomplishment. So it can experience it over and over again."

She added a crucial insight: "This is another reason why we are told to first love ourselves unconditionally before we are capable of unconditionally loving others." In other words, if we are truly each an aspect of a unified whole, then when we love ourselves we are *automatically* loving everything else. Many of the hybrids stated the importance of learning to love ourselves before we can love others, and that insight explains why.

Robert's quote from James Gilliland echoes this: "A consciousness and energy that permeates all life, the one consciousness that encompasses all consciousness on all planes and dimensions throughout the multiverse. The Absolute."

Juju said, "I've read a lot of books on ETs, their concepts, but for me personally I've got to a place where I see God is in everything. Everything has a piece of the God energy; I try to respect all lifeforms as a piece of the divine. But I prefer the term 'Source energy' because 'God' has a kind of father role, which comes from cultural upbringing."

Vanessa: "I view God as Source. The supreme and purest energy source that all comes from. We are all forms of God."

Jacquelin: "I have seven key star families and I've communicated with all of them about how they conceptualize God. The word they use is "One," meaning that everything that exists is a single, interconnected whole. Among the many planets and stars I've experienced and have come from, there's no such thing as worshipping a god. Star beings respect and connect with love, or the One. [...] And in Oneness, the Creator is everywhere; if I touch a tree, the Creator's in that tree, and it's the same for everything. Everything is the One, is the All."

What is the most important lesson you've learned?

From living such extraordinary lives, and dealing with integration on so many levels, what have they taken from it? What has got them through it? What can others learn from their journeys? Some of the learnings are more inner-focused and some are more outer-focused.

Robert: "The most important thing I've learned is how to be more human. I do have all these abilities and amazing experiences, but I still need to ground myself and experience this human existence."

Jacquelin: "To love myself and to live from my heart. By going into our hearts we can remember who we are. Our heads can lead us places that aren't the truth or that can throw us off track. Even people who are in communication with star beings are learning about this. It can get tricky because everyone has filters and we need to be clear about where our guidance or information is really coming from."

Charmaine: "To be open—open-minded and open-hearted; to share my knowledge, experiences and thoughts with others so they may learn from them and gain understanding. Even if negative things happen to you, it can help others by sharing your experiences with them. I believe negativity can always be changed into something positive."

Juju: "It's all about spirituality, it's about interconnectedness, being loving, accepting, holding yourself in the highest vibration, expanding your consciousness, growing.

"Be assertive, be in your truth, in your power, not aggressive but assertive. To evolve, and become who you truly are, and love yourself—and that's vital, as you can't love anyone else if you don't love yourself—you learn that what really matters is your soul essence, and nothing can take that away.

"So work it through, have courage, surround yourself with white and gold light, use healing, stand in your power. But most importantly it's what you think, where you hold your thoughts; hold yourself in a higher vibration of love and gratitude, be deliberate in your thoughts and use them wisely, and you won't attract those negative, fearful things. It's intentional living, choosing and being aware, keeping positive and becoming your authentic self."

Cynthia: "If people could only see the beauty and perfection in our differences, that everything is a piece of art, and let go of wanting everything to be a certain way, they would see the beauty in every single being. They would feel the compassion, they would feel their heart, they would understand who they are and where they came from, and they would stop the judgment and prejudices."

"There is no helping humanity until first, they realize that the material world is an illusion, and second, they get out of their heads and into their hearts. [...] Until humanity realizes how to live in the 'Christ Consciousness,' they are trapped on this prison planet. The simple meaning of Christ Consciousness is to live without fear, greed, judgment or prejudice by looking beyond the physical container to see the Source in every living being. It's that simple."

Vanessa: "My message and my most important lesson is to embrace multidimensionality. I've gone through so many experiences that just shatter frameworks and belief systems; there's no way to integrate them otherwise. That's my first and foremost objective. In embracing that, we're able to access deeper awareness, consciousness, information, and it's about being okay with not knowing, and in that not knowing, we will know."

Methods of Creating Hybrids

Six of our hybrids have a clear idea of how they were created as hybrids. These methods vary from person to person, and yet they have some common themes.

Cynthia was told by her father at age 34 that she was a hybrid. He had worked on a top secret project in the U.S. Army, creating ET-human hybrids. He had drugged her mother before she was pregnant with Cynthia. She was then abducted by these people and impregnated with a hybrid embryo. This embryo was composed of her mother's egg, her father's sperm and two types of ET DNA. She was told she is 38% Anunnaki, 28% Zeta, and 34% human.

Four of the hybrids were influenced by ET DNA while in their human mother's womb.

Vanessa's parents were her human mother and father and she was born in the natural human way here on Earth. When she was in the womb her mother was taken onto a craft and Vanessa was embedded by ETs with galactic coding, which included Sirians from Sirius B, Lyrans, Andromedans, Pegasians, Camelopardians, Zetas and Pleiadians. She is aware that as a soul she had agreed to come to Earth as a hybrid with many galactic DNA elements and energetic imprints from a variety of beings.

Vanessa laid out the four key stages of hybridization on board craft set up for this purpose. A light body of pure gold plasma goes through 'spinning' or 'galactic infusion,' a process of combining DNA and energetic imprints from the various 'parents.' This will begin to set up templates for a cell mass, and the being will be nurtured until they are ready to incarnate fully to Earth parents.

Jacquelin has a heritage of hybrids in her Earth family. Her parents and grandparents were originally Mantis beings who incarnated in this lifetime as human beings. After they passed away they came to her as Mantis beings. When Jacquelin's mother was pregnant with her, she was taken onto a ship where Tall White Zetas implanted DNA into the fetus. This DNA was a combination taken from ET races, from a hybrid man on Earth and from her parents. She watched this procedure taking place from the point of view of her spirit form, while her physical body in her mother's womb was being implanted. This was confirmed at age 20 when, during a meditation, an ET presence known as Quabar said to her, "We want you to know you are from us." The beings told her she carries seven frequencies: Mantis, Tall White Zeta hybrid, Arcturian-Zeta hybrid, Quabar, a dolphin-like race, Reptilian and a celestial/star race which humans don't have a name for.

Juju was born to human parents who were Pentecostal Christians, who would have thought that any unusual visitors to Juju were the devil. They wanted nothing to do with ETs and UFOs. By age six, the beings inserted their DNA directly into her. They said they did it this way so her parents would not have to have any ET contact. She eventually knew she was a Reptilian hybrid after a Reptilian male came into her room and inserted implants behind her eyes, to send back to their kind everything she experiences in this lifetime on Earth. When he touched her she felt changed, and it felt good, and she learned about her previous life as a Fajan star being living on a planet in the Andromeda galaxy. She also learned that as a soul she had decided to connect with Pleiadians, and the insectoid species—the Mantis and the Greys.

Matt thinks his parents made an agreement on the soul level to have and raise a hybrid child. He believes he was genetically altered by ETs while he was a fetus in his mother's womb. He was then born in the usual human way. He had several physical abnormalities which included one of the tubes above his stomach being placed in the wrong direction, having bad asthma for years, very high blood readings and liver problems. He thinks he has DNA from Tall White Zetas, Sirian Warriors (the blue race) and perhaps from some other ET races. He is in touch with some of these beings daily, and feels he is part of this group of beings.

Some of them are less clear about how they were created as hybrids. They gradually came to the realization and conviction that they are hybrids. Charmaine wondered for years why she was being visited and abducted by ETs, and by humans that seemed to be military. She wondered why, when she would sit quietly with her eyes closed, she would see Reptilian eyes, feel Reptilian energy and talk with this being as a special friend. The confirmation of her being a hybrid came in her adult years when she asked the ETs who were visiting her if there was any way they could confirm that she is a hybrid. In response, she had an experience of being changed into her Reptilian form by a group of Reptilian beings and felt complete, powerful, joyful and free from inner conflict. She wonders if some special procedure had been used to facilitate her conception because she was conceived after her mother was told by doctors that she was unable to have any more children.

Tatiana does not know how she was created as a hybrid, but she had seen a being in her room and wondered how she might be connected to him. She related to things which Charmaine had told her about being a hybrid. Tatiana's confirmation came in her adult life through muscle testing by her kinesiologist, which verified that she has more than 50% non-human DNA and that she needed to find out more about this for herself. A second confirmation happened when she was taken up in a tube of white light into a ship. She saw the same man who had previously visited her in her room, and her clothing transformed into that of his Pleiadian people as a symbol that she is one of them.

Robert has four theories about how he was created as a hybrid:

1. ETs implanted an embryo in his mother's womb, with specific DNA from selected people who had been put together over generations to created the genetics they wished, combined with ET genetics.

2. When his mother was pregnant with him she was taken to a ship, where he as an embryo was removed from her and overlaid with ET genetics. These genetics included DNA from one or more ET species and from other human abductees. After this overlay he was returned to his mother's womb.

3. ETs might have made an exact copy of him when he was an embryo, and this copy was imbedded with ET genes and implanted into his mother's womb to replace the original embryo. She was also carrying an identical twin, who mysteriously disappeared from her womb.

4. His former ET self from an earlier incarnation on another planet chose to reincarnate in this life as a human, and brought some of those ET genetics with him. He may have created himself on a soul level, by making this choice. He feels sure that he had agreed to be a hybrid in this lifetime.

No matter how they came into being, these people are each convinced that they are hybrids. They have a unique perspective on human beings and the Earth, and identify deeply with the star beings they are connected to.

The method of their creation was not something they were focused on until we asked them about it. The understanding that this is their nature brought joy, relief and peace—a reaction vastly different to that which what we might expect of a regular human. To have their complex, often conflicted thoughts and feelings finally make sense gave them a feeling of integration and gratitude. The most important thing to them is that they carry out their missions and are of service on Earth.

In Barbara's previous research into ET-human hybrids, she learned mostly about the types of hybrids that did not have a large enough percentage of human in them to be able to live on Earth. They lived their entire lives on the ships or on other planets, and performed many tasks for the ETs in charge. They occasionally had the chance to see their human parents for brief periods of time.

This research included the various reproductive methods in which hybrids were created, the different stages of hybrids (according to how many generations they had been breeding with humans), the types of beings who were creating hybrids, the reasons given for why they were creating hybrids, human male and female reactions to the forced reproductive procedures, and their reactions to seeing their hybrid babies and children.

The research also included information about the few hybrids whom she knew who were human enough to live on Earth, their unusual abilities and skills, their purpose for being here, how they were created as hybrids, and the special work they are doing here.

They all expressed feeling 'different' to their families and to all other people around them. They all had awareness of their true (ET) family and their true home (their ET planet), and had a longing to return there. They each have some psychic abilities which they used in their daily lives. They each had ongoing encounters with their ET beings, and received messages and guidance from them.

Thus there are many similarities between them and the eight hybrids in our study. Our hybrids were created by ET DNA being added to a human mother and father's embryo or child, rather than by enforced mating between a human and a hybrid.

Compared to this new study, she did not hear from her original hybrids nearly as much of a spiritual perspective, nor anything about love, light and oneness, nor as defined a statement of mission, nor as large a cosmic perspective, nor the emphasis on other dimensions (frequencies), nor the emphasis on Ascension.

Purpose

Introduction

Among the many aspects of the hybrid phenomenon which may engage one's fascination, eventually one comes to the central question: why? What is the *purpose* of all this? Why would such a variety of beings, 'from' various places and dimensions, take such an active interest in the planet Earth and its lifeforms? And, what roles do the hybrids play within this larger enterprise?

As we have seen, the answers largely orbit the enigmatic concept of Ascension. Interpretations of this vary considerably, and we will look at that in detail. As for individual roles, this has been a key aspect of the learning journey of each hybrid. Some have more than one role, and they tend to have a variety of enhancements which support their roles. These commonly include psychic and healing abilities.

To explore the question of purpose in detail, this section breaks the subject down into four chapters: Frequency; Ascension; Bridges and Ambassadors; and Missions, Abilities and Services.

To better get to grips with the language and concepts of the hybrids, we first offer an examination of 'frequency' and 'vibration.' The reader may have developed their own working model for the various applications of these concepts, but particularly for those who are struggling, we have pulled together the numerous takes on the subject, and offer some further ways into it. This gives us a solid place from which to start exploring Ascension.

We then look at personal purpose. The hybrids are often referred to as bridges and ambassadors. Those that are clear on this role are offering it to the world in different ways, to various degrees. They use their abilities to help carry out their missions, and often focus this in particular services.

Frequency

Let us try to develop an understanding of what the hybrids mean by 'frequency' and 'vibration.' Frequency is used frequently, and as the glossary suggests, it is another complex facet of this field. In human terms it generally refers to a measure of how often something happens, but here it appears to have multiple definitions and applications. It has mainly been used to mean: different energetic states; dimensions; rates of vibration; measures or patterns of energy, and identifiers for each soul. Let us look at some examples.

Charmaine said, "I have always been very aware of frequencies, being able to hear some that others cannot. [...] Frequencies can be in sound form, energy frequencies, color frequencies, and natural frequencies such as that of the Earth. The military has researched how to manipulate frequencies to cause negative effects in individuals and groups, such as fear and ill health."

She illustrates this in the transcript of her regression, describing being subjected to a variety of frequencies which were used to trigger and measure physiological responses, particularly shapeshifting.

Cynthia pointed out that both races and individuals have identifying frequencies. "Every person has our own frequency, it's called the "soul identity" and carries a frequency that only belongs to that soul." She was also able to identify the sex of a rattlesnake by its feminine frequency.

Jacquelin also uses frequency as an identifier: "I call Quabar "my soul's key frequency.""

Vanessa used frequency in several ways. She spoke of shifting frequency to facilitate astral travel. In terms of light language she said, "It's a different frequency of consciousness and is all about opening the heart chakra. [...] It has so many different uses, but is a way to communicate on a soul level, and bring other frequencies and energies into existence."

She sees it as having multiple uses. "We all work with frequencies and vibrations every day. I hear particular frequencies that indicate ship communication, guide communication and implant updates/healings that take place in my body. My light language work also works with frequencies. Through sound and light codes we are able to shift frequencies into higher alignment to prevent disease and to clear the aura/energy field. More takes place in light language transmission sessions but that is the brief description."

Vanessa has a strong sense of her own multidimensionality and sees this as one of the lessons for humankind, that we are all multidimensional beings who have the opportunity to learn about this. "[Ascension] is coming because we are 'raising our frequencies,' or having more awarenesses of the rest of our multidimensionality."

She noted that the creation of hybrid children involves "collecting the earthly codes/frequencies."

Vanessa further used it in relation to raising frequency in Ascension, saying that the hybrid children are contributing to this, often passively. "Hybrid children have specific frequencies that they deliver through their field to help facilitate shifts in their environment for a particular outcome. Many times this occurs unconsciously and operates at a soul level."

Jacquelin echoed this. "They said that just my frequency being on Earth is enough. We're all here with our frequencies to assist Earth and humanity through the Ascension process."

Jacquelin referred to frequency in a variety of contexts, including her Star Origin Readings. "I [...] give them the frequencies or tone mantras to speak, which brings their star family to them in a bigger way."

She also used it with regard to clarity of communication with your guides. "Just state your intention. I say, "I welcome all those of love and light to assist me, to support me in mind, body, spirit and soul, in all that I am doing on Earth." And say it from the heart, because they can feel the heart intention, which is more important than what is being said. By going into the heart and really feeling and meaning that, they know it because it's a clear and high frequency."

She discussed raising frequency in the process of Ascension. "Hybrids are here to slowly integrate the higher consciousness energy in order to raise the frequency to help humanity evolve, to become conscious and to remember that we are love. We are all One, always interconnected, we can't separate ourselves from them: they are us, we are them. Whether there's a being who's of low or high frequency, it's all *us*. As we are raised into higher frequencies, that perceived duality disappears and there is only love, peace and joy. [...] I see those of lower frequency creating friction to help everyone become or remember who they really are. We are all co-creating this process."

Frequency can also be used to define spatial dimensions. She said, "Dimensions are different frequencies or vibrations, that's all they are. Quabar showed this to me; I travel with them through my consciousness, and at times I travel with my astral body. They show me the dimensions and other stars systems firsthand. They have shown me how dimensions are layered like an onion, and that there is no such thing as time and space, that's all illusion. [...] One time, I rode on a wave with them into what looked like deep space where they showed me the frequencies of Earth, the fundamental vibrational expression of Earth. The vibrations looked like endless ribbons of symbols, which created the physical form of the planet."

Once understood, this can be applied in astral travel. "There are many different vibrational rates of tones and harmonics. If a person can attune themselves to let's say a fairly high frequency, their consciousness can be on Alpha Centauri in a second. So, if someone centers and grounds in joy and love, and then sets their intention to be in another star system, they can go. These are simply states of being, energetic states, which everyone has the ability to experience."

The density of a dimension can therefore be expressed as frequency. "The Earth's density is a low frequency compared to the star being frequencies that I've had the privilege of experiencing. I love Earth, it's a beautiful, amazing planet, but it's very challenging to live in these densities."

Our personal multidimensionality can also be expressed in terms of frequency. "Looking at the bigger framework, we're integrating past lives and future lives to come into a soul balance. The soul balances itself between the different spectrums of frequency. We may be here, dealing karmically with this world, still learning something our soul wants to learn, while at the same time living other lives in other star systems, or perhaps in another dimension where we are etheric, bathing in love, light and joy. All of us are integrating our multidimensional selves to regain our wholeness. This is part of what Ascension is about: returning to love and light. This allows our consciousness to expand, and say, "Now I remember the truth of who I am: I'm not this body, I'm not this personality. I'm a beautiful light of creation, I'm divine love.""

Jacquelin said that the star beings are triggering activations in people by using their ships to "[emit] frequencies through a spectrum of beams. [...] Also, our chakra systems and DNA are being activated by the higher energies flowing onto and into Earth, which can bring us into a place of awakening as well as inner balance. This process raises a person's frequency and expands their consciousness. It also clears away old beliefs and patterns. [...] Humanity has gotten stuck in limiting beliefs and become enslaved; then of course it's easy for others of lower frequency to have an affect on them."

High frequency can be experienced and cultivated through a variety of grounding, connecting and celebrating activities, which can help with one's personal Ascension process.

She summed up her understanding thus: "Frequencies are the vibrational range of energy expressing itself, whether it be in physical or nonphysical form. This is how I define frequency in my second book when discussing star beings, who simply express various vibrations—as we all do. When they speak their own languages or share symbols with me, the vibration of who they are flows through."

Juju has a similarly broad understanding of frequency, and applies it many ways. Her contribution to Ascension is to "bring my fifth-dimensional frequency to Earth, to be part of the mission. My soul comes from a fifth-dimensional place, carries that energy, and being a hybrid allows me to carry more of that frequency. [...] We understood that a lot of other ETs were coming here to help Mother Earth carry that higher vibration. [...] Earth wants to evolve, and with all this shadowy government stuff going on, with negativity, greed, power and control, creating hierarchies, that's very unevolved, 3D thinking. We're trying to move past that. When you realize the beauty of equality there's no need for that. I had a friend at the DEA who learned that frequency towers around the U.S. keep the frequencies capped, like putting a lid over you, preventing your thoughts from expanding. Cell towers send out frequencies that are messing with the natural balance of life. We're trying to break through all that. We don't need that type of technology as we're all telepathic."

Juju focuses on keeping her vibration high, and sees it as central to one's spiritual journey. "The higher your vibrational frequency becomes, the closer you get to the highest, universal truth, but our personal truths are different, and we must respect that. I see 'universal truth' as the highest, most pure knowledge of Source energy, the Creator of All That Is. Each evolutionary step a soul takes towards Source energy, as an increase in one's vibration, opens us to this pure truth. We exist here in physical, third-dimensional form, which grants us very little access to pure truth—compared to those of higher dimensions—so each of us has our own. I believe it is every soul's wish to evolve toward universal truth at some point. There is nothing more exhilarating or more beautiful."

Robert has a physical, grounded attitude to frequency and Ascension. "A lot of us get so detached that all we can explain is the ethereal, and be so knowledgeable on the ethereal, but the point of being a part of this is to help connect the ethereal and the physical, because Ascension is a physical thing. We need to pull it down and ground it. You can't touch the ethereal, it's like grabbing smoke. I try to see the science behind these frequency things."

In his view, the work of the hybrids—who are incarnating as humans in the third dimension—must include a physical, hands-on experience, even if it means dealing with those of a lower vibration. "Our frequency has an effect on those around us for a reason, so we can't just sit at a computer and be a keyboard warrior. Guys: we have to go out there and *do* it, we have to *make* it happen. We've been learning and talking about this stuff for years, and now it's time to do it. It's like we've gone through school, and now it's time to get a job. [...] We have to get out there and deal with it on this 3D level—it's not all love and cupcakes here. Look at the world around you—it's collapsing. I'm seeing things dying all around me. It's a serious situation. We have to get out there—I can't let Joe Blow die because I did the work and he didn't—that's insane. How can someone claim to be such a loving being and not care that Joe Blow is going to die?"

"Is there good and bad between high and low? No, I don't believe so. Vibrations are different, but they're all part of existence—good, bad, high and low; it's all relative to me. [...] Which gets into the whole moral question of why raise the vibration. I think the truth of it is that it was allowed to get so negative here because there's no good or bad, it's just an experience. But the negativity has gotten so bad that humanity literally killed our planet. It's time to act, to step out of the negativity, that's been played out already. Forget all this transitioning to the fifth dimension and all that hoopla, it's just a new expression of life on this planet."

Robert talked about the energetic "transition" event that is heading for Earth, a combination of a galactic superwave and our solar system moving into a more energetic galactic zone. "I believe the hybrids' main tasks are to help raise the vibration and to bridge the gap to ET. Then ET helps train us for this event, so we get a smooth transition. I've no idea what's on the other side but I feel it's going to be awesome; it's going to be a cool light show, which will awaken everyone's minds, and I think it's going to be really positive. I think everyone is going to snap out of these programs, this negativity."

Matt has a clear view of frequency and its relationship to Ascension and hybrids. "Frequencies are different levels of existence. They are what separates the physical from the metaphysical. They are the different layers of reality which are what we call dimensions. Everything vibrates at different frequencies. [...] Ascension is evolution. It is growth. It is our experiences and lessons which have taken us to the next level of our being. Ascension is essentially our frequency existing on a higher level of consciousness. [...] Hybrids can help with the process of waking people up. We can help people come into their power and realize that we are all infinite beings with amazing abilities."

A working understanding of frequency is necessary to make sense of the concepts in this field. To relate to it, one only has to think in terms of mood. We can feel bitterness and anger, or love and gratitude, or tranquility and peace. The difference between rage and ecstasy is a visceral thing, and give us very different energetic states.

As Juju pointed out when asked to define frequency, music has a strong effect on us, and can enhance or shift mood powerfully.

Depending on our activity and the time of day, our brainwaves will operate to a lesser or greater degree in five frequency states—gamma, beta, alpha, theta and delta. These are employed in different types and levels of activity, whether doing, thinking, relaxing, daydreaming or sleeping.

In terms of vibration we can all relate to the concept of good and bad 'vibes.' We know if we feel good in a certain place or not, and we can often clearly sense the moods of individuals and groups.

On the face of it, it is harder to relate to the idea of shifting into higher frequencies and moving from the physical to the metaphysical. The hybrids often refer to the density of the energy field of this planet and of human form. Some of them have had notable difficulties with adjusting.

But we do in fact have several ways into this concept. In our dreams we often shift into less physical forms and can levitate, float and fly. That state can feel entirely natural to us, and on waking we feel a comparative heaviness. Out-of-body experiences, including near-death experiences, allow us to experience being a consciousness only. Hypnotic regression can facilitate this in a more controlled way. Meditation and psychedelic experience can also create states of consciousness which are less rooted in the body.

So we do have access to less dense states, and the practical advice on pursuing one's own Ascension process can help us further relate to the frequency aspects of the lives and missions of the hybrids. The main purpose and effect of 'raising the frequency' is facilitation of the larger Ascension process, and we look at that in depth in the Ascension chapter.

Ascension

When attempting to understand the purpose for ET interaction with the Earth and its inhabitants, the one-line summary appears to be: ETs are creating hybrids to help Earth and humanity evolve. This phenomenon, commonly referred to as 'Ascension,' can be thought of as a process of physical, emotional and spiritual evolution. The ETs which are creating and dispatching hybrids to Earth have in most cases already ascended. They are evolved beings who value evolution and, like cosmic missionaries, are determined to bring celestial enlightenment to others. The hybrids have a variety of missions within this larger mission, and to help them they incarnate with various abilities and inclinations. These abilities can be upgraded by the ETs or the hybrids themselves throughout their journey.

Like a kind of interrogative big bang, questions simply explode out of this core concept—more than the hybrids themselves could answer at this stage.

The purpose of this book is not to study Ascension in detail, but given its apparent centrality to this subject as a whole, let us build an impression of its nature, and understand how we can experience this process ourselves. According to the hybrids, what is it, what are its mechanisms, and how can it be facilitated?

Matt: "Ascension is evolution. It is growth. It is our experiences and lessons which have taken us to the next level of our being. Ascension is essentially our frequency existing on a higher level of consciousness."

Cynthia: "Ascension is all about humanity remembering how to live in their hearts and not their heads; it's about taking their power back through living in the Light with unconditional love."

Jacquelin: "All of us are integrating our multidimensional selves to regain our wholeness. This is part of what Ascension is about—

returning to love and light. This allows our consciousness to expand and say, "Now I remember the truth of who I am: I'm not this body, I'm not this personality. I'm a beautiful light of creation, I'm divine love. [...] Ascension is about growing and evolving as a soul. It's a process, not a one time event. Humanity is in the process of evolving into a higher degree of consciousness and remembering that we are all divine love, that living from the heart and loving is everything. It's also about being authentic in who we are."

Juju: "We all have an innate desire to evolve. My understanding is that Mother Earth herself wishes to move forward and evolve, and so does a huge human soul group, who all want to shift together into a fifth-dimensional existence. Ascension is more about the universe than humanity, it's about the universe expanding. Evolution is going to happen regardless—it's already happening. Humans can choose for themselves—no one is controlling or judging them. If you've learned everything, and are ready to go to a higher dimension, you'll go that way. For some, their soul wants to learn more, it wants a better foundation before ascending. The human soul group is made up of many smaller soul groups, some of which might stay behind—they will have another opportunity. While the rest go to the fifth dimension, they will go to another 3D world and continue learning there."

Vanessa: "Ascension is a process of recalibration to align ourselves with Source so that we can become one with, or come into equilibrium with this energy, and experience eternal nirvana. We're trying to move towards an equilibrium between our vibration and what Source really is. I see it like a canal—a system of balancing levels."

Charmaine: "Our souls have gone through many lives and forms, not all of them are necessarily on planet Earth nor in human form. Although the outer shell changes over each lifetime, grows old and ceases to function, the soul continues. With each reincarnation and experience the soul learns and evolves; we do not remember everything from our past incarnations, only what we are meant to at that time. When it's time for the shell to cease and the soul to go back home, the soul ascends from the current life to space. Information is compiled from that lifetime and compared with previous incarnations to plan what the journey and experiences will be in the next life, before the soul is reincarnated into the next form."

Robert: "A lot of us get so detached that all we can explain is the ethereal, and be so knowledgeable on the ethereal, but the point of being a part of this is to help connect the ethereal and the physical, because Ascension is a physical thing. We need to pull it down and ground it. You can't touch the ethereal, it's like grabbing smoke. I try to see the science behind these frequency things."

"Which gets into the whole moral question of why raise the vibration. I think the truth of it is that it was allowed to get so negative here because there's no good or bad, it's just an experience. But the negativity has gotten so bad that humanity literally killed our planet. It's time to act, to step out of the negativity, that's been played out already. Forget all this transitioning to the fifth dimension and all that hoopla, it's just a new expression of life on this planet."

These summaries suggest some variety in interpretation of Ascension. From being better people, to physically shifting into a different energetic state, to achieving eternal bliss. Perhaps they constitute a potential sequence of events. In any case, the thread is evolution.

And it is clear that Ascension, like enlightenment, is an open door. Anyone can choose to seek it, to walk through it and to share the benefits of doing so. Working on this book has been a direct experience of Ascension, and it is a wonderful experience, despite the occasional bout of growing pains. The more you experience it, the more sense it makes.

The box texts throughout Part II offer practices which can contribute to one's personal Ascension. They offer methods of connecting, communicating, grounding, protecting, healing and expanding. Connecting to your guides, opening your third eye, raising your vibration and staying connected are all things that can be done daily. Manifesting protection is something we all need from time to time, as is healing.

Like enlightenment, sex and dreams, there are many aspects of life that are experiential at their core. Ascension is an active process, and the hybrids share further guidance on personal Ascension.

Robert: "I get guidance on diet, exercise, keeping my thoughts at a high vibration; every thought has to be a loving thought, all day, 100%.

To practice keeping my thoughts loving, I have a technique. First, learn to love yourself, because if you can't love yourself there's no way this is going to work.

To do this I need to be in love all the time, so I had to ask myself: what *is* love, and how do I use it? I go back to a time when I experienced that feeling of deep love, like being embraced by my mother, or my wedding day, whatever experience gave me a physical feeling of love. I focus on reliving that feeling, imagine it in my heart, and try to manifest it. Once you can feel that filling your heart, with every breath in, feel it expand from your heart throughout your body. Then try to maintain that in your interactions. At first it's artificial, but with practice it becomes habit, and with habit it becomes natural, and you become a more loving person."

Vanessa: "We're all hybrids, because we can awaken and work with that DNA. It's about: what is your will? The hybrids come in with more awareness of how this works to help the rest of us, to help others to awaken. Being in your humanity is enough; experiencing your bliss, being in your authenticity, *is* the mission. It's enough to do that. You're already doing a lot for the world when you're in your authenticity. When the hybrids incarnate, their beingness is enough to help humanity—being in their bliss—and that's a big part of the teaching."

Juju: "To evolve, and become who you truly are, and love yourself—and that's vital, as you can't love anyone else if you don't love yourself—you learn that what really matters is your soul essence, and nothing can take that away. So work it through, have courage, surround yourself with white and gold light, use healing, stand in your power. But most importantly it's what you think, where you hold your thoughts; hold yourself in a higher vibration of love and gratitude, be deliberate in your thoughts and use them wisely, and you won't attract those negative, fearful things. Some may see injuries, and can feel sorry for themselves, but that's not standing in your power. You can look back later on at things that were negative at the time, and realize that actually they happened at the right time, because you may not have finished that project or met that person, for example. It's intentional living, choosing and being aware, keeping positive and becoming your authentic self."

Matt: "I can point to three things that helped in my awakening process.

"Meditation is definitely number one. It can calm the 'monkey mind,' the internal dialogue that won't shut up, the rational 'protect me' part of your mind that shuts out things you don't like. It's only focused on the past or the future, so if you're in the now you're out of the monkey mind. You'll never find it talking about what's happening now—never anything useful. Meditation goes deeper, it trains your brain to pick up on subtle energies—you're almost training yourself to be more open. Everyone can transmit, but it's about learning how to use your antennae to receive better. It can also help with intuition and developing your moral sense. It can fine-tune things and make them more accessible.

"Morals are a vital part of self-realization, which is essentially trying to become a better person. You have to take a good look at yourself and see your faults with honesty. For example, stop denying that you do something—when you *clearly* do. You have to ask things like: am I acting from my highest good, or preventing myself doing something I *should* be? The clarity you get from meditation helps facilitate this. It helped me to wake up to see that everything's part of everything. Once I got that my morals changed automatically. Part of it was conscious, but a lot slots into place because you have a different outlook. Once you change, you deal with things in a way that serves you—and other people—better.

"Looking after your body in general is the third key thing. You have to look after the vehicle you're in while you're here. Unless you're doing that the rest of it isn't going to fall into place properly. The meditation and morality is nowhere near as clear if the vessel is impure. But remember that you are not your body. Don't let these bodies obscure the true light being that you are."

Cynthia: "My guides explained it quite simply: humans have been brainwashed into believing through religion and ideology that humans are the only beings in the universe, and in order for humanity to awaken to their truth, they must release their judgments and prejudices. Therefore, many of the hybrids have chosen to be able to shapeshift between human and other races as needed, so that humans will realize they are not their bodies but their souls. [...] There is no helping humanity until first, they realize that the material world is an illusion, and second, they get out of their heads and into their hearts.

"Until humanity learns how to live in the 'Christ Consciousness' they are trapped on this prison planet. The simple meaning of Christ Consciousness is: to live without fear, greed, judgment or prejudice by seeing beyond the physical container to recognize the Source in every living being. It's that simple."

"If you don't like what's happening in the world, then change the way you think and act, and you no longer have to live that way. The third dimension is all about acknowledging the change and becoming the change. [...] You may look at your life and say, "How can I help others, what can I release that no longer serves me?" You want to be the highest you can be, like a plant opening its flower."

Charmaine: "Every action has a reaction and even the smallest thought or positive action makes a difference. You can be a pebble that causes a ripple in the pond, or just be a pebble at the bottom of the pond, but either way the choice is yours!"

Jacquelin: "What can help everyone to move through Ascension with greater ease is to focus on things that bring us joy, which is a high frequency. Walking in nature can ground and uplift us, connecting us to Earth and ourselves. Of course, having a good support system of friends and star beings can also give us support. We can send love and healing thoughts and images to the Earth, ourselves, and all life forms. We can bless the sky, the trees and the stones as we stroll through the woods. We can radiate love to the stars. We can pray, meditate, tone, sing, dance, play and laugh along with everything else that celebrates life. Creative expression and beauty lifts our souls. Writing, gardening, and playing with animal companions and children contributes to global healing. Most of all, living from the heart raises our frequencies and allows us to see that we are One in love."

Vanessa: "My message and my most important lesson is to embrace multidimensionality. I've gone through so many experiences that just shatter frameworks and belief systems; there's no way to integrate them otherwise. That's my first and foremost objective. In embracing that, we're able to access deeper awareness, consciousness, information, and it's about being okay with not knowing, and in that not knowing, we will know. That's similar to what I wrote in my thesis, about the mystery, and being okay with the mystery of life—wanting to know the mysteries, but being okay not knowing. It's such a paradox, like how do you live like that, function like that? It comes down to you being in your power in each and every moment, and being very clear with who you are and what feels in alignment with your highest good in each and every moment."

This is truly a workout for the mind, body and spirit! This guidance could be taken in a different order, but there seems to be a flow to it.

It begins with loving yourself—cultivating a loving appreciation for yourself. This can then be extended out to all other life, and you begin to identify with the rest of existence. This works best when connecting and harmonizing the mind and the heart, learning to live and love with compassion. This can help develop and project your authenticity, which promotes inner satisfaction. Your personal bliss positively affects others simply by existing, and being an example. Cultivating a state of gratitude reinforces this.

In being so open, one must recognize the need for protection and invoke it when necessary. Keeping your energy field clear of negativity is vital, and will help you stand in your power. Living intentionally in this way can be supported by meditation, which focuses, trains and clears the mind. Developing a strong moral sense provides the inner guidance you need to be sure you are acting from your highest good. Looking after your body through good diet, exercise and clean living serves your objectives on every level.

Connecting to your inner light will support your work on developing the Christ Consciousness, connecting to the seed of Source within every being. Living without fear, greed, judgment or prejudice will help you choose action over inaction, and allow the other elements to manifest in the real world.

In your work, you can maintain your personal integrity and health through regular connection and grounding. Celebrating and honoring all of life, of which you are a part, allows you to experience the multidimensional nature of existence, and comes full circle to loving yourself. By loving yourself you are loving everything else, and vice versa.

Whichever view of Ascension resonates with you, a better experience of life itself is available through practices which the hybrids see as being central to the larger process of Ascension. As above, so below.

Bridges and Ambassadors

Two key terms came up time and again when discussing the role of the hybrids: 'bridge' and 'ambassador.' They have slightly varying applications, but there is a general consensus that a key part of their mission is to bridge humans and ETs, and four of them spoke specifically about this. With the term 'exopolitics'—and its engaged aspect 'exodiplomacy'—coming into increasing use, the hybrids could be thought of as a key group of exodiplomats.

Charmaine: "I am here to bridge the divide, to help facilitate bringing the hybrids together with the experiencers and abductees. Further, to bring them together with the rest of humanity, even the skeptics! [...] I believe that one purpose for the creation of hybrids is to bridge the divide between the ETs and humans, taking positive attributes from each race for certain purposes, such as healing, higher intelligence, stronger spiritual connection and so forth."

Robert: "We're accelerating that awakening process in humanity, we're the bridge between worlds. And by being the bridge we have multiple dimensional degrees of effect around the planet. [...] I believe the hybrids' main tasks are to help raise the vibration and to bridge the gap to ET. Then ET helps train us for this event, so we get a smooth transition."

Vanessa: "[Ascension] is coming because we are 'raising our frequencies,' or having more awarenesses of the rest of our multidimensionality. It is coming because we are becoming more universal and unifying. The hybrids can and will be a bridge and link to the process. They will teach their parents about their origins and the ways of being on these other planets. Their experiences and knowledge will teach us how to shift and change."

Jacquelin: "We will continue to integrate hybrids into the cultures on Earth. [...] For me it could never be fast enough, but for humanity, and for the human mind, the evolutionary process has to go at a suitable pace. But it is happening, and new bridges and frequencies are shifting things into the new paradigm, allowing humanity to evolve. It has to be done slowly because humans are not yet open to embracing their family from other star systems."

"We can share with humanity the good that hybrids have to offer and this leads to the good that star beings have to offer. That's key, because it's not about us really, we agreed to do this in service. The bottom line is that we're bridges; this is how I've always seen myself. We are bridging our cosmic families with humanity, so that humans can realize that they are cosmic citizens and, therefore, evolve in a much quicker, more profound way."

"The bottom line is to bridge our cosmic family with humanity. It doesn't serve a purpose to just show off this skill or that skill, there needs to be a positive intention or focus to say, "We're sharing these abilities because you too are connected to the stars and have a star family; isn't it exciting that you can discover that connection?""

The bridge role seems to work the other way too.

Matt: "I have a feeling they want to learn about our world and our consciousness. They exist in one consciousness, whereas our perception is that we're all very separate—even though we're all one really. We have a dualistic perception; they don't understand how that is and want to experience it. It's the opposite of humans, who want to experience oneness."

Robert: "Part of it is incarnating as a human being, coming from another race and experiencing life as a human at this time. That part of the mission is for the beings as well. The Mantis beings have a collective consciousness, so they don't know what it is to have a sense of a separate consciousness. Humans believe we're all individual and we're not connected to anything. So some beings come here just to experience the illusion of separation. That helps them understand humans better."

A number of the hybrids understand they also function as recording and transmitting devices for their star families.

Juju: "With me, the implants they put behind my eyes allow me to send back all experience, a kind of biofeedback. Everything I experience in this lifetime is sent back to them. So right now you're on camera on my homeworld."

Robert: "In a way I think they live vicariously through me—it's a way to experience human life. They download my experience through my Mantis DNA, like turning on the Rob channel. I would say that it's a safe bet that any time someone interacts with me, they're interacting with the beings through me."

Jacquelin: "These beings are able to literally view the world through my eyes."

Two of the hybrids used the term 'ambassador.'

Robert: "Bringing this awareness to humanity is one facet, being something of an ambassador. I can help ground these beings, and when they're ready to introduce themselves to humanity I'm like a buffer zone, I walk between the two worlds, interacting with both."

Jacquelin: "I've been told I was created to be an ambassador here, representing a number of races."

After Barbara related her experience of meeting a Reptilian ambassador, Juju responded, "I'm glad you've had positive experiences with Reptilians, Barbara. I've tried to explain that to people, but I've had to be really careful what I say because it can make me a target. Because too many people think all Reptilian ETs are bad. The one you met, who was an ambassador to Earth, that would be really challenging. I would never want that job."

Given humanity's general attitude toward ET existence, which tends to vacillate between scoffing skepticism and acceptance, it is vital to have representatives for the races which are interacting here. The hybrids are only one degree of separation from the ETs themselves, so if humanity can learn to accept them we will be closer to a radically expanded understanding of reality itself.

Missions, Abilities and Services

One of the defining aspects of a hybrid is their mission. These plug into the main mission of Ascension in different ways. They vary greatly, but key themes are readily apparent. We asked them to sum up their missions. Often these would overlap with their key message.

Tatiana: "To help humanity and the Earth through applied psychology and neuroscience."

Cynthia: "To help hybrids and starseeds remember their star family and mission through DNA activation; to help them come into their powers; to be an example through living in the Christ Consciousness."

Charmaine: "To help humanity and the Earth through health and wellbeing; to help people connect, grow and open up their spirituality; to encourage expression through the arts; to bridge the divide between ETs/hybrids and humanity; to empower and educate; to offer support groups for humanity, experiencers, abductees and hybrids."

Robert: "To bring ET awareness to humanity; to awaken and accelerate hybrids and starseeds; to bring physical dimensions to the phenomena; to heal, and teach self-healing."

Juju: "To be of service to Mother Earth, and the animals specifically; to collect and transmit data back to Faqui; to offer loving fifth-dimensional vibration to all life on Earth towards the evolutionary path."

Vanessa: "To inspire others to be in their fullest power and bliss; to educate humanity on ETs, multidimensionality and other realms of existence."

Jacquelin: "To teach people how to communicate with animals and nature. To share a message of love, equality and oneness. To bring ET awareness to humanity."

Matt: "To heal people and help them come into their power; to teach them how to heal themselves and find their own paths."

All or most of them say they are here to: help anchor higher frequencies on Earth to aid Ascension; act as a bridge between humanity and the ETs; help raise human consciousness; and protect life on Earth.

Connection, communication, empowerment, enlightenment, liberation, inspiration, raising consciousness, healing, protection and care for people, animals and Mother Earth. The focus seems to be on evolution, health and positive relationships, and the interaction of these things. In fact this list features all the things required for healthy relationships, with ourselves, each other and the living world. Though in this case, those relationships extend beyond our planet and its inhabitants.

As we learned in the interviews, the hybrids come in with various abilities which facilitate their missions. Most of them use their gifts, and some are able to make a living by providing services which draw upon them.

Tatiana: Psychic abilities; intuition; revitalize dying plants; uplift people through communication and listening; energize and inspire people through dance.

Services: Teaching dance.

Cynthia: Psychic abilities; channeling.

Services: Making sculptures for starseeds of their star family that contain high frequencies that activate their DNA—helping them remember their powers and mission; Counseling starseeds (teaching them about their powers and how to protect themselves from negative forces while completing their missions).

Charmaine: Psychic ability; healing; telepathy; astral travel; shapeshifting; intuition; animal communication; channeling.

Services: Nutrition advice; Emotional Freedom Technique; Life Coaching; Reiki healing; angel attunements; workshops, lectures and interviews.

Robert: Visualization; healing.

Services: Creation of 2D and 3D consciousness-amplifying technologies (CATs); healing.

Juju: Psychic abilities; intuition; shapeshifting; healing.

Services: Reiki practitioner; author; teacher.

Vanessa: Psychic abilities; healing; telepathy; astral travel; bilocation and light language.

Services: Starshine Guidance Sessions; Past Life Akashic Record Readings; Magic of Pegasus Healing Sessions (Includes: Reiki, color and sound healing); Light Language Healing Sessions.

Jacquelin: Psychic abilities; intuition; animal communication; healing.

Services: Star Origin Reading; Soul Recovery; Psychic Reading, Developing Intuition; Spiritual Awakening; Past Life Reading; General Reading About Your Animal; Behavioral Issues; Soul Recovery; Tracking Lost Animals; Life After Death (Messages from Animal on the Other Side); Past Life Reading; Healing; Apprenticeship Program: learning how to communicate with animals.

Matt: Psychic abilities; healing.

Services: Reiki remote healing.

Most or all of the hybrids have or can do: psychic ability; telepathy; astral travel and healing.

We have personally shared some of their gifts, including Cynthia's sculptures, Matt's Reiki, Robert's CATs, Jacquelin's Star Origin Readings and everyone's teachings. These can have a profound effect, and often come with an undeniable extra-dimensional quality.

In his Star Origin Reading, Miguel experienced a strong sense of presence, like a group consciousness—just as he did in his first regression session with Barbara. This also manifested during music sessions, which he found 'raised his vibration'—a concept described in detail by Juju—and the entire room seemed to fill with bright white light and a strong presence. Thereafter he began playing energizing music whenever he needed a lift in the writing and editing process. He was further inspired by Jacquelin and Juju to take more time to be in nature, to reconnect to plants and animals, and even to develop his workspace into a high-vibration area full of sculptures, images and crystals which uplift. He found everyone's texts to be inspiring and liberating, and with every reading they elicited feelings of overwhelming love and appreciation.

For Barbara too, knowing each of our hybrid friends was a profoundly inspiring experience. In her Star Origin Reading with Jacquelin she resonated deeply with her original incarnation in the celestial realm, and subsequent incarnations as one of the dolphin beings, Mantis beings and Pleiadian beings. From Cynthia she learned and began her practice of sending out love energy to all others from her heart. From all eight hybrids she received remote healing energy for a serious physical condition she had, and she recovered remarkably well. She is full of appreciation, admiration and love for each of these exceptional beings.

We would encourage readers to make contact with the hybrids through the meethehybrids Wordpress site if they believe they can be of service. They are open to all genuine enquiries and will help where they can.

Guides and Star Family

All the hybrids experience some level of conscious connection with their guides/star families. Guides are often part of the star family, whether one's 'parent' race or not. But they can also receive information and support from angelic/celestial beings, members of the soul group, human spirits, animals or other beings. Each hybrid may have a mixed group of guides.

As well as ET guides, Charmaine spoke of a wolf spirit that she could see from early childhood, whose spirit, energy and traits she draws upon when needed. She also has a connection with an Egyptian boy who was a childhood friend in an earlier incarnation in ancient Egypt, and a Native American Indian. In her experience, one is not restricted to a fixed set of guides, they can come and go as necessary throughout a single incarnation. If you put out the request for support with a particular aspect of your journey, a new guide can come to you.

What roles do they play?

Guides offer different types and levels of support: information (for the self and others); encouragement and emotional support; and healing.

Information

Vanessa spoke of being shown her own creation by a guide. "I have one guide in particular, a Pleiadian-Sirian woman named Anika who told me that she was my mother in my first incarnation on Earth, in Lemuria. I actually was able to watch my creation."

Guides can often help to outline purpose and role.

Jacquelin: "A long time ago I asked Quabar what my mission is, and they said, "You can do whatever you want to." And I asked them, "Am I on my path?" They replied, "There *is* no path, the only path is love." They said that just my frequency being on Earth is enough. We're all here with our frequencies to assist Earth and humanity through the Ascension process."

Cynthia: "In early 2003 my guides explained that my soul had agreed to come into a hybrid body in order to assist starseeds to fully awaken to their true mission on Earth. By 2005 I was making sculptures of benevolent beings that would carry an aspect of the soul of that being to assist the starseeds in what they needed most."

"My guides explained it quite simply: humans have been brainwashed into believing through religion and ideology that humans are the only beings in the universe, and in order for humanity to awaken to their truth, they must release their judgments and prejudices. [They] always tell me the first thing to do is to get people out of fear and into their heart, to remind them how to live in the Christ Consciousness, and the rest will fall into place."

Matt: "My guides, angels and star family all help me to stay on course and help me to find things that I need to know or be aware of."

There is a firsthand component to some of the information sharing.

Jacquelin: "Dimensions are different frequencies or vibrations, that's all they are. Quabar showed this to me; I travel with them through my consciousness, and at times I travel with my astral body. They show me the dimensions and other stars systems firsthand. They have shown me how dimensions are layered like an onion, and that there is no such thing as time and space, that's all illusion.

"These frequencies exist within us, they're within and without, as above so below. I call it traveling with my consciousness, but there's no time and space, it's all right here, right now. It's a state of being. Quabar has taught me about this firsthand over many years. One could say I take a ride with them into these various frequencies. I feel like I'm on an amusement park ride. It's always fun. One time, I rode on a wave with them into what looked like deep space where they showed me the frequencies of Earth, the fundamental vibrational expression of Earth. The vibrations looked like endless ribbons of symbols, which created the physical form of the planet."

Charmaine related that she had been taught healing techniques directly from tall Greys on a ship, so the information can take the form of training.

Juju described an experience with her star family, Greys and insectoids, who trained her to 'blink' one of their ships from point to point, and to make a smooth entry into the waters of the San Francisco Bay. She was also taught, by a Grey guide, how to send pure white love energy to a hybrid baby for growth and balance.

During many conversations in and out of the formal interviews, Jacquelin would be speaking aloud with her guides. She remarked that she carries on two conversation tracks simultaneously, with ourselves and her guides. At times information would come through so fast that she would ask them to slow down while she made notes. She always showed gratitude for the information.

Juju remarked that, "During this conversation I have my guides with me to give me extra information that I don't have."

Cynthia would often pause when sharing information, and then pass on what her guides were clarifying for her.

As far as choice goes, it seems the hybrids are at liberty to take what they consider useful to them. Jacquelin said, "I consider their guidance, but most of all I listen to my heart and my soul to be clear on who I am and what I want to do."

Support

Emotional support is important to the hybrids, who say they can feel lonely and alienated at times.

Juju shared her sense of isolation. "It's kind of sad as I'm the only one from my planet; it's a lonely existence, being separate from my home planet all my life. But there are many ETs here from all over, and I feel like they're my extended family. [...] The Greys and insectoids treat me like family because they know my people don't come here. They pick me up, take me places on ships. They treat me like one of their own. [...] I'm praying for the time when I can go back home—I was ready over ten years ago. I'm doing what I can here, but I would much rather be at home."

Matt echoed this. "I'm happier now, but still feel I don't really belong. I have a longing to be back there, and I'm looking forward to going back one day. I get the feeling that once I've done what I'm supposed to do I can go back."

Encouragement in their missions is a common experience, including their 'bridge' role. Charmaine said, "I've had information downloads from the Galactic Federation which has mostly been over the last two years; they have sent strong messages to say: go forward, bring together those communities, and get the word out about hybrids being here on Earth, as well as ET species and agendas."

Healing

Some reported major healings from their star family. Juju was helped with her kidneys and eyes. "One time I was on the ship and I had an incision in my back as part of a medical procedure. I think they helped heal my kidneys as I had problems before then, which cleared up after. [...] When I was younger they did something to my eyesight. I had to get glasses in my teens, and one day I found that the glasses were blurry and I had 20/20 vision again."

Cynthia's guides have worked overtime. She has had life-saving interventions relating to her lungs and her vascular system, received protection from murderous government agencies, and been given important advice on herbal treatments.

Races noted for their healing abilities are the Nebulan Healers, the Mantis and the Andromedans. Cynthia also talked about receiving healing on board Archangel Michael's medical mothership. Vanessa pointed out that the hybrid children coming through are natural healers.

Several of the hybrids have also stated that their star families assist them in the healing work they perform on others.

What kind of connections do they share?

Most of the hybrids maintain a regular or constant connection with their guides.

Jacquelin: "I communicate with my star families on a regular basis. I will often reach out to them for support, love and information. And they will often contact me telepathically to share information or to let me know that they are present."

Robert: "The Mantis beings are always with me. I've been told by people who can see the energies that they can see ten Mantis beings around me all the time. I don't feel their presence that often as it's such a part of my field. For the most part they don't want to interfere with me, they want me to figure things out for myself, and they guide me in various ways. [...] If I want to connect to them I just turn it on, and if I want some privacy I tell them to bugger off.

But probably there is no such thing as private thoughts. It's taken some getting used to, learning to separate my thoughts from theirs.

Charmaine: "The ETs are always with me, but the human and animal spirits come and go as I need them. Either I call on them or they step in."

Juju: "My star family is always with me. Also, I am close with a number of ETs that check on me and help me learn new things. I constantly have to ask myself if things I'm experiencing are my imagination, or if it's coming from my guides. What works for me is being aware of the time. The creative mind takes time to create something, whereas truth is instantaneous. If it's instant knowing I run with it, if it's taking three seconds to develop, it's my imagination." [...] When you expand in consciousness you can begin to distinguish where the information is coming from, whether it's your higher self, or ETs. Like distinguishing between dreams and actual events."

Tatiana also noted the way in which she differentiates between her own thoughts and a communication from the beings. "I know when it's me or them, from the language. It's always encouraging, positive. If I ask something I'm worried about, they come back with very positive messages, more positive than I am generally. [...] It comes in very deeply, it feels very truthful for me."

Charmaine had some interesting reflections on the connection with one's star family, particularly with regard to children. "I had a permanent ET connection as a child; it was only later that I realized no one else was connected to them. Most children have 'imaginary friends' but lose them when they begin to get suppressed, primarily by their parents. It's not just human or animal spirit beings, they may also be seeing ETs, perhaps being abducted. If their parents just want the child to shut up about it, what does the child do with that? If they could explore that instead it would be much healthier. We're all spiritual, and by suppressing a child you're cutting off their spirituality, forcing them to lead a life of being spiritually disconnected, which causes emotional and mental problems throughout their life; this in turn leads to many of the problems we have in the world. We need to be a whole being, and not sever the connections which make us a whole being."

On engagement with them she said, "They can still look after you even if you don't engage, if you don't want to be spiritual. But the more you ask for assistance and knowledge, the more they will engage. They won't lay it out on a plate without you doing anything, but you can have more if you are open to it."

How do they communicate?

Charmaine talked about the variety of ways that guidance comes in. "They pass on knowledge at the right times and in a way you're susceptible to. Dreams are common, as is an instant knowing. It may also manifest in art. If you just sit and relax with a pencil or paintbrush it can just start flowing through you. And there can be a direct input of information. When I was a teenager I started doing tarot card readings, and had an accuracy that shocked people. I just had the information immediately."

In the middle of a flow about limiting beliefs, Jacquelin interjected, "Star beings are around me right now, having a group discussion about this, which is fun."

Meditation was mentioned often with regard to communication. Matt described how, after getting into a state of deep relaxation, he found himself in a situation in which he was given information symbolically. "I was taken somewhere, like someone's home. They had an old-fashioned grindstone and a man was sharpening a sword. I asked him why he was doing that, and he said, "We're preparing you for war.""

Juju also requests contact through sightings of craft. "I'm always asking them to show themselves, and sometimes they'll guide you to look at a star and give you a real quick blip, but it's a risk to them as our government has devastating weapons. So it's nice just to get a blip or a streak."

Communication via star and/or light languages came up with several of the hybrids, notably Vanessa, Jacquelin, Robert and Juju.

Vanessa in particular works with light languages, and wrote her masters thesis on the subject, which she is now expanding into a book. "Sometimes I channel my guides, and they speak in different cosmic or angelic languages, and sometimes it's my higher self, it's coming from my own soul. Light language is a heart-centered communication system that is truly universal. There are different light languages, dialects if you will, that come from maybe Lyra or Sirius and other star systems. It's a way to talk directly with the heart space, without cognitive, logical language, because words get in the way sometimes. It has so many different uses, but is a way to communicate on a soul level, and bring other frequencies and energies into existence.

"At times when downloads come in, I can feel different beings around me, conversing with me and giving me the information. At other times I've felt open communication from myself to them;

often my energy is going up into the ships, almost like a bilocation experience. Sometimes when driving I've felt myself in their space; with me, but not in my car."

Vanessa said that her contacts with her star family can take place either astrally or physically, and are all voluntary. "But sometimes I do say, "No thank you." Two nights ago I was asked to go on a specific mission with them, but said I was really tired, so no. He laughed, he was very okay with it."

Cynthia has a rare connection with the beings. She began making sculptures of ETs, and went through a series of stages of channeling "soul aspects" of the relevant ETs into them. "The first few were from memories of being with a Zeta-human hybrid baby and human-looking beings from the Galactic Federation and the Sirian Warriors of Light. Then I began to go into trances, making beings I had no recollection of, such as the Andromedan race called the Buddic tribe of Andromeda, as well as a variety of Zeta races, and the Salamander beings. By the second year, I began hearing telepathic voices directing me on how to make their features. By the third year, I was experiencing new benevolent beings that would either physically appear to me, or I would see them in the etheric realm, or sometimes in my third eye as if I was seeing them on a computer monitor."

Guides are very important to each of the hybrids, and they benefit greatly from the interaction and support they offer. They deeply appreciate the presence of these beings whom they can often relate to better than the humans they live alongside.

How can they be contacted?

Jacquelin gave us clear, simple guidelines on bringing in our guides: "Just state your intention. I say, "I welcome all those of love and light to assist me, to support me in mind, body, spirit and soul, in all that I am doing on Earth." And say it from the heart, because they can feel the heart intention, which is more important than what is being said. By going into the heart and really feeling and meaning that, they know it because it's a clear and high frequency."

The Heart

In the wisdom of the hybrids there are many parallels with Buddhism, but there is one particular distinction. The focus here is on opening the heart, more than "taming this mind of ours." It seems that the heart is truly the heart of this subject.

Cynthia: "Protection is one of the easiest abilities, but it is important to always believe in ourselves, our abilities. We do this simply by surrounding ourself with the Light of Source, and filling our hearts with unconditional love—first directing it to self, then to all others. The darker, more negative a person, the more it is important to share your love and Light with him or her. This puts protection around yourself while also increasing your power and diminishing the power of the dark over you. The more we use our love and Light, the more our DNA is activated."

"After all, Ascension is all about humanity remembering how to live in their hearts and not their heads; it's about taking their power back through living in the Light with unconditional love. [...] Ascension is when the soul has learned all the lessons from the thousands of lifetimes in the third dimension and has moved into the heart for resolution."

"The only effective way to work with humans is to first get them out of judgment and into their hearts. [...] If people could only see the beauty and perfection in our differences, that everything is a piece of art, and let go of wanting everything to be a certain way, they would see the beauty in every single being. They would feel the compassion, they would feel their heart, they would understand who they are and where they came from, and they would stop the judgment and prejudices."

Charmaine: "[The most important thing I've learned is] to be open; open-minded and open-hearted, to share my knowledge, experiences and thoughts with others so they may learn from them and gain understanding."

Robert: "To practice keeping my thoughts loving, I have a technique. [...] I go back to a time when I experienced that feeling of deep love, like being embraced by my mother, or my wedding day, whatever experience gave me a physical feeling of love. I focus on reliving that feeling, imagine it in my heart, and try to manifest it. Once you can feel that filling your heart, with every breath in, feel it expand from your heart throughout your body. Then try to maintain that in your interactions. At first it's artificial, but with practice it becomes habit, and with habit it becomes natural, and you become a more loving person."

"I'd also ask: where does your information come from? Mine comes from my mind and heart; the beings do guide me along, point me in the right direction, but they never tell me anything directly. I'm dubious about beings that go around giving information a little too freely."

Juju: "Cynthia Crawford also encourages abductees to summon love in their heart, and send it to the beings. If they are not good, they will leave. They can't take that. It changes your experience. If you hold yourself in light, you will see and feel that experience more clearly. If people feel fear and anxiety, if they feel victimized, they are lowering their vibration. And they are really bringing to themselves what they fear."

Vanessa: "Light language is like speaking in tongues. It's a different frequency of consciousness and is all about opening the heart chakra. It's all accessed and interpreted through the heart space. [...] Light language is a heart-centered communication system that is truly universal. There are different light languages, dialects if you will, that come from maybe Lyra or Sirius and other star systems. It's a way to talk directly with the heart space, without cognitive, logical language, because words get in the way sometimes."

"In my sessions for my clients [...] I go into the heart space and transmit the codes that are intended for the healing at that time, similar to how Reiki or other energy healing modalities work. Then I relay to them the awarenesses I received through various chakra points and clairvoyant visions. For example, I may receive information in my heart space like a heaviness during a specific portion of the sessions, and that will indicate something that is going on in their personal life, like a break-up or death in the family, or a sacral chakra awareness if someone just miscarried."

Jacquelin: "Sharing my gifts helps to raise humankind's consciousness and frequencies in a way which opens the heart."

"I consider their guidance, but most of all I listen to my heart and my soul to be clear on who I am and what I want to do."

"I have a practical emphasis in my work, giving the message that we're all one, and helping to awaken others on how to live from the heart. Those are my key messages. My main focus is on being the most loving being I know how to be."

"Just state your intention. I say, "I welcome all those of love and light to assist me, to support me in mind, body, spirit and soul, in all that I am doing on Earth." And say it from the heart, because they can feel the heart intention, which is more important than what is being said. By going into the heart and really feeling and meaning that, they know it because it's a clear and high frequency."

"Ascension is a process of growing and evolving as a soul. Humanity is gradually ascending into a higher degree of consciousness and remembering that living from the heart and loving is everything. It's also about being authentic in who we are. Every soul chooses their own pace with their Ascension process."

"Again, it's not about the mind understanding it all, it's about what the heart feels and knows. The heart is very wise. What does your heart say? What does your soul say? The mind always wants to create a framework, the mind and ego always want to know the answers. They separate whereas the higher consciousness creates unity."

"[The most important lesson I've learned is] to love myself and to live from my heart. By going into our hearts we can remember who we are. Our heads can lead us places that aren't the truth or that can throw us off track."

"It's easier for animals to love unconditionally because they have retained their heart centers and intuitive abilities. The animals taught me how to love in a better way, and the star beings taught me how to love in a clearer way."

"Ascension is about living from our hearts not our heads, and remembering who we are and that love is everything."

There are multiple meanings and applications here. The heart can represent or facilitate: intuition, love, openness, acceptance, connection, protection, communication and clarity.

The existence of the hybrids is itself a lesson in being open to other lifeforms. If we can accept the hybrids, we can accept the star beings, and if we can do that, surely we can accept other human races and groups. Humans tend to trust and favor 'in-groups,' those with which we identify and share interests. The oneness, openness and acceptance that the hybrids talk about is all about opening the heart and connecting with those beyond our in-group, which is everything else that exists.

Let *that* sink in.

Loving ourselves is mentioned numerous times, and again relates to oneness. If we are all one, then we cannot love others unless and until we love ourselves.

The hybrids speak of a clarity that comes from the heart, in discerning truth, keeping them on the right track with their missions, hearing their inner voice and communicating with their guides and star families.

Vanessa's study and practice of light language has shown her that it is "heart-centered," and facilitates a kind of universal communication by being so pure. Jacquelin's approach to calling in her guides requires channeling the request through the heart for the same reason.

Robert has developed a practice that raises his vibration through filling his heart with love and transmitting it through his body first, and then out into the world. Cynthia has two protection techniques, both of which require summoning love in the heart then directing it outwards.

Ascension is a process which is seemingly both a cause and an effect of love and unity, and working with and from the heart is central to this. Jacquelin and Cynthia both underlined the point that it is about living from our hearts instead of our heads and understanding that we are all one.

Can Anyone Have ET Contact?

After the book was written the question of whether ET contact is available to anyone came up, so the participants, including Barbara, were asked to write a summary of their thoughts and guidance.

Jacquelin: Yes, everyone has the ability to communicate with ETs. If they are fearful, that's what would block the communication. I've been teaching people how to communicate with ETs and animals for many years and most people can do it. Those who can't are blocking, perhaps due to fear, or not wanting to recall a memory.

ETs come through in whatever way they can—dreams, telepathically, signs, visions. They intend to communicate, not to create fear. They come through in gentle, loving ways.

People can develop relationships with ETs. They are our friends, mentors, family. By using intuition anyone can develop the skills to communicate with ETs.

Vanessa: Yes absolutely. I feel that as each person evolves on their divine path at some point their star brothers and sisters will contact them. A way to invoke benevolent ET contact is by purely asking for it/stating the intention and living from the heart space. I have found that we often make contact with our ET guides and family when we are on a path of compassion and seeking truth and bliss. If it is part of the soul agreement to have interactions with other types of ETs with questionable agendas, then that contract will take place at some point.

Juju: In my understanding, ET contact is fundamental to life, just as is eating, breathing and being loved! The question remains with the individual themselves.

1. Do they want contact?
2. Would they recognize it when they have it?

Everyone's expectation and perception of contact is different. Ask yourself: what do you consider ET contact? For example, if you just meditated and looked down at your seat to find a praying mantis on your chair, would you get it? Would you make that connection with that being and say "Hi!" or "Thank you!"?

Ask yourself also: which species are you trying to contact? Even for starseeds, some of the ETs can be startling and may give us a 'negative experience' only because of how we respond to them! So be clear in your asking, and set your intentions. You can attract self-serving ETs or you can attract loving, caring ETs that will be more gentle in their approach with you (contact during dream time, blinking their ship lights at you from space, only allowing you to remember small pieces at first, etcetera).

Cynthia: When I asked this same question of my guides, the answer was, "You must be in your heart and want contact to understand the integration of star beings with humanity." It won't work if a person is just curious. If they do not understand how to use their 'Light' and are not able to unconditionally love all beings, then they won't be able to have contact. When I tried to have conscious contact, it took me three weeks because I was holding onto resentment and anger. So, when I finally gave in and said, "I promise to love you unconditionally and release all anger," suddenly a being materialized before me.

Matt: I think that anyone can have contact with ETs and I don't believe there are set requirements. I think it can happen for anyone who is open-minded enough for them. I'm not sure about the type of contact you might have, but I definitely think it is doable.

Barbara: Many people ask me, "How can I have contact with extraterrestrial beings?" They may not be aware of having had encounters with these beings but they would like to have contact. In my own personal experience I successfully used a technique which had been suggested to me by an extraterrestrial being during a channeling by one of my experiencer clients.

In 1994 I was preparing for my fourth year of researching crop circles in England, and I strongly wanted to know how the genuine crop circles were made and by whom. In the channeling the being suggested I could ask to be taken for the making of a crop circle. The day before I flew to England for my annual crop circle visits I talked out loud to the crop circle makers, with total earnestness and passion. I did not know who they were or what they were like or if they were ET beings of some sort. I trusted that intelligence and creativity was involved in the forming of these exquisite patterns laid down in fields of growing crops. I enthusiastically praised them for their coming to Earth and giving us the beautiful 'gifts' of crop circles, which awaken us, stir our curiosity, expand our thinking in cosmic directions and energize us. For 45 minutes I continued praising them and asking them to please take me for the making of a crop circle. Three weeks later I asked again, in my mind, and my wish was granted. The last night of my stay, three beings came into the room of my bed and breakfast and took me through a wall, through the open air and into a small craft, and I soon witnessed the making of a crop circle. I was the first to discover it the next morning, and it looked just like it had in my experience.

This technique of concentrating and talking to the beings out loud and asking them for the contact you want, can be very effective if you really mean it and if you feel it strongly with your emotions and your heart. It may be that you only get one experience with them, so ask wisely. If you had made a soul agreement to have ongoing contact, then it can start small and grow from there.

I advise honoring them with expressions of respect and love, and asking for only benevolent beings to come to you. You too may very well have the contact you desire.

Robert provided detailed instructions on achieving contact in his 'contact protocol.' To save readers from having to refer back, we include it here.

Contact protocol

To be consciously meditating is the contact state. There is a feeling to it, and if you can maintain that while awake, that's contact consciousness. I also call it 'singularity consciousness.'

I base this system on the law of equal exchange. It takes a lot of energy for the visitors to get here, so if we request a meeting with them, we need to do the best that we can, with the resources available to us, to match that energy. I call this my 'contact gas tank.' The concept is simple: fill up the tank to have contact. It raises your vibration and lets you spend energy for the intention of positive contact. One very important thing: the energy you put into this is the energy you get out.

How to fill the contact gas tank:

1. Do not purposely harm a single living thing. Take the bugs and spiders outside the house. Water a weed growing out of the cracks in the concrete. Be consciously appreciative to all life you come in contact with. (Thank you for this experience little spider, but you

live outside.) By doing this, the visitors will see that you respect and appreciate all contact with life on your world. This means you have the ability to respect and appreciate life from other worlds.

2. Be mindful of your thoughts. Try to look at the positive in everything, even things you don't like. For example, a friend just painted their wall the ugliest color you have ever seen, yet you still tell your friend, "It looks great buddy," because you don't want to hurt their feelings. Train yourself to not have that first negative thought; instead try to think, 'I'm happy my friend enjoys this.' The visitors are extremely telepathic—they hear everything you are thinking. Imagine how people around you would act if they can hear what you are thinking. So start training yourself now.

3. Perform at least one act of kindness to a stranger every day. The visitors can see how you treat others.

4. Love—the most powerful emotion in the universe. Love yourself, throughout the day for as long as you can maintain it. With every breath you take, feel love in your heart. Feel it throughout your body. When you're out and about, feel love for everyone you see. Stop for a moment and breathe in love, connect with all living things, and connect to their existence. Love—anything else is fear.

Some of these tasks may not seem to have any relevance to contacting beings from another world, but they do. It seems that when I follow these steps the best that I can, I tend to get a more interactive experience.

Expect first contact with the species you resonate with the most. It will initially happen in your sleep, when you are half conscious. They are so advanced that they know you better than you know yourself. If they sense fear they'll leave you alone.

To initiate it, let go of all expectations, fears and concerns. It's a physical feeling, and you'll know when it feels like the time is right. Eventually you'll have the urge to say, "I'm ready."

NB. To all the tech people out there, do not go into this to learn of technology. These beings are not just more technically advanced than us, they are more spiritually advanced as well. From what I've learned, the benevolent beings couldn't care less about technology, they are most interested in mentoring us in matters of spirituality. Be patient, the information on technology will come. They need to know you're responsible enough to experience their technology before they give it to you.

Personal Journeys

Around a month into the interviews, it was turning into such a wild, personally expanding ride that I suggested to Barbara that we keep notes on our journeys and write them up for the final part of the book. We discuss how we got into such an unusual subject area, and what the experience of working with these beings and concepts has given us, so far.

Miguel's Journey

What makes someone decide one day to write a book about hybrids? And how did it begin as a book project and end up as a vision quest? Ufology has been a lifelong interest, but it was revived in spectacular fashion during a vacation in 2009 when my partner and I had a life-changing UFO sighting over the Azorean island of Graciosa. We were stargazing one August night and saw what at first seemed to be a satellite tracking across the sky. It then began to brighten and swell rapidly, as though it were a torch turning towards us. My partner said what I was thinking: "God, it's like it's *looking* at us." It then shrank back down and continued, before brightening again, even larger, and suddenly shooting off in a vast streak of light across the heavens. It was *exactly* like the Starship Enterprise going to warp. Many readers will sympathize with the way that such an experience imprints on you, and leaves you forever more trying to get to the bottom of the mystery.

In 2013 I was writing a novel about truth, exploring a wide variety of its aspects, from lie spotting, to truth and reconciliation commissions, to the denial inside a crumbling marriage and beyond. One character particularly intrigued me, as he seemed to have access to some truly deep, dark secrets. Most writers will be familiar with the way that some characters come to life, and begin to tell you who they are—and so it was with Albert. He hinted of connections to the black budget world, and I wanted to know more. I soon found myself researching the topic of UFOs afresh. I compiled a large volume of books, documentaries, lectures and interviews—in print and online—and immersed myself. I wished to create a framework into which all the reported phenomena might fit, to see if the big picture would come into focus. The further I explored, the more maddeningly nebulous it became, but I resolved to understand it, and turn it into a novel.

But that was not my only inspiration. For at least 20 years I've been having a series of particularly vivid UFO-related 'sci-fi' dreams which seem to be somehow real in a way that normal dreams are not. They're not just clear and lucid, but within them I have an unusual depth of knowing, a real sense of backstory. There are continual close encounters with craft, most of whom are unlike any I'd seen in pop culture or ufology. I began to wonder if I might be stepping into the lives of others, whether parallel selves or other souls entirely. I used my notes on those dreams to form the backbone of a much larger story, encompassing the entirety of ufology and venturing into spiritual and political realms. The work of Richard Dolan on the 'breakaway civilization' concept provided excellent background material, as did the testimony of a great number of brave souls who have come forward at great personal and professional risk.

I was particularly struck by Karla Turner's book *Taken*, and the stories of the eight women interviewed. I then discovered Barbara Lamb's conference lectures on YouTube, and was deeply moved by the experiences of the women who were discovering that they had hybrid children, and were being taken at night so they could interact with these infants. It was the mixture of love, heartache, bittersweet joy and often disempowerment that hooked me empathically, and I realized I'd found the emotional center of ufology. The novel that came out of that phase was centered around hybrids, and as I wanted to honor their lived experience, I contacted Barbara with a view to gaining more insight.

When we spoke, she shared with me the fact that a group of hybrids she knew personally were considering how to bring their experiences and understandings to the wider human community. I evidently spent the whole night percolating, as upon waking I filled eight pages of my journal with notes on my response to the idea. I then produced a discussion paper, blending cost-benefit analysis and strategy document, which was heavy on safeguarding issues.

Just as with the original research for the novel, I felt very protective towards these people. I have yet to fully understand why I feel that so strongly, but I suspect that, as with so many other facets of this subject, there is far more to it than meets the eye.

Of key importance, I felt, was the issue of the hybrids taking control of the discourse, giving them their own voice so they could speak without distortion, without being badgered by the cynical, belligerent types that spend their time insulting other people in online comment sections.

I shared the paper with Barbara, and after a long discussion about the issues raised, I suggested that we consider collaborating on the book which you are now reading.

My original intention was to be a silent witness, an objective social scientist recording the details of their reality to share with the wider world. That seems cute at this point. Instead it's been a dramatic, ongoing personal expansion, and one which stands as the greatest conceptual challenge of my life. Prior to beginning this work, I was out on one of my 'cycling meditations' and the thought appeared in my mind: 'the barrier *is* the way.' The thing that prevents you going forward is the opportunity to *truly* advance, if you can find and engage the resources to overcome it. In my previous life as a researcher and campaigner in sustainability I overcame numerous challenges that had initially seemed laughably insurmountable, so I knew that with energy and strategy you and your colleagues can succeed. And yet this is, you may have discovered, a challenge of a different order.

The first thing I had trouble with was the response of Juju and Jacquelin to the idea I initially held that the hybrids and others could help defeat those that hold back human development and liberation on this planet—what Hunter S. Thompson termed 'the forces of old and evil.' Both of them said words to the effect of, "There *are* no sides." I thought, 'What do you *mean*, no sides? There are *always* sides.' The entire campaigning enterprise rests on the fact that there are conflicting views on a given policy, and that each side seeks successful mobilization of resources in order to achieve their desired outcome. Some strands of campaigning involve efforts to meet in the middle, but often it is a zero-sum game. If I am a campaigner at heart, a man fighting to create peace and justice in a world run by shallow, psychotic villains, how do I process the idea that these sides are illusory? But is that even what is meant?

And then there were the ideas of frequency, vibration and light. One cannot get terribly far into a conversation with a hybrid without encountering these concepts on some level. And try getting your mind around the business of transitioning from 3D to 5D. The average reader will no doubt sympathize to some degree—and I hope we've helped to make these things somewhat clearer.

As things turned out, in addition to the duties of lead author, editor and production department, I was chiefly responsible for the transcription work, turning around 50 hours of interviews into the initial core of the book. The processes of listening repeatedly, writing up, editing and proofing all gave me a deep familiarity with the material, and non-stop opportunities to process and integrate it. The layers of information began to knit together subconsciously, and trigger a succession of what appear to be conscious realizations. But for those aspects which are experiential in nature, such as frequency, vibration and light, something—whatever it is—had more surprises in store.

During the second interview with Juju—and following an informal Skype chat with Robert the previous day—I began to feel what I can only describe as a kind of cellular acceleration, or effervescence. Juju and Barbara were talking, and I was staring at my hands, wondering what the hell, when Juju commented, "You have a strong aura around your hands, Miguel." 'Good God,' I thought, 'This thing's actually for *real?*' That was the first time I had that body shock, that moment of realizing that something paranormal was genuinely occurring: this person could *see* energy. It's one thing to be open to it, to support these people and hear them out, it's another when they casually demonstrate something that regular humans don't tend to. I reflected that Robert had said the previous night that he acts as an accelerator for people, just by being in contact with them. Was I actually having my frequency raised by ET-human hybrids?

When I shared this experience with Juju she said that I would be opening up more and more, and that I should invoke protection so that I'm not open to everything, because not every kind of energy is going to be positive towards me. I said I didn't know how, and hoped that I would find some technique for that. The next day I was again out cycling, and spontaneously received a vision of Master Sananda, of whom Cynthia had produced a beautiful sculpture. He was in the center of my chest, hands pressed together in prayer. He then dissolved, to be replaced by an image of a quartz crystal ball which I had recently bought in Glastonbury. It began to spin, and as it did so it began to radiate, then *blast* out, a dazzling white light. 'There it is,' I thought. '*That's* my protection. Now I can visualize it.'

Juju's and Jacquelin's connection to nature, and focus on keeping their vibration high, led me to fill my window ledge with plants which changed the energy in my living space. Discussions on crystals with Matt, Charmaine and Robert prompted me to indulge my love of them and add to my collection. Over the course of this project my workspace has transformed into a high vibrational zone of Buddhas, gods, angels, animals, crystals and mandalas. It is vivid, inspiring, calming and supporting, and has helped keep the vibration of my input high. Little by little, I was beginning to experience their world.

And yet I was still confounded by the 'no sides' concept. It seemed to run against the grain of my identity. But, as with some of the other concepts, I was given a stunning experience which offered a personal understanding. It began with meeting Charmaine at the 2015 Glastonbury Symposium. We talked about health matters, and she recommended a healer who lived near my parents in the South East of England. I decided it was worth a shot, and at short notice drove down on the Friday. It was wonderful to see my family for the first time in 19 months, and also meet up with an old school friend with whom I'd shared many stages of life, and experiences. On the Sunday—my birthday—I drove over to Charmaine's house and met the healer, Alan. I mentally asked any friendly, interested entities to work through us both to assist the healing. Moments later, Alan said that there was a spiritual being present. Shocked but not entirely surprised, I asked if it was an ET of some kind, and using kinesiology he dowsed its nature by asking questions and receiving the answer from his body. "It's not ET ... it's angelic ... it's an Archangel ... *oh*. It's Archangel Michael. That *is* interesting. I've only met three or four other people who have Michael around them." That *did* give me goosebumps. I then shared with him two angelic experiences I'd had in the past, one of which may have been a life-saving intervention.

The next day I asked Barbara about the possibility of doing a regression to go back to my angelic experiences. Prior to my birthday experience I had felt great resistance for some indefinable reason. We arranged to do a regression the following day.

When we got to the session, which was my first, I did my utmost to go with it. Even via an imperfect Skype connection, Barbara was able to send my body to sleep while keeping my mind active. But as I discovered, it's a different type of active. Normally my mind is a full-on debating chamber, with a variety of opinions and emotions being thrown around. But in regression there is only one voice.

Thought comes slower, clearer. There is more signal, less noise. I came to understand that the first angelic experience, which involved a meeting and apparent download in a tent in 1993, was primarily about opening my consciousness, proving to me the existence of other beings—and other realms and states of existence—by giving me direct experience. And it seemed that I had some significance to these beings.

Then I went to the second experience in 1994. I was in the back of a car as we hurtled along at night, when a car pulled out of the oncoming stream of traffic to overtake. One moment I was being blinded by the headlights as the car was on top of us, and the next, I was aware of nothing but white light. I had no form, I was simply a pinpoint of consciousness, and I then became aware that floating in the air before me was an angel with its wings spread. It was a dazzling spectacle, which still makes me pause to take it in. The vision lasted just a few moments, then all sound seemed to be sucked backwards, and my consciousness was dumped back into my body. It took me a few moments for me to realize that we had somehow avoided a collision, and that the driver and other passenger up front were not discussing angels, so I kept it to myself. In the regression, I understood that that experience was about protection. Whether or not the angel edited events so that we did not get destroyed in a car wreck, I don't know. But what was clear, again, is that they were demonstrating that I was significant to them in some way. Perhaps it was a reminder to me.

The final question I pursued in the regression was my sense of mission. Why, from the age of four or five, did I have an inner knowing that I was here to do something important? What has been the driving force behind it? What am I involved in? Is someone else pulling my strings, whispering in my ear? When I set out this intention, I became aware of space, stars, then myself, in a sitting position, and I seemed to exist at a vast scale. Behind and beneath me, like a cosmic beanbag, was a field of consciousness made up of countless pinpoints of light. As I paid attention to this field, I began to hear a rising susurration of voices as it paid attention to me. Every voice seemed to be addressing me, and it grew louder as I listened. It was a wonderful communing, like a surprise birthday party. I burst out laughing at the sheer joyous surprise of it. It was exhilarating and enlightening. I felt more connected than I have ever felt, and it was all good. I have believed for some time that the whole of existence is a single consciousness in infinite manifestation (and that humanity's ignorance of this is the central cause of our misery), and that communion entirely reinforced that sense.

Then my awareness shifted, as though I were looking over my shoulder toward the field. At my back, stretching out of sight into the distance, was a row of silhouettes, some bipedal, some not, some just fields of energy, and it hit me that they were my previous incarnations. A series of thoughts came one on top of the other: 'So each incarnation reviews the life it has just lived, then determines what it would like to work on in the next incarnation. So, to the question 'Who am I doing this for?' the answer seems to be: *me*. And when I select my mission in the next incarnation, form follows function, so I select an appropriate form—the body is simply a tool (which makes racism look especially pointless). So if all this is just rolling ever onward, none of us need beat ourselves up over what we achieve or do not achieve in each lifetime—all we can do is do our best and understand that it is a never-ending series of lessons.'

There were other important realizations concerning my connection with other intelligences, but by the time I surfaced from the regression I felt more at peace than I ever had. While straight. And I finally felt I had some insight into the perspective that "there are no sides." In the grand scheme of things, the multidimensional mechanisms of creation, the cycles of existence, the shifts in mission and form, we are all playing so many roles throughout our journeys that defining anything as one side versus another only works from the narrowest perspective. There *are* sides, but they are simply roles we choose, and agree to play at the pre-incarnation soul level. Cynthia talked about such ideas in detail.

Juju said, "Light doesn't oppose, it offers what it is. It's available. There's no fight or war in the light, those are products of lesser energies." But if we are all playing roles, then isn't it *all* positive energy in some way? When Jacquelin talked about friction creating a pearl, she apparently supported this view. As ever, I was trying to rationalize a mass of complex ideas and experiences to create a framework that anyone could understand and make use of. Those playing the role of the light in this 'world of polarities' could use this material to create more light. But again, 'good' and 'bad' are relative terms. To those wanting to poison the planet and make the rich richer and the poor poorer, anyone opposing them is downright evil.

While pondering this the next day I decided to book dowse, taking a book from my shelves and opening it at random to see if it held something I needed to hear. The book was *National*

Geographic's Essential Visual History of World Mythology, and I happened to open it at a page on The Bhagavad Gita. Out of the whole work, the editors of this book picked out the tale of Krishna telling Arjuna about karma yoga, which they described as "essentially performing acts or duties without any concern for results." Bam! There it was—exactly what I needed to read at that moment. It gave me a new take on the 'no fight' concept. I could simply offer this work to the world and let go of any attachment to outcome, or the idea of using it to strike back against the darkness. The book, and myself as an author, must be as the light, offering only what it is.

This concept also gave me a new attitude to the question of proof. I was initially concerned that the book should be persuasive enough to crack the seals on any mind, no matter how determinedly skeptical. But now I saw that as a distraction, and was reminded of what was once billed at a conference as 'the policy food fight.' In my renewable energy days I was a cheerleader for a particular policy which I saw as the best tool to democratize energy and create educated stakeholders out of the world's householders, farmers, communities and so on. But the policy debate was falsely advertised as a dispassionate process of choosing the 'best' policy for a given jurisdiction. It took me a while to realize that this was merely a distraction from the real point: who gets control—of energy production, of revenue streams, and of the discourse around energy production itself. So when I look at the debates around 'proving' UFOs and ETs are 'real,' it's actually a distraction from the real matter: what are the implications of ETs interacting with humans? And it should surprise no one that the stakes are identical: who gets control. This has major overlaps with the energy debate, and comes down to money and power. Arguably, so does every policy debate.

But what is at stake here, that I am most concerned with, is human consciousness. When certain people insist that UFOs and ETs do not exist, and are certainly not interacting with humanity, those people are generally materialists, or attached to another worldview that is threatened by the existence of, and interaction with, beings with often superior intelligence, understanding, abilities and technology. The issue of why this subject is suppressed is well rehearsed by now, but in my view it centers on control of the population. The ET reality has such a dynamic effect on those who experience it that their minds are freed from the limitations of human cultures and those who control them. For the arch-materialists, little can be as threatening as enlightenment, and liberation from materialism.

While I no longer feel a need to convince anyone of anything, I will share my sense of whether or not the information is legitimate. If we conceptualize knowledge as the experience of information, then this book offers only information—at the level of immediate perception. As I have laid out above, being open to experience can begin granting it in various ways, and sooner than you might think.

What I feel legitimizes the information is the insight. Only experience creates insight, bullshit does not. If one makes up a story about their best friend dying, they simply retell it over and over. But the person who experiences that apocalyptic personal tragedy will spend years, perhaps decades processing it, trying to make sense of it, learning to live with it, finding new ways to think about that person and the relationship, wondering where they might be now and so on. Eventually, important understandings will emerge, and the ongoing experience changes who they are and how they see the world. The same is true of ecstatic experience, and all experience to some degree. Only that which actually happens can truly gift us with insight. And in the conversations with the hybrids I was continually struck by the insight that they have produced over time. Occasionally one person's insight would echo that of another, but often they would be unique to that person and their journey. To that extent, I am confident that each person believes what they are saying, and it is real to them.

So if they are not lying, could they be delusional? Could someone be living a fantasy of such scale and complexity and still function in society? To the best of my knowledge, they have all made it this far without such a state of delusion becoming evident.

It occurred to me during this process that demanding proof that meets contemporary Western scientific standards is effectively getting stuck on the material, which is *exactly* missing the point—this is spiritual and experiential, hence the Ascension instructions. I recall an old acquaintance being deeply influenced by Carlos Castaneda's books, and when I raised the matter of their disputed authenticity, she said that the importance of the work was the ideas and practices within—they had made a difference to her life and that's what counts. As it happened, she taught me the technique for making a dream lucid—looking for one's hands—which within a week had given me a wonderful lucid dream, into which I summoned her. Later the same day I found myself in the exact spot in Leicester Square in London where the dream had commenced, and as that fact hit, I happened to look across the square towards the Odeon, and saw a female Hare Krishna devotee. She looked up at me at the same moment and made a beeline for me. With the briefest greeting only, she held up a book on astral projection. Stunned, I told her that I'd just done that for the first time, not three hours earlier, and it began on the exact spot on which I now stood. Without missing a beat she said, "Yes, you have mystical powers."

The point is: being open to both taught wisdom and the wisdom of personal experience can be of benefit to yourself and those you influence, actively or passively. If you are ready to work with new ideas and techniques, you can have transformational experiences. I have read the entire book at least a dozen times through the drafting and editing process, and each time something else comes clear, as though for the first time, and has a positive effect on me. I trust this will be the same for every reader, which is profoundly meaningful for all of us who have contributed to this work.

In my second regression with Barbara, wherein I explored my mission in this incarnation, I found it expressed as: "to discover and share beautiful truths." I learned that I know I am fulfilling my mission "when my soul breathes deeply." This experience has been so powerful and multidimensional that it would take years to digest and an entire book to unpack properly, but suffice to say: my spiritual lungs have never been so full.

Barbara's Journey

From my earliest days, I hoped to somehow be helpful to people in my life, yet I did not feel drawn to any of the 'helping professions.' I received a Bachelor of Arts degree in Philosophy from an Ivy League women's college in New England, married a Protestant Minister, had children, became a Dance Therapist, a Tai Chi teacher, eventually became licensed as a Marriage and Family Therapist, co-directed a large counseling center, and explored using deeper states of consciousness in my therapy work. Eventually I received five years of intensive training by the International Association for Past Life Research and Therapies, and began incorporating past life regressions into my therapy practice with some of my clients. During all of these years I paid no attention to the UFO/extraterrestrial phenomenon, assuming it must be only a subject for science fiction.

In 1983 at a workshop conducted by Helen Wambaugh Ph.D, I experienced a regression to the state of being when I was a conscious soul getting ready to come into this lifetime. When Helen suggested, "Now be aware of the main purpose for you entering into this lifetime," I immediately understood that it was, "To show people how it *really* is." What I meant by that is that we are all souls coming from the spirit realm into various lifetimes, and there are countless souls, human and otherwise, doing this time and again. I did not know that they are what I subsequently learned were called extraterrestrial beings, but I knew they existed, and I was committed to informing people about them. For several decades I had no idea what this commitment would lead to.

At the beginning of my final module of training to be a Past Life Regression Therapist, in 1988, my trainer mentioned briefly that those of us professionally using regression therapy might at some time have someone come to us who had been confused or traumatized by unusual, non-human beings visiting them. They may report being taken away by the beings for a short while, and might want us to assist them with regression work so they could know the details of what had occurred. She did not mention extraterrestrials or UFOs, but I was stunned to hear this and experienced cognitive dissonance. Right after she said this, I heard a loud emphatic voice in my head saying, "Pay attention to this Barbara, you will be doing this!"

I was even more stunned by this experience, and subsequently found myself trying to find out about the UFO/ET phenomenon and determine whether or not I thought it was real.

One morning in 1991 I found myself thinking, 'Okay, I think these encounters between ETs and some humans are happening, and I could help them with hypnotic regression therapy.' I had learned enough to feel convinced that millions of people worldwide were having UFO sightings and ET encounters. Two hours later I was in a metaphysical bookstore and the woman behind the counter recognized me as a regression therapist and asked if I would work with her 21-year-old daughter, who was highly traumatized by strange non-human beings coming into her room at night and doing strange things to her. I agreed, and we did a series of regressions to six ET encounter experiences, each with a different species. These beings performed various procedures with her, including healing a serious ear infection and using her reproductive material to produce a hybrid baby. She had also been healed of severe lower back pain by a beam of blue light coming down from an ET craft, and her sister had witnessed this and verified it. After our sixth session she came into my office smiling and looking confident; she announced that she was feeling honored and privileged to be chosen by these beings, was no longer afraid of them and welcomed their coming to her again. I was astonished!

What a fine introduction to this phenomenon this was for me! I decided I felt prepared to help anyone else who might come to me for this kind of work. Little did I know I would go on to work with a series of 1,700 people, for a total of 2,600 regressions over the last 24 years, as of this writing. I began my monthly Experiencer Support Group in 1994 and this group is still convening. I introduced the conducting of such groups to the International UFO Congress during the 1990s, and this offering has been included in many UFO conferences since then. I greatly enjoy giving presentations on ET encounters to conferences and other groups, as well as radio, television and film interviews. I endeavor to 'normalize' the subjects of ET-human contact and ET-human hybrids, and to treat them with the honor and respect I believe they deserve.

As I became more deeply involved in this work in the 1990s, I began having my own personal ET encounters. The first one I vehemently asked for: to be taken for the making of a crop circle in England. At that time I was actively researching the crop circle phenomenon in England each summer, and had been having the great privilege of talking to an ET from the binary star system of Antares, who was channeled through one of my experiencer clients. In 1994 he told me I could be taken by ETs for the making of a crop circle, if I wished to. I followed his suggestions for making contact, and was taken one night by ETs in a small craft and witnessed the making of a crop circle, which synchronistically I was the first person to find and go into the next day.

A few years later my car and I were taken from a California freeway by friendly beings who 'downloaded' from my brain what my experiencer clients learned about their ET encounters and how these encounters were affecting them. The main being gave a significant amount of information when answering questions posed by the woman regressing me, Dolores Cannon.

A couple of years after that, a male Reptilian being appeared in my living room during the middle of one afternoon. I went right over to him and held his hand for several minutes. In a subsequent regression to that experience he said he had been bred as a "friendly ambassador" and was giving me my own contact while conscious and awake in the daytime, so that I would completely trust that peoples' ET encounters were true.

My last encounter, in 2008, also happened in the middle of the afternoon, when I was taken up through the roof of my house to an ethereal area of pinkish-peach-colored mist where a dozen beautiful, tall, willowy, almost transparent beings told me how pleased they were that my co-author Nadine Lalich and I had just completed writing our book, *Alien Experiences*. They emphasized that, "It is time now" for people on Earth to know about other beings in the universe and to recognize that there is much interaction between us.

Through the excellent people I have worked with in regressions, I have learned about a large variety of ET species, many of the procedures they do with humans, the healing they do of humans, the teaching and training they conduct, and the raising of consciousness they inspire. I have also learned about how they create ET-human hybrid beings—through a variety of methods involving human females and males—and the relationships many of these people have with their hybrid children who live on the ships. I gradually began to think some of my clients and a few other people I knew may be hybrids themselves. Some of them suspected this or were given verification by the ETs with whom they were having encounters. Being invited to give a lecture at the national MUFON Symposium in 2011 inspired me to comb through my files and do additional research on the ET-human hybrid phenomenon. I was absolutely fascinated with the information I found.

Before this time I had serendipitously met Cynthia Crawford at a large UFO conference and I immediately had the intuition she was a hybrid because of her unusually large (and beautiful) eyes, and her unusual energy. I said, "I hope you don't mind, but you remind me of a hybrid." She said that she is a hybrid, and from that moment on we became special friends. A year or two later someone introduced me to another woman at a conference, and I immediately said, "I hope you don't mind me saying, but you remind me of a Mantis being," and she said, "Good for you—I *am* a Mantis being!" A third woman came into my awareness, and she turned out to be a Reptilian hybrid.

Gradually, it became clear to me that my favorite aspect of the fascinating ET phenomenon was the hybridization aspect. I was especially grateful for the opportunity to know fellow humans who have a significant proportion of ET DNA in them and are living here as humans and continuing to have contact with the beings they came from. I was thrilled when I was invited to attend a private gathering of hybrids and experiencers near Palm Springs,

California, which was followed by another in Laramie, Wyoming, and a third near Phoenix, Arizona. This group was named the Institute for Human-Cosmic Interaction or IHCI, with the mission of educating the public about human interactions with ET beings and ET-human hybrids. Knowing these hybrid people was truly inspiring for me, and I was tempted to eventually write a book about them. Finding the time to do this seemed impossible because of the fullness of my schedule and life, but my wish continued.

During the past several years I regressed several women who had been told by the ET entity Bashar (channeled by Darryl Anka) that they had hybrid children, even though they did not remember having had ET encounters. In each case they were very excited about their hybrid children and wanted to get to know them. Some of these women wanted to raise them here on Earth, or at least to meet them in person and get to know them as much as possible. This longing matched some of my male and female regression clients who also wanted to have as much of a relationship with their hybrid children as would be allowed. They were told that these children did not have a large enough proportion of human in them to be able to survive here on Earth, and therefore had to live their lives on the ships. Two women in my experiencer group were so dedicated to their hybrid children that they set up a website, hybridchildrencommunity.com, and are now trying to find a large piece of rural property in which sufficiently human hybrid children may come from their spaceship and live safely.

With all this background and experience I was thrilled when Miguel Mendonça invited me to collaborate on a book about ET-human hybrids living among us on Earth. I recommended that we interview Cynthia, Robert and Jacquelin, whom I already knew and liked enormously. Cynthia suggested Jujuolui and Vanessa. Miguel found Charmaine, Matt and Tatiana in England. I could have suggested two additional hybrids whom I know, but we knew that we would already have plenty of material for a first book.

Each has expressed gratitude for our involving them with this project, and we have appreciated their openly sharing who they are and what they know. They appreciate being given a respectful platform through which they can share their unique perspective from the ETs and their experience of living here as hybrids, particularly their missions on Earth. Each of them is an absolutely lovely being, and shares genuine unconditional love, higher frequency, goodwill and spiritual inspiration. They seem sincere, normal people, and yet they are exceptionally talented in their healing and inspirational work, their intuitions, their knowledge and their wisdom. Some have expressed that being interviewed for this book has helped to clarify some of their Earth-life experiences, their ET visitations, where they come from in the cosmos, who their true families are, and the importance of their being here in this lifetime. I think it is wonderful that they are connecting with each other and are hoping to have gatherings of many more hybrids and Star Children.

For me they have brought into my daily experience a deeper appreciation for nature and for all living beings, for cultivating the highest frequency possible, for coming from the heart and expressing more love, for enlarging my cosmic perspective and my appreciation for all life in the cosmos and in other dimensions. From them I have learned much about the Ascension process, which I had heard of but hadn't formerly understood or been interested in. I appreciate their accurate yet nonjudgmental perspective on humanity, even with all our dysfunctions and foibles and atrocities, which helps me with my former disappointment and disgust about our not having evolved yet past war, greed, selfishness, competition and hurting others. I see it all in a more helpful perspective now.

I savored the regressions which I conducted for a few of our hybrids and for Miguel, helping them to know the details of certain key experiences they had had. As with all regressions I have done involving ETs or interdimensional beings, I have learned and appreciated even more than I had done before.

My Star Origin Reading from Jacquelin was a special treasure for me. I resonated strongly with some of the elements she saw for me, including the celestial realm of light which I had originally incarnated in, which matched some rare special moments of bursts of light inside me which I have experienced in this life. I truly felt the Mantis beings which she saw around me, and I felt delighted with her speaking their language, and her giving me my name for me to say aloud when I want contact with my true family. I was delighted to hear that I had been a Mantis being in some previous lifetimes. For many years I have felt a strong love for the Mantis beings, without knowing my own history as one of them. I am also gratified to know I have had some Pleiadian lifetimes, as I have identified with them for thirty years or more.

I am immensely appreciative that Jacquelin has the abilities to 'see' where in the cosmos our souls originally incarnated and some of the beings we have been in previous lifetimes. It confirms the results in my regression work that have shown that many people have had previous lives as extraterrestrial beings. I am gratified to know of the beings I was a member of in some of my past lives, and this information matches the sincere interest in and affinity I have felt for these particular races of beings. What an extraordinary ability she and our other hybrids have!

Of special meaning to me is the experience of having two strokes in the middle of this project, which necessitated my canceling many plans, including leading my annual crop circle tour in England, and a few other highly anticipated events. For a few weeks as I was recuperating, the single thing I did professionally was doing long Skype interviews with our delightful hybrids, and having conversations with Miguel for four or more hours at a time. Even with the geographical distances and time zone differences between all of us, we had intriguing, fascinating exchanges. With each interview I felt special energy, higher frequencies, inspiration and a sense of enlightenment. I had my confidence restored in my professional abilities, and my decision to stay in this life was reinforced. I believe this participation was a major component of my successful recuperation, along with the healing transmissions from the hybrids which caused feelings of new blood vessels being formed in my head. I learned helpful perspectives and felt love from each of our hybrids. I am grateful for this entire project and for the wonderful hybrids I am cherishing in my life.

The few thousand regressions to ET encounters which I had conducted before I met our hybrids stretched my mind and opened up new vistas of understanding for me. Even more so, I grew exponentially further in perspective and appreciation when talking with each of the hybrids in our study. I suddenly realized that my previous perspective of ET-human interactions looked like a 'kindergarten' level of perspective and understanding compared to the 'graduate school' level of perspective I was learning from our hybrids: with their emphasis on Oneness, Unconditional Love, cosmic understanding of the Source, and Ascension. Now I am convinced more than ever that in addition to the more 'self-serving' ETs who interact with and frighten humans, the universe contains gloriously benevolent, loving, spiritually advanced beings in various dimensions who send their emissaries as hybrids to assist and enlighten humanity. Working with our hybrids has been an amazing journey!

The Big Picture

This book will offer every reader a different experience. It contains a wealth of information that everyone will learn something from. We all learn in a unique way and different things will resonate at different times. It is most likely that if you read this book ten times you will have a different experience each time, but on each occasion the material may come together a little more. The hybrids said numerous times that they offer no more than their piece of the puzzle—what they understand today. If we attempt to put these pieces together, what kind of picture forms?

The core seems to be:
We are not alone.
Homo sapiens is a hybrid species.
Reality is multidimensional.
Psychic phenomena are real.
We are in a process of multidimensional evolution.
Time is an illusion.
All things are connected.
God is everything and everyone.
We are all immortal souls.

Right there we have answers to most of our biggest questions. The nature and structure of ourselves, and reality itself, has fascinated and tormented humanity since our earliest expression on this planet. Those who have claimed to be the sole arbiter of such 'truth' have commanded and abused enormous power, and division over the answers has cost the lives of untold millions of people throughout history. The hybrids do not offer it for personal gain but for the education and liberation of others.

On the central matter of Ascension, opinion was split between those who believe it to be a shift from the physical to the metaphysical, and those who believe it is simply, as Robert put it, "a new expression of life on this planet."

What seems clear is that Ascension is fractal in nature. Every being is working on their own Ascension, and it is playing out at every scale. Which implies that the more work we do personally, the more we contribute to Ascension at larger scales.

If we pull out of this 'cosmic' focus, we realize that the heart of this message has been circulating on the planet Earth for millennia. Love and unity has been preached by many, and it feels like the fundamental truth of existence. Those who advocate greed and power tend to use it to justify their own lusts. The source of those appetites may be complex, but it suggests a spiritual and moral poverty. The message of love and unity, when pure in intention, is not acquisitive or self-serving. It has no agenda. It is simply a way of being that serves the flourishing of all.

Either people resonate with that or they don't. For those who don't, the hybrids often remarked that people are free to evolve at their own pace, and learn as much as they want to, *when* they want to. Each incarnation is simply one set of experiences that we can have. Cynthia said many times in both interviews and conversations that, "We are only here for the experience." Robert observed, "There's no good or bad, it's just an experience."

Jacquelin commented on the dualistic roles we play in this shared experience, saying, "Those who choose to focus on the darker side of the spectrum, their soul has chosen to play that role for the sake of duality, for contrast, and also as a push, in a similar way that a pearl is created through friction. I see those of lower frequency creating friction to help everyone become or remember who they really are. We are all co-creating this process."

In terms of a 'dark side' of the hybrid program, no one denied it exists, but there were different takes on it. Some said they avoid giving it attention as they don't want to attract it. Some said it's a matter of perspective and understanding, that it may be a more positive, benevolent phenomenon than people realize. And some said that they have practices for keeping it at bay, often involving raising their own vibration and surrounding themselves in white light. When we think of this at a larger scale, we come back to the idea that our Ascension is everyone's. As above, so below.

The joy of this is that even if one has trouble expanding their reality to accommodate non-human races, they can still draw upon the spiritual wisdom contained in these messages. At the most basic level, one can improve one's experience of everyday life. It can be liberating to be mindful of ideas that transcend the physical, such as, "We're only here for the experience," or, "I'm not this body, I'm not this personality. I'm a beautiful light of creation, I'm divine love."

These enlarge our reality and our sense of self, allowing us to avoid becoming ensnared in the drama of human lives. In a culture that has become increasingly materialist in outlook and values, these principles offer a view of existence that works to undo the attachments and dependencies that cause so much suffering. This includes life itself. If we believe that we only get one life, that can build in a mass of angst, based on: are we getting everything we want while we can? Some may take comfort in the idea that life isn't permanent, and that suffering does end eventually, but one can be just as comforted by the idea that this life is not all there is.

The next phase of personal expansion begins when we accept that these other beings really do exist, and are interacting with humanity on various levels. From channeled messages and psychic guidance, to visitations and the hybrid program, the contact has physical and metaphysical levels. As the section on 'Can Anyone Have ET Contact?' sets out, there are multiple ways of connecting directly with star beings. It is a matter of where your energy and intention is, and how ready you are. There is also the matter of what kind of soul agreement you already have in place.

This raises a sticky point. The hybrids often mention soul agreements, which suggest that our path is to an extent predetermined. But what if we don't like it? If we do get contact with self-serving ETs—that we've agreed at the soul level to interact with—but want it to stop, what should we do? Should we tough it out and see what is to be learned, or should we raise our vibration, invoke protection and be rid of them? Perhaps the contact forces us to grow through the experience of having to deal with them, in the way that most negative experiences in life are opportunities to be resourceful and grow? If we are indeed only here for the experience, then we should embrace this positive attitude and not be too hung up on the process. Like everything else, it comes and goes.

In this expanded view of reality, what is permanent is the soul, and its journeys across time and space. Cynthia's picture of Source dividing itself into Source-selves in order to learn everything anew is consistent with the idea of the soul's journey. In human form those souls appear to be separate, but at times it can feel as though we are part of a unified consciousness. Anyone who has ever sat among a legion of fellow fans at a game and roared together when your team scores, or sung along with thousands at a concert, has experienced a form of group consciousness.

Larry Dossey's book *One Mind* examines in depth, from multiple angles, the idea of "an all-encompassing, infinite dimension of shared intelligence." He shows that many of us experience this in different ways, including premonition, shared thoughts and emotions over distance, 'miraculously' finding lost objects and so on. The nonlocality of consciousness is comprehensively demonstrated to exist among humans, a conclusion reached by innumerable scientists, seers and sages.

The primacy of consciousness is explored in the outstanding book *Mind Before Matter*, edited by Trish Pfeiffer and John E. Mack. In short essays, 20 thinkers from various fields set out the implications of consciousness being primary, rather than secondary—derivative of matter.

Both of these studies of the nature of consciousness agree with the material shared by the hybrids, particularly their abilities relating to psychic phenomena, soul agreements, traveling astrally through higher dimensions, and connecting with their guides over any distance.

If we are immortal souls, part of a unified consciousness from which all else derives, then a very different experience of life is available to us. We are truly one, and are all the Creator. Mystics, seekers and saints down the centuries have come to this understanding through transcendent personal experience. To know the divine is to know our true selves, and vice versa.

If we take on board the ideas that humankind is a hybrid race—and that our souls have almost certainly had incarnations as non-humans—then the trip gets wilder still: we are *all* star beings.

The implications of this are enormous for the human future—imperiled as it is through our accelerating destruction of the natural environment on which we depend. In a world where we all understand that we are the same consciousness—ultimately part of the same unified soul—where is there a need to take more than we need? We are only taking it from ourself.

In a world where we are learning about diverse aspects of our collective self, differences are to be celebrated and learned from with appreciation.

As the Creator, we have unlimited potential to create our own reality. And with liberated minds and open hearts we can experience it in any way we choose.

Would we still act in harmful ways toward others? Would we still need to play a role in creating harm? Perhaps in getting to the point of understanding oneness we have crossed the threshold, and we enter a kind of heaven. A shared heaven only makes sense if we are one when we enter it.

As the reader you will have your own interpretations of the experiences and understandings that have been shared. The joy is in finding the things that resonate, the ideas and practices that work for you. The core of it is entirely relatable—being loving and connected. But here, the message happens to come from the cosmos, via beings who are part ET. Yet they are also us. As Jacquelin said, "There are no *sides*, because whoever we think of as another side is still *us*."

Recommended Reading

Andrews, A. and Ritchie, J.	Abducted: The True Story of Alien Abduction
Boylan, Richard	Close Extraterrestrial Encounters: Positive Experiences With Mysterious Visitors
Browne, Sylvia	Life on the Other Side
Browne, S. and Harrison, L.	The Other Side and Back
Bryant, A. and Seebach, L.	Healing Shattered Reality: Understanding Contactee Trauma
Cannon, Dolores	The Custodians: Beyond Abduction
	The Three Waves of Volunteers and the New Earth
Carroll, Lee	Kryon series
Colli, Janet Elizabeth	Sacred Encounters: Spiritual Awakenings During Close Encounters
Dennett, Preston	Extraterrestrial Visitations: True Accounts of Contact
	UFO Healings
DeRohan, Ceanne	Right Use of Will series
Dossey, Larry	One Mind: How Our Individual Mind Is Part of a Greater Consciousness and Why It Matters
Fowler, Raymond E.	The Andreasson Affair: The True Story of a Close Encounter of the Fourth Kind
	The Watchers
Gilbert, Joy S.	It's Time To Remember: A Riveting Story of One Woman's Awakening to Alien Beings
Greer, Stephen	Extraterrestrial Contact: The Evidence and Implications
Hopkins, Budd	Intruders: The Incredible Visitations at Copley Woods
	Missing Time

Howe, Linda Moulton	Witnessed: The True Story of the Brooklyn Bridge UFO Abductions Glimpses of Other Realities
Jacobs, David	The Threat: Revealing the Secret Alien Agenda
	Walking Among Us: The Alien Plan to Control Humanity
Kuita, Jujuolui (ed.)	We Are Among You Already: True Stories of Star Beings on Earth
Lalich, N. and Lamb, B.	Alien Experiences: 25 Cases of Close Encounter Never Before Revealed
Laszlo E., Grof S., Russell P.	The Consciousness Revolution
LaVigne-Wedel, Michelle	The Alien Abduction Survival Guide: How to Cope with Your ET Experience
Lewels, Joe	The God Hypothesis: Extraterrestrial Life and its Implications for Science and Religion
Littrell, H. & Bilodeaux, J.	Raechel's Eyes, Volumes I and II
Mack, John E.	Passport to the Cosmos: Human Transformation and Alien Encounters
Marciniak, Barbara	The Bringers of the Dawn: Teachings from the Pleiadians
Nidle, Sheldan	Your Galactic Neighbors
Oram, Mike	Does It Rain In Other Dimensions? A True Story of Alien Encounters
Pearce, Stewart	The Angels of Atlantis: Twelve Mighty Forces to Transform your Life Forever
Perry, Yvonne	Light Language Emerging: Activating Ascension Codes and Integrating Body, Soul, and Spirit
Pfeiffer, T. and Mack J. E. (eds.)	Mind Before Matter: Visions of a New Science of Consciousness
Quiros, CristiAnne	Exo-Psychology Research: A Phenomenological Study of People Who Believe Themselves to be Alien-Human Hybrids

Ring, Kenneth	The Omega Project: Near-Death Experiences, UFO Encounters and Mind at Large
Royal, Lyssa	The Prism of Lyra: An Exploration of Human Galactic Heritage
	Visitors from Within: Extraterrestrial Encounters and Species Evolution
Rodwell, Mary	Awakening: How Extraterrestrial Contact can Transform Your Life
Romanek, Stan	Messages: The World's Most Documented Extraterrestrial Contact Story
Russell, Peter	From Science to God
Slattery, D. R. and Grey, A.	Xenolinguistics: Psychedelics, Language, and the Evolution of Consciousness
Smith, Jacquelin	Animal Communication: Our Sacred Connection
	Star Origins and Wisdom Of Animals: Talks With Animal Souls
Smith, Yvonne	Chosen: Recollections of Abductions Through Hypnotherapy
Sparks, Jim	The Keepers: An Alien Message for the Human Race
Strieber, Whitley	Hybrids
	Communion
	Confirmation
	The Secret School
	Transformation
Turner, Karla	Taken: Inside the Alien-Human Abduction Agenda
Walden, James L.	The Ultimate Alien Agenda: The Re-engineering of Humankind
Wells, Sixto Paz	The Invitation
Wilson, Katharina	I Forgot What I Wasn't Supposed to Remember: An Expanded View of the Alien Abduction Phenomenon
	The Alien Jigsaw

Made in the USA
Charleston, SC
01 March 2016